NEW MEXICO

Calvin A. Roberts
and Susan A. Roberts

University of New Mexico Press
Albuquerque

Dedicated to Laura and Dave

Library of Congress
Cataloging-in-Publication Data

Roberts, Calvin A., 1946–
    New Mexico / Calvin A. Roberts, Susan A. Roberts. — 1st ed.
      p.   cm.
    Bibliography: p.
    Includes index.
    ISBN 0-8263-1048-6
    1. New Mexico—History.   I. Roberts, Susan A., 1943–
II. Title.
F796.R644   1988
978.9—dc 19   87-30086
                                                         CIP

Contents

New Mexico

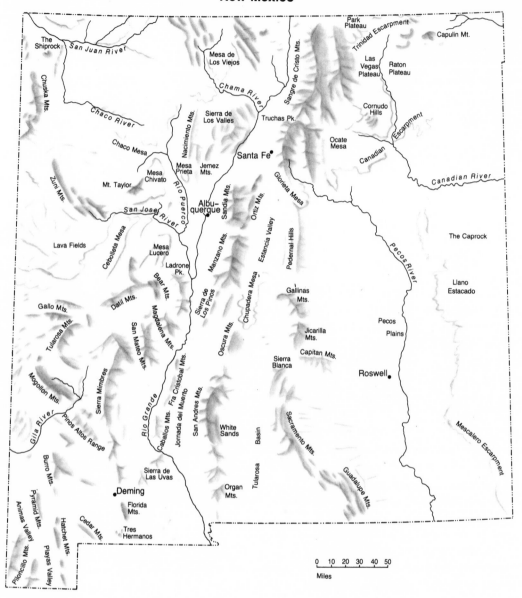

The Shiprock
San Juan River
Chuska Mts.
Chaco River
Chaco Mesa
Zuni Mts.
Mt. Taylor
Lava Fields
Cebolleta Mesa
Mesa Lucero
Gallo Mts.
Tularosa Mts.
Datil Mts.
San Mateo Mts.
Magdalena Mts.
Mogollon Mts.
Gila River
Sierra Mimbres
Pinos Altos Range
Rio Grande
Caballos Mts.
Fra Cristobal Mts.
Jornada del Muerto
San Andres Mts.
Burro Mts.
Pyramid Mts.
Animas Valley
Peloncillo Mts.
Hatchet Mts.
Cedar Mts.
Playas Valley
Deming
Florida Mts.
Tres Hermanos
Sierra de Las Uvas
White Sands
Organ Mts.
Tularosa
Basin
Sacramento Mts.
Guadalupe Mts.

Mesa de Los Viejos
Chama River
Nacimiento Mts.
Sierra de Los Valles
Mesa Prieta
Jemez Mts.
Santa Fe
Mesa Chivato
Rio Puerco
San Jose River
Albu-querque
Sandia Mts.
Ortiz Mts.
Manzano Mts.
Ladrone Pk.
Bear Mts.
Sierra de Los Pinos
Chupadera Mesa
Oscura Mts.
Estancia Valley
Glorieta Mesa
Pedernal Hills
Gallinas Mts.
Jicarilla Mts.
Capitan Mts.
Sierra Blanca

Park Plateau
Trinidad Escarpment
Capulin Mt.
Las Vegas Plateau
Raton Plateau
Sangre de Cristo Mts.
Truchas Pk.
Cornudo Hills
Ocate Mesa
Canadian
Escarpment
Canadian River

Pecos River
The Caprock
Llano Estacado
Pecos Plains
Roswell
Mescalero Escarpment

0 10 20 30 40 50
Miles

1
The Land and Its Early People

Two themes dominate New Mexico's long and colorful history: the land's often inhospitable living conditions and the isolation of its inhabitants from the outside world. While modern technology and the passage of time have helped to tame the environment and to lessen New Mexico's isolation, the land and its people retain a special identity.

Always a large and at times an ill-defined area, New Mexico today measures 391 miles from north to south and 352 miles from east to west. Encompassing a total of 121,666 square miles, it ranks in area as the fifth largest state in the United States. But size has not been the determining factor in where and how the people of New Mexico live; instead, they choose their habitats according to other geographical conditions, such as land surface, rainfall, altitude, and temperature.

New Mexico's land surface can be divided into four distinct provinces: plains, mountains, plateau, and basin and range. The plains province, an extension of the Great Plains which form the western fringe of the North American lowland, covers the eastern third of the state. Located here between the Pecos and Canadian rivers is the Llano Estacado, or staked plains, which comprises some of the earth's flattest land. The mountains province, a region of high and rugged peaks typical of the Rocky Mountains to which it belongs, runs through north-central New Mexico to a point just south of Santa Fe. As a part of the Colorado Plateau, the plateau province of high and usually level land extends across the northwestern part of the state.

The largest of New Mexico's four provinces—the basin and range—forms the land surface of the remainder of the state and is home to most of the state's people. Extending across the southwestern, the central, and the south-central portions of New Mexico, the basin and range province consists of mountain ranges separated from one another by broad, dry basins. Among the more important basins in this province are the Rio Grande Valley, the Estancia Basin, the Tularosa Basin, and the Plains of San Agustin. Among the many mountain ranges here are the Sandia and Manzano mountains, to the east of Albuquerque; the San Mateo Mountains, to the west of Socorro; the San Andres Mountains, between Socorro and Las Cruces; the Sacramento Range, between Alamogordo and Roswell; and the Mogollon Mountains, in southwestern New Mexico.

Although terrain is an important factor in determining where and how New Mexicans live, an even more vital condition is the availability of water. Despite its size, New Mexico has only about 250 square miles of surface water. Furthermore, rainfall favors some parts of the state over others, dumping forty inches of annual moisture on the Sangre de Cristo Mountains in the north and higher than average amounts on other mountain ranges, while the eastern plains and the flat, high plateaus annually receive moderate rainfall between twelve and seventeen inches. However, drier areas of the state, including much of the Rio Grande Valley, often record fewer than ten inches of annual precipitation. Here are areas that are very nearly true deserts.

When the rainfall occurs can be almost as important for New Mexicans as the amount of rainfall, and fortunately, New Mexico receives its moisture at the best of times. Three-fourths of the rainfall arrives during the June-to-September growing season, while the remainder comes mostly during the winter when snow covers the mountains and rain falls in the lower elevations. The spring runoff from melting mountain snows flows into the streams and rivers, which enables people to live in parts of New Mexico that would otherwise be too dry to support a sizable population.

The most important rivers in the state are the Rio Grande, the Pecos, the Canadian, the San Juan, and the Gila. The Rio Grande, the third longest river in the United States and New Mexico's most important lifeline, flows north to south through the center of the state. Along with the state's other rivers, it supports life by making irrigation of crops possible in areas of little rainfall; indeed, people have lived and irrigated crops in the Rio Grande Valley for hundreds of years. In this century dams on the Pecos River have controlled flooding and facilitated farming on thousands of acres of land, much of it located near Carlsbad and Roswell. Since 1940 the Conchas Dam on the Canadian River has provided water for irrigating land near Tucumcari; and irrigation also occurs, though with less success, along the San Juan and the Gila rivers.

In addition to surface water, New Mexicans have increasingly relied upon ground water held in underground lakes and aquifers. Today the state derives more than half its water for irrigation from ground water; and many cities and towns, including Albuquerque,

The Physical Features of New Mexico

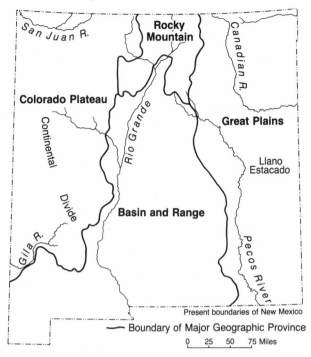

draw their water from underground sources. Nonetheless, water remains, as it has always been, a major concern for New Mexico. While New Mexico's rainfall is often unreliable, more damaging are the periodic droughts that hit the area. In addition, scientists disagree about how much ground water remains in various parts of the state. Some predict that people in certain parts of the state will exhaust their water supplies within the foreseeable future.

Two other geographical factors of consequence to New Mexicans are altitude and temperature. From its highest point—Wheeler Peak, near Taos, stands 13,160 feet high—to its lowest point—Red Bluff, on the Pecos, reaches an elevation of 2,817 feet—New Mexico is generally a land of high altitude. Eighty-five percent of the state has an altitude greater than 4,000 feet. Its high altitude makes the state's climate more northern than its latitude would dictate otherwise, because each 500-foot rise in altitude is equivalent to moving one hundred miles nearer to the North Pole at sea level. In turn, New Mexico's differences in altitude create six distinct life zones, with each one possessing climates, plants, and animals that are different from those found in the other life zones. While the area above 12,500 feet supports few plants or animals, the lowest life zone is a land of cacti, lizards, and snakes. A mild or moderate temperature is typical of most of the state. At the same time, temperatures over the course of a single day may vary as much as 40 degrees Fahrenheit. New Mexico's dry air quickly gains temperature during the day and loses temperature at night.

The Land and Its Early People

Geographical conditions in New Mexico have long dictated ways of living. Today New Mexicans boast of their state as a "land of enchantment," reveling in its crisp, clean air, its glorious sunsets, and its ever-changing landscapes. They may escape to the mountains and reservoirs for recreation; but these diversions often hide the reality that the land—and its water problem, especially—frequently discouraged settlement. Although rivers were America's first highways, they provided no source of transportation through New Mexico. The earliest peoples were forced to travel across the land on foot, and later explorers and settlers possessed only horses, mules, and oxen. These conditions tended to isolate New Mexico from other population centers, thus making it, for most of its history, a remote area largely unaffected by outside forces.

New Mexico's first inhabitants came to a land quite different from what it is today, and they were concerned about neither living conditions nor isolation. Attracted to a wet and cool New Mexico covered with grasslands and forests, these early peoples were big-game hunters, living here between twelve thousand and eight thousand years ago. They arrived in pursuit of the mammoth and mastodon, as well as extinct forms of the sloth, bison, antelope, camel, and horse. How they reached the Americas is the story of the arrival of the first Americans, who most likely migrated to Alaska from Siberia, crossing a land bridge created when water locked in the last ice sheet of the Ice Age caused sea level to drop three hundred feet. Arriving in the Americas more than twelve thousand years ago, these early people spread out, following the animals they hunted and, in some instances, moving into areas abundant with wild fruits, nuts, and berries. They migrated across North America, traveled down into and through Mexico, into Central and South America, and moved on to the Caribbean islands.

Typical of big-game hunters everywhere, each group of hunters in New Mexico made distinctive spearpoints for killing game, utilizing such stone as quartzite, flint, obsidian, jasper, and chert. Differences between spearpoints enable archaeologists to identify the big-game hunters, with each group named for the place where each spearpoint was first found. Two groups of big-game hunters named for sites in eastern New Mexico, where they were first identified, are Clovis Man and Folsom Man. The older of the two is Clovis Man, identified by a spearpoint found in 1932 near present-day Clovis, New Mexico. Little is known about Clovis Man except that these people were big-game hunters, who hunted and killed the giant mammoth, the musk-ox, the sloth, and the two-thousand-pound, wide-horned ox.

The first evidence of Folsom Man surfaced in 1908, when George McJunkin, a cowboy and former slave, discovered bison bones, in which spear points were embedded, in an arroyo near present-day Folsom, New Mexico. McJunkin's discovery finally

Desert Culture projectile points

prompted archaeologists in 1928 to dig up the first Folsom site, where they found more bones of animals hunted by these early people. They also found finely chipped spearpoints—which proved to be smaller and more finely chipped than the subsequently discovered Clovis points—and other artifacts that helped in determining how Folsom Man lived. Much like Clovis Man, Folsom Man hunted, in particular, the giant bison, an animal that provided materials for clothing and shelter as well as food. The hunters' homes were campsites along the trail of the bison. By using carbon-14 dating to determine when these big-game hunters lived in New Mexico, scientists dated Clovis Man at about 9200 B.C. and Folsom Man approximately a thousand years later. Thus, both Clovis Man and Folsom Man lived about ten thousand years ago, at a time when they and other big-game hunters trailed their sources of food through New Mexico.

The big-game hunters continued to live in New Mexico as long as their food supply was plentiful; in time, however, big-game animals disappeared. One likely reason for their disappearance was a change in climate, for when the Ice Age ended, the weather in New Mexico and elsewhere grew drier and warmer. New Mexico's grasslands dried up, and animals began to suffer from lack of food and perhaps from disease as well. Also, the early peoples probably overhunted their prey. With the big game gone from the Southwest, many hunters moved, perhaps to that area of the United States known today as the Great Plains, where

The Land and Its Early People   5

they could find enough game—albeit smaller—to continue their basic living patterns as hunters.

To fill the vacuum created by the withdrawal of the big-game hunters, people from the west spread across the Southwest and into the western part of present-day New Mexico. Known as desert dwellers, these people practiced ways of living that make them part of what is called the Desert Culture. These desert dwellers passed through two stages of development. Living between eight thousand and five thousand years ago, the first-stage desert dwellers hunted deer, antelope, rodents; fished; and gathered seeds, nuts, and berries.

Second-stage desert dwellers, who lived in the Southwest between five thousand and two thousand years ago, became agrarians. After noticing that seeds left behind in a certain place one year had grown into plants by the following year, the desert dwellers purposefully began to leave seeds in places where they returned the next year. Thus, the desert people added gardening to their ways of living, and while they still moved around and lived in natural shelters such as caves, they began to build some shelters of brush.

The people of the Desert Culture are known for two items, the basket and the milling stone. Baskets were used to gather, to store, and even to cook food by dropping heated stones into liquids. Milling stones were used to grind seeds into flour. Archaeologists have found thousands of artifacts, including countless baskets and milling stones, which provide evidence that the desert dwellers lived throughout the Southwest.

As time passed, the peoples of the Southwest changed their ways of living to include the adoption of a sedentary life-style, as opposed to the nomadic existence of the big-game hunters and the desert dwellers. The people began to settle in places where they built permanent homes. However, not all of the early peoples of the Southwest changed their lives in the same ways or at the same time, for such changes depended, in part, upon learning new ways of doing things, often from the people of other cultures. Nevertheless, three important sedentary cultures emerged from the Desert Culture, with each developing distinctive ways of living; and people from two of these three cultures lived in New Mexico. The third culture, the Hohokam, lived in Arizona.

Of the two cultures found in New Mexico, the Mogollon—whose name comes from the mountains and the rim where their remains were found in west-central New Mexico and south-central Arizona—were the first to acquire more advanced ways of living. Indeed, the proximity of the Mogollon to the people of Mexico benefited them in learning new ways of doing things. As early as 3000 B.C., the ancestors of the Mogollon were growing a type of corn also cultivated by their neighbors in Mexico; at about the same time, Mexico provided them with squash. After adding the

Early Cultures in New Mexico

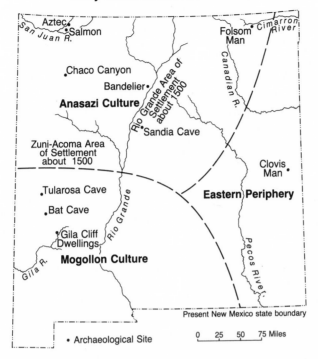

red kidney bean to their diet between about 1000 and 400 B.C., the Mogollon began to use pottery in approximately 300 B.C., again borrowing from Mexico both of these additions to their culture.

Having become a culture of true farmers by 300 B.C., the Mogollon began to build permanent homes by digging round or oval pits two to four feet deep and then covering these pits with timber and dirt roofs. These pit houses, built closely together, formed villages. In growing their crops in the mountain valleys, the people cultivated corn, squash, beans, and perhaps some cotton. Pits dug both inside and outside the houses provided food storage areas, and one larger pit house probably served as a religious center in most villages. Some pit burial remains reveal the Mogollon practice of placing offerings, most often pottery, in the graves. Each pot was intentionally broken, archaeologists speculate, to release the pot's spirit, which was thought to be part of the maker.

Since the Mogollon were safely removed from other peoples, they had the luxury of developing their own culture, which most likely reached its peak in A.D. 500. With mountains on three sides, a desert on the fourth, and villages built on high ground, they must have felt quite secure. Yet the Mogollon spread out from their homes in the mountains, moving into new mountain valleys and coming into contact with other peoples, with whom they shared their corn, squash, beans, and pottery.

The Land and Its Early People

To the north of the Mogollon lived the second of New Mexico's two important cultures that emerged from the foundation of the Desert Culture. These northern people, the Anasazi—a Navajo word meaning "the Ancient Ones," or alternately, "enemies of our ancestors,"—developed more slowly than the Mogollon. The Anasazi lived on the Colorado Plateau, in what is today the Four Corners Area, where four states—New Mexico, Colorado, Utah, and Arizona—come together. And because the Anasazi lived in the same general location for more than fifteen hundred years, archaeologists know a great deal about them and have determined how the Anasazi changed their living patterns during different time periods.

From A.D. 1 to 500, the people of the Anasazi Culture are called Basketmakers because of their great skill in making baskets for gathering seeds, nuts, and berries. Their baskets were so tightly woven that they could be used for carrying water and cooking food; but the Basketmakers, however skilled, still had no pottery at a time when the southern Mogollon Culture was reaching its peak. To hunt, the Basketmakers used a weapon called the atlatl, the Aztec word for a spear-throwing device used by many early peoples. By effectively lengthening the arc of the throw, the atlatl enabled hunters to send their spears and darts much greater distances than when thrown only by hand. Basketmakers also kept two types of domesticated dogs; human burial sites have yielded both a collielike dog and a smaller black and white, terrierlike dog.

From A.D. 500 to 700, the Anasazi Culture was a Modified Basketmaker Culture; for the Anasazi settled down while they were still hunting small game. They built villages of pit houses, and with their knowledge of crop-growing gained from the south, they cultivated corn, squash, and beans. To process corn into meal for corn cakes, they used a flat stone called a metate and a grinding tool called a mano. During this period the Anasazi also learned how to make pottery, which facilitated the cooking and storage of food. The Anasazi still made baskets, and they continued to weave the fibers of yucca plants into sandals, rope, and other useful items.

Still another important development affecting the Modified Basketmaker Culture was the introduction of the bow and arrow, which most likely came from the north. The bow and arrow proved to be more effective than the atlatl, and the Anasazi became more skilled as hunters while simultaneously increasing their skill as farmers. By A.D. 700 the Anasazi fit into the pattern of other Southwestern peoples, most of whom had similar ways of living. They knew about farming, hunting by bow and arrow, and pottery-making; lived in villages, most often in pit houses built in part below the surface of the ground; and maintained a religious center in their villages.

Seventh-century pit house

From A.D. 700 to 1050, the Anasazi Culture was a Developmental Pueblo Culture. During this period the Anasazi began to build rows of adobe houses above ground, sometimes arranging them in U-shaped or L-shaped rows. Centuries later, these villages of surface houses came to be called *pueblos,* a Spanish word meaning "town." Near the center of each group of houses was a pit house, called a kiva, which served the community's religious needs. To enter and leave the kiva, the Anasazi used a ladder that extended through an opening in the mud-covered roof. As time passed, kivas became an ever more important part of the culture, and except on rare occasions, they were open only to men, who met in the kivas to consider religious matters and other issues vital to the people. While women were likely excluded from the kivas, archaeologists believe that women owned the houses and most of the furnishings; in this matrilineal culture, property was handed down from mother to daughter.

Because this period seems to have been fairly peaceful, the Anasazi could polish their existing skills and develop new ones. Among their old skills was pottery-making, which they now improved upon to produce finer pottery. Among their new skills was cotton-growing and later, weaving cotton into cloth to make summer clothing. They also tamed the turkey and wove turkey feathers into blankets. The hard cradleboard for holding babies was introduced into their culture at this time, most likely coming from the Mogollon area. Using this cradleboard caused the back of infants' heads to become flattened, and the flattened head grew to be so popular that the entire physical appearance of the Anasazi changed within a few generations. Normally long and narrow, the

The Land and Its Early People   9

Anasazi skulls after their transformation by the cradleboards looked short, wide, and flat at the back.

The Anasazi's greatest achievements, however, occurred between A.D. 1050 and 1300, during a time that archaeologists variously call the Classic Pueblo Period, the Great Pueblo Period, or the Golden Age. During this time in the development of the Anasazi Culture, some of the people used stone masonry to build multistoried apartment houses, while others created great cliff dwellings. In expanding to the south and to the southeast, the Anasazi became the dominant culture in what is today the American Southwest.

The Anasazi built their largest apartment houses on the floor of Chaco Canyon in northwestern New Mexico. Their most imposing structure, Pueblo Bonito, meaning "Pretty Town," got its start after A.D. 900, and the Anasazi continued to work on it in stages until its completion in about A.D. 1130. Four stories high once it was finished, Pueblo Bonito covered more than three hundred acres, contained over eight hundred well-plastered rooms, and housed perhaps as many as twelve hundred people. Today

Pueblo Bonito at Chaco Canyon

the ruins of Pueblo Bonito and other pueblos on the floor of Chaco Canyon serve as a reminder of the extraordinary achievements of the Anasazi during the Classic Pueblo Period. Both Chaco Canyon and Aztec, another Anasazi site in New Mexico, are now national monuments.

The ruins of the great cliff dwellings, which provide yet another reminder of Anasazi achievements at the height of their culture, are most dramatically preserved in Mesa Verde National Park. Mesa Verde, which means "Green Table," is a flat-topped area that rises above rugged canyons in southwestern Colorado. Evidence exists that the Anasazi moved to Mesa Verde sometime during the Modified Basketmaker Period (A.D. 500 to 700) and that they built large apartment houses on top of the mesa during the Classic Pueblo Period. But after A.D. 1200, evidently because of pressure from their enemies, most of the Anasazi at Mesa Verde left their mesa-top community homes, with some moving to caves and others building cliff dwellings. Cliff Palace, the largest of the Mesa Verde cliff dwellings, contained more than two hundred rooms and some twenty-three kivas.

In addition to building the remarkable homes they lived in during the Classic Pueblo Period, the Anasazi constructed complex water control and road systems. Earlier they had built reservoirs and check dams to store the water from summer rains; now, at Mesa Verde, the Anasazi began to dig ditches for irrigating their crops. At Chaco Canyon they designed a system of dams, walls, and ditches, first to catch the water as it ran down from high places, then to direct it into the ditches, and finally to carry it through gates and into the fields. At both Mesa Verde and Chaco Canyon, irrigated and improved crops consumed fewer working hours and freed the people for other pursuits.

At Chaco Canyon the Anasazi also built a network of roads, ranging in width from ten feet to thirty feet and distinguished by borders and hard surfaces. These roads—including, where necessary, stairways and ramps to carry the people up to and down from the cliffs—connected pueblos in the canyon with settlements outside it, with some even stretching beyond the communities that were part of the Chaco area. No one knows precisely why the Anasazi built so many roads and such wide roads, but most likely they were constructed to accommodate trade with other areas, to facilitate the travel of large numbers of workers from one town to another, and to aid in the performance of religious rites. During this period the Anasazi built their great kivas in Chaco Canyon.

With religion evidently consuming more of their lives, the Anasazi also devoted more time to arts and crafts than during any previous period. Each group of Anasazi made pottery that was unique in both shape and pattern, painting fine line designs on black-on-white pots. They also painted murals on the walls of kivas, wove beautiful textiles, and increasingly adorned themselves with ornaments made of shell, turquoise, and other materials. From Mexico they imported parrots and macaws.

Despite their many achievements, the Anasazi's Golden Age did not last forever; in fact, the decline of the Classic Pueblo Culture in Chaco Canyon may have begun as early as the late 1100s. Although it occurred elsewhere at the close of the 1200s, the end of this period witnessed the abandonment of one pueblo after another. No one knows exactly why the Anasazi abandoned the pueblos, but archaeologists believe that there may have been several reasons, including the presence of roving bands of Indians, disease, disagreements, and even fighting among the Anasazi themselves. It is certain, however, that farming, which had always been difficult for the northern pueblos, received a devastating blow in 1276, when a great drought hit the area, a drought that was to last for twenty-three years.

Most likely, then, a combination of problems, highlighted by a food shortage, caused the people to leave the great pueblos. As a part of the resulting migration of people in search of new homes, the northern Anasazi generally migrated southward, moving into areas that already had a settled population. In New Mexico these areas were the Zuni country, the western mountainous region, and the Rio Grande Valley—all of which had a permanent water supply. Because people already lived there, the arrival of new settlers caused such problems as overcrowding and a decline in architecture, arts, and crafts.

In calling this period after A.D. 1300 the Regressive Pueblo Period, archaeologists view it as a time in which pueblo cultures moved backward rather than forward. Yet this transitional period was also a time of some achievement, as evidenced by the work of those who lived at what is today known as Bandelier National Monument, a Regressive Pueblo site near Los Alamos. Once again the people built large pueblos, mostly on the floors of valleys; and Pecos, located east of the Rio Grande, was the largest of these pueblos. Some of the buildings in these new pueblos, frequently as tall as five stories, stretched along streets. Other new pueblos, with their rows of multistoried buildings centered around open plazas, marked a break from the design of earlier pueblos, emphasizing a way of laying out the towns that became common only after 1300. Open courtyards housed the kivas, which differed from pueblo to pueblo, varying in shape from round to rectangular. Variety also characterized a pottery that was quite different from that of the Classic Pueblo Period. Almost entirely gone was the black-on-white pottery, replaced by black and white-on-red pottery, which varied widely in shape and design from one pueblo to another.

The Regressive Pueblo Period ended as yet another major change in pueblo life occurred after 1450. Once again, pueblos

Evolution of Indian pottery: *lower left,* mud bowl (A.D. 450); *upper right,* black on white (A.D. 1000); *lower right,* black on red (A.D. 1000); and *upper left,* multicolored bowl (A.D. 1200)

Cliff Dwellings at Bandelier National Monument

were abandoned and the people moved, a migration that after 1500 left New Mexico with two population centers, one in the Rio Grande Valley and the area eastward to Pecos and the other in the Zuni–Acoma area. The people who lived there were the ancestors of the present-day Pueblo Indians, whom the Spanish explorers and early settlers first met as they moved into New Mexico during the sixteenth century.

The Indian villagers found by the Spanish explorers, when they arrived in the Southwest in the sixteenth century, lived in some seventy-five to eighty pueblos stretching from the Piro villages of the middle Rio Grande Valley northward to Taos and westward to the Acoma, Zuni, and Hopi villages. The Spaniards were especially impressed with the way in which these peoples built their houses, for each story of the multistoried buildings rose above and behind the rooms of the level below it. Looking like giant stairways, the two- to five-story buildings reminded the explorers of Spanish towns; hence, the name *pueblos*. Most pueblos encountered by the Spaniards housed between two hundred and three hundred people, although some were larger; and a total of about thirty thousand pueblo inhabitants, including the Hopi in present-day Arizona, lived in the Southwest during the 1500s.

The Spaniards named the inhabitants of these towns Pueblo Indians, but the Pueblos were not a single tribe, for while they shared similar living patterns, beliefs, customs, and skills, they did not speak a common language. The Indians of New Mexico's nineteen present-day pueblos speak three different languages. The Zuni people speak Zuni; the inhabitants of Laguna, Acoma, Santo Domingo, Cochiti, Santa Ana, San Felipe, and Zia speak Keresan; and the peoples of the other nine pueblos speak one of the three tongues among the Tanoan language family. Tiwa is spoken at Taos, Picuris, Sandia, and Isleta; Tewa, at Santa Clara, San Ilde-

Taos Pueblo

New Mexico's Indians Today

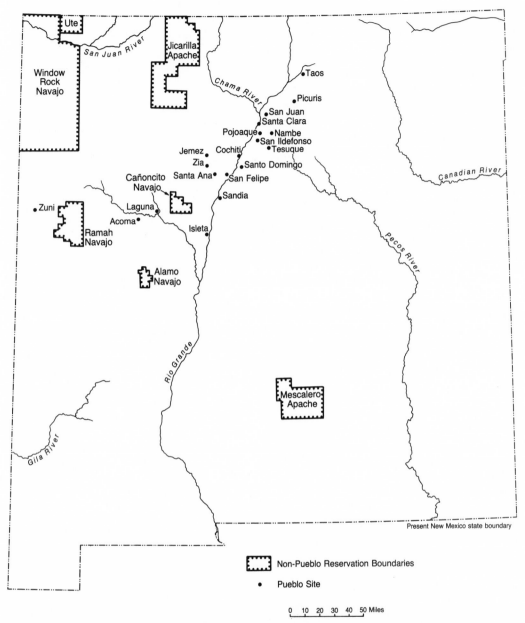

Non-Pueblo Reservation Boundaries

• Pueblo Site

0 10 20 30 40 50 Miles

fonso, San Juan, Pojoaque, Tesuque, and Nambe; and Towa, at Jemez alone. For centuries these language differences have helped to foster feelings of separation and independence among the various Pueblo peoples.

But the Spaniards found that the Pueblo peoples shared similar ways of living, including the architecture and functional use of each pueblo. Lower-story rooms, which served mainly as storage areas, were entered by way of pole ladders placed through narrow openings in the roof, while ladders outside the buildings

The Land and Its Early People

Kiva wall paintings at Kuaua (Coronado State Monument)

led to each higher story. Equipped with small outside doorways measuring three or four feet high and two feet wide, upper-story rooms provided sparsely furnished living space for the family, with additional living space available on the outside terraces during good weather. Inside the living quarters was a centrally located fireplace and perhaps an area set aside for grinding corn. The sun itself helped to provide much-needed winter heat, for the Indians saw to it that many pueblo buildings had a southern exposure.

The Pueblo peoples used what was readily available as building materials. The villagers to the west used soft sandstone, while those in the Rio Grande Valley, who had no such supply of stone, used adobe as a building material. Adobe was made by stirring water into a soil mixture of clay and sand; walls were built by spreading the adobe mixture over a framework of sticks and brush. To provide for their domesticated animals, the Pueblo Indians designed dug-out areas for their small, shaggy dogs and built large turkey pens holding as many as one hundred fowl, whose feathers were valued as a weaving material. Although all the pueblos had kivas, their size and location varied from pueblo to pueblo, with the pueblos built around plazas usually having two kivas in each plaza. On the walls facing the plazas were painted religious murals or designs.

The polytheistic Pueblo religion reflected the daily forces that affected the lives of the villagers—the sun and moon were Pueblo gods; and clouds, thunder, and wind were Pueblo spirits. The Pueblo peoples conducted religious ceremonies throughout the year. During the summer months religious rites centered on the growing of crops, for the people needed rain and a good harvest. During the winter, however, the focus of the rites shifted

A garden at Zuni (1930s)

to such concerns as hunting, curing, or war. In some pueblos kachinas, regarded as the spirits of ancestors, played an important role in these ceremonies. The people believed that these messengers of the Pueblo gods were capable of controlling the weather, bringing rain, and ensuring good health.

The concern for rain and crops reflected the Pueblo peoples' primary means of survival—farming. In the Rio Grande Valley the Pueblo Indians practiced irrigation, digging ditches with their wooden tools to carry water to their crops. Since such projects entailed a great deal of work, irrigation farming became a community project, with the men tilling the soil and planting the crops and the women joining the men during the harvest. Pueblo Indians who lived outside the Rio Grande Valley, such as the western pueblos and those east of the Manzano Mountains, practiced dry farming to overcome the lack of water. They tilled the soil deep so that it retained some moisture, or they planted crops by arroyos to catch runoff from rainfall or melting snows.

In their fields the Pueblo Indians grew corn, beans, and squash. Corn, the main crop, grew in many colors—blue, red, yellow, white, pink, and dark purple—and after it was ground, it was made into flat corncakes, the mainstay of the Pueblo diet. At harvest time the villagers enjoyed fresh vegetables, but they carefully dried most of the crops on roof tops to sustain them during the rest of the year and in future times of bad harvests. The women often supplemented the diet by gathering wild fruits, nuts, and berries, while the men hunted deer, antelope, squirrels, rabbits, and gophers. Some hunters from pueblos near the plains went to hunt the buffalo, returning with hides and dried meat called jerky. In making full use of what their land afforded them in all their endeavors, the Pueblo peoples used more than seventy plants for foods, medicines, and dyes.

The division of labor designed to secure food for survival reflected the presence of developed social structures within the tightly knit pueblo communities; but just as the pueblos were independent from one another, there existed differences in their social structures. For the Pueblo villagers to the west, the basic social unit was the clan, a group of blood relatives who traced their blood relationships through the female line. In these pueblos with their matrilineal societies, the women owned the land, houses, fields, and stored food; and property, of course, was passed through the female line. A mother and her husband, their daughters and sons-in-law, and their grandchildren often shared a household, and within such an extended family, the eldest female commanded the greatest respect.

The pueblos of the Rio Grande Valley placed less emphasis on the clan, with some pueblos developing patrilineal societies for tracing blood relationships and determining property ownership. In these pueblos the most important position within the social structure was occupied by the *moiety,* a term that means one-half or either of two fairly equal parts and reflects the division of the pueblos' inhabitants into two groups. In some pueblos the moieties represented the summer people and the winter people, with each being responsible for the religious rites that fell within its half of the year. To aid them in carrying out their responsibilities, the moieties in each pueblo had separate chambers—a squash chamber for the summer people and a turquoise chamber for the winter people—in which they planned ceremonials and stored religious items.

The Pueblo peoples were also quite skilled craftspeople, practicing basketry, beadwork, weaving, and pottery-making, among other arts. Pueblo men wove cloth out of cotton for use in making the women's long dresses and the men's loincloths. Pueblo women fashioned their pottery without the aid of a potter's wheel. Using the coiling method instead, the women first rolled clay into ropes and then wound these clay ropes around and around, forming the pot into its desired shape and size. After scraping, drying, and smoothing the pot, the potter painted designs with vegetable or mineral dyes before hardening it by fire fueled with wood or animal dung.

The skills and life-style of the Pueblo peoples did not escape the attention of the Spaniards, who described in detail the Pueblo ways of living they encountered as early as the 1500s. Less readily identified and understood by the first Spaniards, however, were New Mexico's nomadic Navajo and Apache Indians, who made up the largest non-Pueblo Indian groups encountered by the

Spaniards in the Southwest. Besides sharing a seminomadic life-style, the Navajo and the Apache were related by language, with each belonging to the Athabascan language family. Originally from Canada, these Indians migrated to the Southwest for reasons that remain unknown and arrived at a time still undetermined. Some archaeologists believe that the Navajo and Apache arrived in the 1200s, upsetting the Anasazi at Chaco Canyon and Mesa Verde, while others place their appearance in the Southwest just before the arrival of the Spaniards.

Although the evidence pinpointing their arrival is unclear, members of three Athabascan-speaking tribes still live in New Mexico today. The Navajo, with its 125,000 members representing the largest Indian tribe in the United States, live in present-day northwestern New Mexico and northeastern Arizona on a reservation that covers about 16 million acres, or about 24,000 square miles. The Mescalero Apache live east of the Rio Grande, between Alamogordo and Roswell, in the south-central part of New Mexico; and the Jicarilla Apache live west of the Rio Grande in the north-central part of the state. A fourth Apache group, the Chiricahua, lived in southwestern New Mexico until the late 1800s. While the Athabascan-speaking tribes developed greater cultural differences among themselves than did the Pueblo peoples, the Navajo and the Apache used the same word to describe themselves—*Diné*, meaning "The People."

When they arrived in the Southwest, the Navajo lived primarily as hunter-gatherers, but they also acquired cotton cloth and other items from the Pueblo Indians in exchange for animal hides and jerky. In time, the Navajo became more settled than their Apache cousins, although they did not totally relinquish their nomadic way of life, tending to move about with the seasons and building separate houses for their families in the places where they lived during the year. The typical early Navajo house, or hogan, used three upright poles to form a framework upon which logs were placed horizontally and which was then plastered with mud. A covered entryway completed the round, windowless structure.

In addition to building hogans, the Navajo also began to farm, a skill learned from the Pueblo Indians. The Navajo mostly grew corn; indeed, the very name *Navajo* may come from the Tewa word meaning "arroyo of the cultivated fields." Similar in still other ways to their Pueblo neighbors, the Navajo, like the western pueblo groups, had a matrilineal society. They divided into clans, with each Navajo remaining a lifelong member of the clan of his or her mother. Several hogans built closely together would house an extended family; yet these clusters of hogans did not constitute a village, for the Navajo simply did not live in villages.

As in the case of their Pueblo Indian neighbors, religion

Navajo sand painting, 1935

played a central role in the life of the Navajo, who believed that supernatural beings possessed the power to do good or evil. The shaman, or medicine man, was in charge of such Navajo religious rites as curing the sick or sending the men to war. Sand paintings, an important part of the curing ceremony, represented one of the more colorful features of Navajo religion; and they were more detailed and achieved a higher quality than either Pueblo or Apache sand paintings. Using dry colors from ground-up plants and minerals, the shaman and his helpers let the dry colors sift through their thumbs and forefingers onto a layer of clean sand, usually located on the floor of the sick person's hogan. Depicting events in the lives of the Holy People, some sand paintings were one or two feet in width, while others measured fifteen to twenty feet wide. Created from memory, the sand painting fit the curing ceremony chosen by the family and was destroyed before sunset on the day of its creation.

Like the Navajo religion, the Apache religion believed in the good and evil powers of supernatural beings. Most Apache rites were curing ceremonies directed by a shaman, who employed supernatural powers granted to him by the Mountain Spirits, or

New Mexico

Gáhan. A representative Apache curing ceremony included four masked dancers posing as the Mountain Spirits as well as a shaman, whose songs summoned supernatural aid on behalf of the ill. Of course, the Apache practiced rites other than those for illness; for example, the Mescalero Apache's ceremony celebrating the coming of age of young girls was a particularly joyous ritual.

Upon arriving in the area, the Apache groups in New Mexico spread out over a large area, and no one Apache group saw itself as a single, united tribe. Instead, the Mescalero had five tribal bands, the Chiricahua had three, and the Jicarilla had two. In turn, each band divided itself into local groups containing ten to twenty extended families. Since there was no central tribal organization, unity within the band rarely occurred, and in most cases the local group acted on its own as a hunting party, raiding party, or war party.

In moving from place to place, the Apache in New Mexico lived mostly by hunting and gathering. Since movement precluded permanent homes, the Mescalero Apache and the Jicarilla Apache lived in tipis, which were cone-shaped tents made of animal skins that resembled the shelters of the Plains Indians. The Chiricahua Apache, on the other hand, lived in wickiups, which were huts built around oval-shaped frames covered with grass and brush in the summer and with animal hides in the winter.

Mescalero Apache Mountain Spirit Dancers perform the *Gáhan* ritual

The Land and Its Early People

Once they had reached New Mexico, each larger Apache group lived in a separate area, although it took the Spaniards many years to be able to differentiate among them. The Mescalero—whose name most likely came from the mescal, or agave plant, which they ate—lived in the southern part of present-day New Mexico. The Jicarilla Apache lived in what is present-day northeastern New Mexico and southeastern Colorado; and like the Navajo, they learned some farming techniques from the Pueblo Indians, planting corn, for example. The Chiricahua Apache, called the Gila Apache by the Spaniards, moved about in present-day southwestern New Mexico and southeastern Arizona, and they eventually gained renown as one of the most skilled groups of Indian warriors in the United States. Given their locations, then, the Athabascan peoples surrounded the sedentary Pueblo Indians of present-day New Mexico.

Thus, when the Europeans encountered New Mexico's Indians, they met peoples who had been in the Southwest for varying lengths of time and had different life-styles. Of foremost interest to the early Spaniards were the Pueblo Indians, the descendants of the great Anasazi Culture which had flourished at Chaco Canyon and at Mesa Verde. The Spaniards found among the Pueblos a culture rooted in nature and adapted to the land of New Mexico. The Spaniards were slower to identify the non-Pueblo Indians, and they dealt less effectively with the nomadic Athabascan-speaking peoples who were relative newcomers to the Southwest.

2
The Spanish Explorers

After 1500 the newcomers arriving on the upper reaches of the Rio Grande were drawn to the land of the pueblos by the siren's song of fabled golden cities and untold wealth. While searching for riches, the Spanish explorers crossed vast, inhospitable expanses of uncharted territory to reach the interior of the North American continent. Their arrival in New Mexico was not, however, an isolated occurrence, but was simply another episode in the Age of Exploration, that great burst of European energy during the fifteenth, sixteenth, and seventeenth centuries, which carried Spanish, Portuguese, English, Dutch, and French adventurers to far-flung new lands, including the Americas.

The origins of the Age of Exploration lay in the European desire to trade with India and the Far East for spices, perfumes, rugs, dyes, medicines, and precious metals. The trade itself, which was already well established by the end of the great crusades, was unsatisfactory to most European countries because Italian merchants monopolized trade with the East, a trade that moved overland and took many, many months. To break the Italian monopoly and to reap rewards for themselves, other Europeans began the search for alternative, namely, all-water routes to the East. In benefiting from a national school of navigation and a location that allowed its sailors to catch the prevailing winds both en route and upon return, Portugal took the lead in the search for an all-water route around Africa to Asia during the 1400s. After progressing along the west coast of Africa in stages, Portugal at last found that route: in 1498 Vasco da Gama sailed around Africa's Cape of Good Hope to India, returning home with a cargo of spices worth sixty times the cost of the expedition.

By the time the Spanish monarchs Queen Isabella of Castille and King Ferdinand of Aragon entered the search for an all-water route to India, it was evident that Portugal would control the route that carried ships eastward; so they turned to Christopher Columbus, who believed that he could reach the Far East by sailing westward from Europe. An Italian by birth, Columbus first approached Isabella and Ferdinand with his proposal in 1486, but was turned down. He met further rejection at the courts of Portugal, England, and France before the Spanish monarchs finally agreed in 1492 to sponsor his voyage. Of course, Columbus never reached the Far East; instead, he made four different voyages to lands that came to be called the Americas. The voyages of Columbus and his successors at the Spanish court led to the exploration of the Central and South American coastlines and the founding of permanent Spanish settlements on the Caribbean islands of Hispaniola, Cuba, Jamaica, and Puerto Rico.

From their Caribbean settlements Spaniards expanded to the mainland and into the interior of the Americas within a relatively short period of time. For upper-class Spaniards, the new lands offered opportunities for adventure, recognition, and wealth that were no longer available in Spain. In the eyes of the Catholic church, the native inhabitants of the Americas were souls crying out for conversion to Christianity. Therefore, conquistadors set out to conquer great empires for country, for God, and, of course, for themselves—motives which later historians summarize as "glory, god, and gold."

The first great conquest began innocently enough in 1517, when Francisco Hernández de Córdova, who had been part of a slaving expedition to the Yucatan peninsula, returned to Cuba with stories of great inland Aztec cities filled with gold. Córdova's tales so excited Spanish officials in Havana, Cuba—then the major Spanish city in the Americas—that Hernando Cortés left Cuba in February 1519 with the intent of conquering the Aztec empire. By the time it ended, this expedition of eleven ships, six hundred soldiers, some priests, and sixteen horses would establish Cortés as one of the greatest of all the conquistadors.

Stopping first on the Yucatan peninsula, Cortés made his way to Vera Cruz, where he established a settlement. From there he and his party moved inland, replacing Indian symbols of worship with Christian ones. And facilitating the movement of the party was Malinche, or Doña Marina as the Spaniards called her, an exiled Aztec princess who spoke both the Aztec and Mayan languages and served as interpreter and mistress for the intrepid Cortés. On more than one occasion Doña Marina's quick wits saved her lover from death. In November 1519 Cortés entered Tenochtitlán, capital of Emperor Moctezuma's great Aztec empire, and shortly thereafter, the emperor became his prisoner. Although forced to withdraw from Tenochtitlán in June 1520, Cortés attacked again in December, and by August 1521 the once mighty Aztec empire lay at his feet. In the process of their conquest, the

Spaniards destroyed three-fourths of Tenochtitlán, which Cortés himself called the "most beautiful city in the world."

On the ruins of Tenochtitlán the Spaniards built a city they named Mexico City, after Mexica, the name that the Aztec people had given to themselves, and they named the land they had conquered "New Spain of the Ocean Sea." Thanks to the efforts of Cortés, Spain now had a great mainland empire with uncounted wealth, especially in silver; and Spain added even more riches with Francisco Pizarro's later conquest of Peru (1532–1535). From the mines of New Spain and Peru, Spain obtained more gold and silver than all the other European countries combined had found in the lands that they conquered. In addition, its mainland acquisitions gave Spain control of millions of Indian souls awaiting conversion to the true faith; and Franciscan, Dominican, and Jesuit priests came to the Americas to complete their salvation.

The excitement caused by the acquisition of New Spain and its great wealth spurred further exploration not only to the south but to the north as well. Attention focused immediately on Florida, where Juan Ponce de León had died in 1513 while seeking the "fountain of youth." Hopes of finding riches in Florida now drew more Spaniards, and while the expeditions proved to be fruitless, they did not end Spanish exploration in what is today the United States. Indeed, a failed expedition to Florida initially drew the attention of Spanish officials to New Mexico, the region north of New Spain.

Headed by Pánfilo de Narváez and consisting of four hundred men, the expedition sailed for Florida in 1528. Although Narváez repeatedly heard tales of rich Indian villages located in Florida's interior, he found no gold and silver, only unfriendly Indians and lethal fevers. Disheartened, the 242 surviving members of the expedition retreated to the coast, built five boats, and set sail along the coast of the Gulf of Mexico for New Spain. Before it could reach its destination, the little fleet was destroyed by storm and shipwreck; and eighty survivors from two of the boats were washed ashore near Galveston Bay, in present-day Texas. Among the fifteen men still alive in the spring of 1529 was Álvar Núñez Cabeza de Vaca, originally the royal treasurer for the Narváez expedition and now a captive of coastal Indians.

In September 1534 Cabeza de Vaca, two Spaniards, and a black Moorish slave named Estevan escaped from their Indian captors and began their famed march westward, making their way from village to village by acting as healers. They walked across Texas and probably through parts of New Mexico and Arizona before ending their journey in April 1536 on the northern frontier of New Spain. As the only known survivors of the Narváez expedition, they solved the eight-year-old mystery surrounding the disappearance of Narváez and his four hundred men.

Of even greater interest to officials in New Spain were the

Romantic view of Cabeza de Vaca crossing the Southwest. Actually, the Spaniards wore deerskins

survivors' accounts of the northern lands they had crossed, for the four men were the first non-Indians to travel across the great interior of the North American continent. Spaniards listened intently as Cabeza de Vaca described a land of little farming and few settlements, whose inhabitants treasured some beads, turquoise, coral, and arrowheads made out of "emeralds" and told occasional tales about people far to the north who lived in large houses and traded in turquoise.

Although Cabeza de Vaca described an impoverished land, Spaniards preferred not to believe him; after all, they had found great wealth in New Spain and Peru. Might not a city said by Indians to hold great wealth lie farther inland in Florida than Narváez had traveled? Perhaps the Indian villages with large houses to the north of Mexico City would prove to be another Peru, and the lands to the north might well hold the legendary seven cities of gold.

As Spaniards contemplated the northern lands, they recalled the fable of the seven cities of gold, a story with both European and American origins. One European legend maintained that as the Moors overran Portugal in the 700s, seven bishops fled westward by sea, and somewhere in the Atlantic they were said to have set up church districts in very rich lands. On the American side of the Atlantic was an Aztec legend which claimed that the Aztec people had come from seven caves far to the north; still other tales described a land of gold and silver that lay forty days journey to the north. To discover the truth of these stories, Spaniards would have to undertake northern expeditions.

One high-ranking Spanish official whose imagination was fired by Cabeza de Vaca's accounts was Antonio de Mendoza, viceroy of New Spain. Determined to find out for himself what the northern lands held, Mendoza organized a small fact-finding party to journey northward. Depending upon what the party found, Mendoza could then decide whether or not to send out a full-scale expedition. Leading the party was Fray Marcos de Niza, a Franciscan priest who had been with Pizarro during the conquest of Peru; acting as guide was Estevan, the black Moor who had accompanied Cabeza de Vaca; and escorting them was a party of Indian helpers.

Setting forth in March 1539, the party first traveled up the west side of New Spain, then northeast across the desert of present-day Arizona. Because the party moved slowly, Fray Marcos sent Estevan ahead, instructing him to mark a path for the expedition to follow, to make friends with the Indians along the way, and to look for cities of gold. To keep Fray Marcos apprised of his progress, Estevan was to send back crosses of varying sizes to signal what he found—small crosses to indicate little of value and large crosses to announce that something of value lay ahead.

While the party was still moving through Arizona, Fray Marcos received from Estevan a very large cross; and excited by the apparently good news, Fray Marcos and company hurried forward, only to learn that the Moor was dead. Estevan, who was three days ahead of the main party, had been killed upon entering Hawikuh, one of the Zuni villages just inside present-day New Mexico. Although no one knows for sure why Estevan was killed, some historians believe he may have demanded turquoise and women that the Zuni were unwilling to give to him. Others say he may have possessed a gourd rattle like those carried by enemies of the Zuni; still others suggest that Estevan, who was black and wore feathers and rattles, may have looked like a wizard to the Zuni. In any case, Estevan made such an impression on the Zuni that they remember him in their legend telling of the death of "one of the Black Mexicans" from "the Land of Everlasting Summer" (Mexico).

No one knows for sure if Fray Marcos then traveled on to Zuni after learning of Estevan's death. Perhaps Fray Marcos never got close enough to see Zuni, or he may have been close enough to see the villages in the distance, perhaps with New Mexico's sun shining so brightly on the walls that they took on a "golden" hue. Whatever happened, the friar told Mendoza that he had seen

Ruins at Hawikuh

Zuni, that it was a settlement of seven villages altogether larger than Mexico City, and that the villages of Zuni were the golden cities called Cíbola. Cíbola, meaning "buffalo cow," became the name that Spaniards now applied to that area north of New Spain which supposedly contained great wealth.

With Fray Marcos's report in hand, Mendoza hurriedly set plans in motion for a full-scale expedition to Cíbola. One reason for acting quickly was the fact that Hernando de Soto—a veteran of the conquest of Peru and a wealthy Spaniard who had heard the tales of Cabeza de Vaca—had already sailed for Florida with the intention of exploring eastern North America. Completely unaware of the distance separating Florida and New Mexico—such was the knowledge of North American geography at the time—Mendoza feared that the de Soto expedition would get to Cíbola before his own. A second reason for acting quickly was to forestall the plans of the inveterate conquistador Hernando Cortés, who wished to lead another expedition.

To explore Cíbola, Mendoza chose Francisco Vásquez de Coronado, the young governor of Nueva Galicia, a western province of New Spain, and a man of means who was willing to help in financing the expedition. Together Mendoza and Coronado spent approximately 4 million dollars (by today's standards) in outfitting an expedition that included a naval fleet, which was to sail up the Gulf of California with support supplies while looking for a water route to Cíbola. Once preparations were completed, Coronado headed north on 22 February 1540 with 250 horsemen, 50 or more men on foot, the wives and families of several soldiers, and several hundred Indian helpers who were to tend the expedition's cattle, sheep, mules, and extra horses. The soldiers were variously armed, with some carrying guns. Because he had made the trek before, Fray Marcos served as guide; and five other friars accompanied Coronado as well. The presence of the priests was in keeping with Mendoza's special instructions to Coronado's force, namely, that the Spaniards were to Christianize the Indians they met, not slaughter them.

The Coronado expedition spent a hard six months traveling to Zuni, arriving at Hawikuh in July 1540. One look at Zuni—with its six villages, not seven, and its huts of mud, not gold—revealed to the Spaniards in the most explicit terms that they had not found the seven cities of gold. And in addition to what must have been indescribable disappointment, the people at Hawikuh did not welcome the intruders with open arms. Only after Coronado's men had forcefully subdued them did the Zuni make peace. Although the Spaniards found a needed supply of corn and beans inside the villages, they did not locate any precious metals, only a few bits of broken stone. With disappointment surely turning to anger, Coronado's men might well have taken out their frustrations on Fray Marcos, but the thoroughly discredited friar beat a timely retreat to Mexico City.

Once encamped at Zuni, Coronado sent out small parties to scout the surrounding area and to search elsewhere for the fabled cities of gold. Having heard of a land called Tusayan, Coronado sent a group under Pedro de Tovar westward to investigate, but while Tovar came across the Hopi villages in present-day Arizona, he found no riches. However, he returned to Hawikuh with tales of a great river farther west, and to learn more about this river, Coronado next dispatched a party under García López de Cárdenas. Traveling farther to the west than Tovar, these explorers found a great river and a canyon so deep that it defied the efforts

One section of a mural depicting the Coronado expedition

of three soldiers to climb down its walls to reach the river. Cárdenas and his men were nevertheless the first Europeans to see
what are known today as the Colorado River and the Grand
Canyon. A third group of explorers sent out by Coronado, under
the command of Melchior Díaz, traveled to the lower Colorado
River in an attempt to meet the supply ships commanded by
Hernando de Alarcón. As it turned out, Díaz found only letters
left behind by the fleet, which had departed for New Spain after
finding no traces of either Coronado or Cíbola.

Coronado found the reports from the west so disheartening
that he might have called a halt to the expedition, but tantalizing
news about a land to the east convinced him to continue his
search. The harbinger of the encouraging news was a resident of
Pecos Pueblo whom the Spaniards called Bigotes, meaning "Whis-
kers." Upon hearing of the arrival of outsiders, Bigotes had traveled
to Hawikuh to see the Spaniards for himself, and once there he
told Coronado about the plains and buffalo herds to the east,
about Acoma Pueblo, and about the Tiguex villges along the Rio
Grande. Again Coronado sought to verify the report by sending
out an exploratory party, this one under Hernando de Alvarado.
Traveling eastward, Alvarado and his men saw Acoma, Tiguex,
Pecos, and the plains, and they hunted buffalo. Returning to
Hawikuh, Alvarado suggested that the expedition winter on the
Rio Grande at Tiguex, near present-day Bernalillo, and Coronado
ordered the main party to the river.

Acoma Pueblo

New Mexico

Kuaua Pueblo, a Tiguex village (Coronado State Monument)

In itself, the report of the Alvarado party might not have prolonged the Spaniards' stay in the northern lands, but at Tiguex the Spaniards heard the kinds of tales that had initially lured them northward, reports of a rich land on the plains to the east, a land called Quivira. The teller of these tales was a Pawnee captive of the Pecos Indians whom the Spaniards called El Turco, or "the Turk," because he supposedly looked like one. Alvarado had found El Turco at Pecos and brought him to Tiguex, where he described to Coronado a land so rich in gold that the Spaniards would have trouble carrying it home. But as winter set in, Coronado knew a march to Quivira would have to wait until spring.

In the meantime, the Spaniards appropriated the earthen houses of Alcanfor, the southernmost Tiguex village, and demanded food and blankets for the winter. Facing months of being forced to accede to the demands of their arrogant visitors, the Tiguex Indians revolted; but like the one at Hawikuh, the struggle was fierce, short-lived, and one-sided. The Indians could not overcome Spanish weapons, and when the battle ended, two villages lay in ruins, both sides had suffered losses in killed and wounded, and the inhabitants of other Tiguex villages fled into the winter cold. Coronado had disobeyed Mendoza's orders, for he had killed rather than Christianized the Indians at Tiguex.

When spring came, Coronado headed eastward across the Llano Estacado, or "Staked Plains," guided by El Turco and Isopete, a Wichita Indian captive from Pecos. The Spaniards pushed through the Texas panhandle and into present-day central Kansas, where their journey ended near what is now the town of Lyons. There stood Quivira—in reality, only the grass huts of the Wichita Indians, whose chief wore a copper, not gold or silver, plate around his neck because it was the only metal he owned. Once again, the tales of wealth had proved false, and El Turco now admitted to having tricked the Spaniards in an effort to help the Pueblo Indians get rid of their unwanted guests. Coronado learned from Isopete that El Turco had also begun plotting among the Wichita to kill the Spaniards. In reprisal the Spaniards garroted their unreliable guide, who, even as he faced death, continued to promise that riches lay just beyond the horizon. In appreciation for his aid in uncovering El Turco's treachery, the Spaniards let Isopete remain at Quivira as a free person.

Now that the plains venture had clearly miscarried, Coronado led his men back to the Rio Grande, where they spent the cold winter of 1541–42. Although its sense of failure was great, the expedition was about to experience still more trouble. While engaging in a horse race with a friend, Coronado suffered serious injury when his saddle girth broke and his friend's horse trampled him, injuring his head. By the spring of 1542 Coronado was well enough to quit New Mexico for good, and he returned with his expedition to New Spain. The only Spaniards to remain behind were three priests, who were excited over the prospect of opening a new mission field for the Catholic church. All three likely died at the hands of Indians.

Back in New Spain, Coronado reassumed his post as governor of Nueva Galicia, but his problems were far from over. In 1544 he stood accused before the court on charges of having mismanaged the expedition. Among other things, the government charged him with great cruelties toward the natives of New Mexico, gambling, and the misuse of funds. Convicted, stripped of his office, and fined five hundred pesos, Coronado became a broken man. Gaining little solace from the subsequent reversal of his conviction by New Spain's highest court, he quietly served his last days in a minor post in Mexico City before dying in 1556.

A failure in his own estimation and in the eyes of Spanish officials who had expected him to find new riches for Spain, Coronado nonetheless added greatly to the geographical knowledge of North America. He and his men were the first Europeans to see the Colorado River and the Grand Canyon, the first to explore the land of the Pueblos, and the first to recognize the continental divide as the great watershed of North America. In addition, the information gathered by Coronado and his men aided later Spanish advances to New Mexico. Still, it would be almost forty years after Coronado's return to New Spain before Spaniards would send any new expeditions northward. Coronado's description of a land devoid of riches partly accounted for the lack of interest, as did a preoccupation with the discovery of new sources of silver northwest of Mexico City. The silver rush that ensued brought to the area of present-day northern Mexico

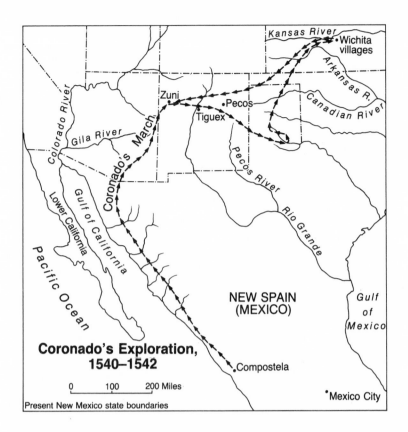

Kansas River
Wichita villages
Arkansas R.
Zuni
Pecos
Tiguex
Canadian River
Colorado River
Gila River
Coronado's March
Pecos River
Rio Grande
Lower California
Gulf of California
Pacific Ocean
NEW SPAIN
(MEXICO)
Gulf
of
Mexico
Coronado's Exploration,
1540–1542
Compostela
0   100   200 Miles
Mexico City
Present New Mexico state boundaries

people eagerly searching for more silver and eventually farmers who brought the land under the plow.

Yet even in the absence of new expeditions, the Spaniards never completely lost interest in the lands explored by Coronado. After all, they knew that there were souls along the Rio Grande to be saved for the Catholic church. They also hoped that the northern lands might reveal the fabled "Northwest Passage" connecting the Atlantic and Pacific oceans, which Spain hoped to be the first to find. And finally, the Spaniards had not given up altogether their dream of finding riches in those lands, a dream revitalized by the silver discoveries beyond Mexico City. Perhaps, some said, a rich "new" Mexico lay somewhere on the northern interior. And as more and more Spaniards called the northern lands the "new" Mexico because of the riches they might yield, the name New Mexico remained.

Renewed interest in the north led to four brief expeditions during the 1580s and 1590s, none of which followed the path of Fray Marcos and Coronado across Arizona. By 1580 the Spaniards had concluded that the sparsely inhabited deserts of eastern Arizona offered little, and they had recently learned of a route into New Mexico that went up the Rio Grande. Setting forth in 1581, the first expedition to follow the new path possessed primarily a missionary purpose. Its leader was Fray Agustín Rodríguez, who had heard of a land to the north with souls to save

The Spanish Explorers

while he was stationed at Santa Barbara on New Spain's northern frontier. After successfully petitioning the viceroy for permission to explore the land along the Rio Grande, where he hoped to expand the work of the Catholic church, Fray Agustín left Santa Barbara on 5 June. In his party were two other priests, an escort of nine soldiers under the command of Francisco Sánchez Chamuscado, and a number of Indian servants. The friars and soldiers first moved down the Conchas River and then up the Rio Grande Valley, visiting the pueblos along the river as far north as Taos. To the west they visited Acoma and Zuni, and to the east they crossed to the plains and saw the buffalo.

In his excitement over the land of the Pueblos, one of the friars, Fray Juan de Santa María, left the others to carry news of the expedition's discoveries back to New Spain. The other two friars, Fray Agustín and Fray Francisco, decided to remain at Tiguex, and soon they dispatched the soldiers home. These soldiers, minus a tired and ill Sánchez Chamuscado, who died en route, reached New Spain in April 1582 and told of the land they had seen and of the priests who had stayed behind. What neither they nor anyone else knew was that Fray Juan de Santa María had been killed by Pueblo Indians who feared he was sending for more unwanted Spaniards, while the two friars at Tiguex had been killed for their meager possessions.

With the fate of the friars still unknown, the Rodríguez–Chamuscado expedition aroused such immediate interest in New Mexico that a second expedition was on the Rio Grande heading north by 9 December 1582. This expedition had two leaders and two motives. Fray Bernardino Beltrán, the religious leader of the expedition, hoped to find and, if necessary, to rescue Fray Agustín and Fray Francisco. Businessman Antonio de Espejo, the secular leader who also paid for the fourteen-soldier escort accompanying Fray Bernardino, hoped to find mines and a "lake of gold" rumored to be in the area. Fray Bernardino succeeded in establishing the unfortunate fate of the missionary friars at Tiguex; the Espejo branch of the party pursued its treasure hunt. And although Espejo and his followers found neither the elusive mines nor the "lake of gold," the searchers wandered westward into present-day Arizona, where they found copper and some silver before returning to New Spain. Having failed in his self-appointed task, Espejo nonetheless told a tall tale of wealth in New Mexico, a story that grew more and more colorful with each telling.

As the reports of the Fray Agustín and Espejo expeditions circulated in Spain as well as in New Spain, they served to refocus official interest in New Mexico. As a result, Spain's ruler, King Philip II, issued instructions to the viceroy in 1583 that would pave the way for actual Spanish colonization of New Mexico. Under orders from the king, the viceroy was to find someone to settle, pacify, and bring the Catholic faith to the area. But even

King Philip II of Spain

while plans for such an undertaking were still in preparation, two other groups entered New Mexico.

The first group that moved up the Rio Grande was led by Gaspar Castaño de Sosa. As the lieutenant governor of the province of Nuevo León, Castaño de Sosa had taken charge of the province in the absence of the governor and had begun on his own to plan the settlement of New Mexico. What was most remarkable about the lieutenant governor's actions was his intention of starting a colony without permission from the crown, an act which was in apparent violation of a royal edict that specifically required a grant to settle new lands. In reasoning that New Mexico had been crossed and recrossed by many Spaniards and therefore was not technically new land, Castaño de Sosa simply wrote officials to declare his intentions, and in July 1590 he set out for the Rio Grande.

In the party traveling into New Mexico were 170 townspeople from Almadén, a small silver-mining town whose inhabitants were left in desperate straits once the silver had played out. They were easy prey for the enterprising lieutenant governor, who faked an assay of rock samples reputedly from New Mexico in order to trick the townspeople into believing that they would find silver in New Mexico. Taking along their personal possessions and live-stock, the good citizens of Almadén found themselves on the Pecos River in October 1590, and two months later, after as-cending the river, they reached Pecos Pueblo. From Pecos Castaño de Sosa's "colony" explored the Rio Grande Valley, always keeping an eye out for the expected silver. Once they had tired of the nomadic life, the Spaniards set up their headquarters near Santo Domingo and settled down in their new home.

The Spanish Explorers

Ruins at Pecos Pueblo

This new settlement, however, proved short-lived, for in March 1591 fifty soldiers from New Spain arrested Castaño de Sosa and took him downriver in chains. Brought before the courts of New Spain, Castaño de Sosa stood trial for settling in New Mexico without a direct grant of authority. Castaño de Sosa was convicted and expelled from the Americas, and he died while fighting a shipboard uprising en route to his place of exile in the Far East in 1593. Castaño de Sosa was later cleared of wrongdoing by officials in Spain, and had he lived, he might have returned to New Mexico legally in the official role of governor. Nonetheless, his expedition made history. The carts that carried the goods of the would-be settlers into New Mexico were the first wheeled vehicles to travel over territory that would one day be part of the United States. In addition, the Castaño de Sosa venture supported an increasingly popular idea that New Mexico might prove to be a land worth colonizing.

The fourth and final incursion into New Mexico before the land was legally settled occurred in 1593–94. It got underway when Captain Francisco Leyva de Bonilla, after chasing a band of Indians far northward, persuaded a small group of soldiers to follow him into New Mexico in search of gold. Thus, what began as a pursuit of marauding Indians beyond the frontier of New Spain ended in a quest for the fulfillment of the age-old dream of wealth. Traveling up the Rio Grande, Leyva and his men reached the pueblo of San Ildefonso, where they stayed and lived off the people. In their anxiety to get rid of their unwanted guests, the Indians resorted to an old trick, telling Leyva that there were riches in the cities on the eastern plains. The great canard of Quivira had reappeared, and the Leyva party, like the Coronado expedition before it, pursued its dream by heading east. Out on the plains the soldiers met their deaths, probably very near where Coronado had ended his trek. Their fate would remain a mystery until an Indian who had accompanied the soldiers to the plains returned to the Rio Grande Valley and reported the story to New Mexico's first official Spanish governor some five years later.

Even before Francisco Leyva de Bonilla's trail was cold, however, the viceroy of New Spain had begun to lay plans for colonizing New Mexico—a decision which was the result of years of interest in the region, spawned initially by Cabeza de Vaca, Fray Marcos, and Coronado and later by Fray Agustín, Fray Bernardino, Espejo, and Castaño de Sosa. These explorers had prepared the way for the next major development in New Mexico's history—its permanent settlement as a colony of Spain.

3
Early Spanish Settlement, 1598–1680

At the end of the sixteenth century the time of exploration and illegal expeditions in New Mexico gave way to a period of colonization, for while the explorers and interlopers had discovered no treasure, they had found in New Mexico a land worthy of settlement. To be sure, a few Spaniards retained their tarnished dreams of riches, but their search now became a less important activity on the Rio Grande than the desire for permanent settlement and missionary work among the Pueblo Indians. In officially sanctioning the new priorities for New Mexico, King Philip II of Spain in 1583 ordered his viceroy in New Spain to find the right person to colonize New Mexico, and fourteen long years later the viceroy chose Don Juan de Oñate as the man for the job. Oñate, who first petitioned the viceroy for a grant to settle New Mexico in 1595, had waited two years for final approval of his appointment as governor and captain general of the province. Along with his new titles, Oñate received the authority to apportion land among the settlers who would accompany him.

Several factors had favored Oñate's selection as governor, including the fact that he came from a wealthy and distinguished family. Born in 1552 in New Spain, Oñate grew up in a family whose wealth came from successful silver mines near Zacatecas; and his marriage to Doña Isabel Cortés Tolosa, a descendant of Mexico's conqueror Hernando Cortés, brought Oñate even greater wealth and influence. In addition, twenty years of service as a soldier fighting Indians in New Spain gave Oñate valuable experience as a military leader. Finally, Oñate had grown restless in looking for something new and challenging to do since the death of his wife in the 1580s.

Had he been less than wealthy, Oñate could not have undertaken the settlement of New Mexico. In fact, he had to agree to assume most of the bill for the expedition, including the pay-

Don Juan de Oñate's coat of arms

ment of the expenses of the soldiers and settlers and the purchase of supplies and livestock. The government paid only the expenses of the friars going to New Mexico to convert the Indians to Christianity. Clearly, as far as Spanish officials were concerned, the most important reason for the expedition was to spread the true faith. In addition to saving souls and founding a colony, Oñate was instructed to explore and map the coasts and harbors of New Mexico, a task consistent with the Spaniards' belief that the Pacific Ocean lay only a short distance westward from the lands crossed by earlier explorers. Oñate was also told to search for an all-water route through the Americas, the long-sought "Northwest Passage."

The colony that set forth from Santa Barbara on 26 January 1598 contained 400 men, 130 of whom had wives and children and 129 of whom were soldiers. Ten Franciscan friars also joined the trek northward. Two-fifths of the colonists headed for New Mexico were born in Spain; nearly one-third were born in New Spain; and the remainder came from places either not identified or located in other parts of Europe or the Americas. The expedition utilized 83 carts and herded 7,000 head of livestock.

After slowly pushing to the Rio Grande, Oñate and company then followed the river's course northward until, by the middle of April 1598, they were within twenty-five miles of present-day El Paso. Continuing their march up the river valley, they reached the land of the Piro Indians, who gave them much-needed food and water. The Spaniards named this place Socorro, meaning "succor," and it was here that Oñate left the main party and moved on with an advance group, visiting several Indian villages, including San Juan near present-day Española. The people of San Juan, reported by earlier explorers to be friendly, welcomed the Spaniards.

On 11 July 1598 Oñate made San Juan, which was located in a small valley near the point where the Chama River flows into the Rio Grande, the site of the first Spanish settlement in New Mexico. The Spaniards named this first colony San Juan de los Caballeros, meaning "San Juan of the Gentlemen," for this was the way in which Oñate and his group regarded themselves. The main party reached San Juan in mid-August, and within two weeks the foundation for a church was laid. Within a few months, however, the Spaniards moved to the west side of the Rio Grande, attempting to put some room between themselves and the San Juan people and to gain space for expansion. Here the Spaniards built their second settlement, known as San Gabriel.

From the very outset Spanish settlers found the land of New Mexico uninviting, and they did little to improve it. While they should have been working at living on the land as it was, the settlers spent their time in looking for wealth that was nowhere to be found. Even Oñate had brought along mining equipment in case he found gold or silver; and indeed, some Spaniards evidently expected to find silver lying visible on top of the earth, where it could simply be picked up. Once it was clear that there were no riches to be found in this inhospitable land, the colonists quickly became disillusioned and had to be disciplined by the governor. This was not, however, a story unique to Spanish America. Events occurred in much the same way at Jamestown, Virginia,

Site of San Gabriel near Española. Base reads: "Oñate's Capital, 1598, First in U.S."

nine years later, when the first settlers of that English colony spent their time in digging for gold. It took the firm hand of Captain John Smith to save that colony, just as over a decade earlier and two thousand miles to the west, Oñate had acted to save the colony of New Mexico with his own strict and unpopular rules.

In addition to the unrest of discontented colonists, trouble with the Pueblo Indians threatened Oñate's venture. Although the San Juan people remained friendly and helpful, the Acoma people were anything but accommodating. They lived in their "sky village" atop sheer walls several hundred feet above the plain, and since the pueblo could be reached only by toeholds dug into the walls, the Indians felt that they were safe and secure even from the Spaniards. They found an opportunity to test their strength against the Spaniards when, in early December 1598, Juan de Zaldívar, Oñate's nephew, arrived at Acoma with a party of soldiers. En route to join Oñate, who was traveling westward in search of the Pacific Ocean—thought to be near New Mexico—Zaldívar and his soldiers succumbed to the Indians' promise of supplies and climbed the walls to the village. Once Zaldívar and his men were inside Acoma, the Indians fell upon and slew most of them. Some Spaniards died while trying to jump to the plain below, although three survived by landing in the wind-swept sand at the base of the walls.

When Oñate received the news, he wept at the loss of his nephew and his men, and then his sorrow turned to outrage and a determination to act. He knew that if he did not subdue Acoma by force, people at other pueblos would sense Spanish weakness, a sign that would end any hope for the colony's survival. Thus, on 12 January 1599, Oñate dispatched a punitive force of seventy men under the command of Vicente de Zaldívar, Juan's brother.

Arriving at Acoma on 21 January 1599, Vicente ordered the people to surrender immediately, but the Indians, secure in their sky village, refused. The main force attacked the next day, drawing the defenders' attention while Zaldívar led eleven soldiers up the rock behind Acoma and gained a foothold in the village. Now pressed on two sides and faced with a small cannon that the Spaniards employed with skill, the Acoma people fought desperately in an uneven struggle. When the battle was over, much of Acoma smoldered in ashes, and between six hundred and eight hundred Indians lay dead. The survivors stood trial before Oñate, charged with the December massacre and with armed opposition to the new masters of New Mexico. Their fate was a harsh one. Men and women alike were sentenced to twenty years of work under Spanish supervision—a polite way of sentencing them to slavery—and all males over the age of twenty-five also had one foot cut off. Sixty young girls were sent to Mexico City to live out their lives in convents, while young people under the age of twelve were placed in the care of Catholic priests. Oñate had

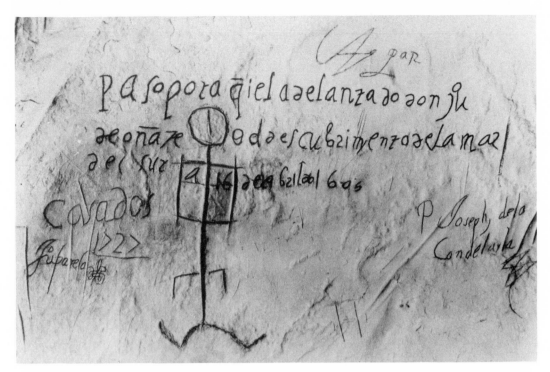

Oñate's carving at Inscription Rock near Grants

made his point—opposition to Spanish rule would bring swift retribution.

Still, nagging difficulties continued to plague the colony of New Mexico. In addition to the disappointment over finding no riches, food became a problem because even though the settlers did some farming, they never produced enough to feed themselves. Indeed, shortages of all kinds plagued the Spaniards, and although Oñate requested and received reinforcements from New Spain, the new soldiers, friars, and supplies did not arrive at San Gabriel until December 1600. Only then did Oñate feel that the colony was strong enough to permit him to undertake further explorations, which was one of his duties as governor and captain general of New Mexico.

In 1601 Oñate and eighty men explored the land to the east of San Gabriel. Guided by an Indian named Jusepe, who had accompanied Francisco Leyva de Bonilla to the plains and lived to report his fate to Oñate, the third expedition to Quivira, like its predecessors, failed to find the wealth promised in the legends. And when Oñate returned to San Gabriel, he found the settlement nearly deserted. The colonists, tired of the hard life and the governor's strict rule, had packed up and made their escape down the Rio Grande. The fate of Spanish New Mexico hung by a thread.

Yet Oñate did not give up, undertaking in 1604 further explorations to the west, where he hoped to find the Pacific Ocean and perhaps the "Northwest Passage" as well. Instead, he found

Early Spanish Settlement　　　43

the Colorado River, which he followed to the Gulf of California. Meanwhile, the reports of the refugees from New Mexico who had returned to New Spain raised doubts in official circles about the colony's success. The debate over the fate of the colony and its governor raged until Oñate was finally forced to admit defeat. After all, his service in New Mexico had not fulfilled his dreams of becoming either rich or famous. Greatly disappointed and much poorer than at the start of the venture, Oñate left office under suspension from the king, officially resigning his dual posts as governor and captain general of New Mexico on 24 August 1607.

Nine years had passed since the founding of the colony, and Spanish officials now looked with dismay at the state of affairs in New Mexico. For a brief time the king considered giving up on New Mexico once and for all, but then word came that the Franciscan friars could already count eight thousand Indian converts to Christianity; and to abandon these new converts was out of the question. Thus, on 1 November 1609, the king made New Mexico a royal colony under the direct control of the crown. Now the government would pay the colony's expenses and conduct its future as a field for missionary work.

Assuming the office as New Mexico's first royal governor was Pedro de Peralta, who traveled in 1610 to San Gabriel, which served as a reminder that Oñate had planted a Spanish colony in New Mexico. Shortly after his arrival, Peralta moved the citizens of San Gabriel to the site where the Spaniards would build a new capital—Santa Fe, meaning "Holy Faith." Santa Fe's location had the advantage of being at the center of many of New Mexico's pueblos, although it was far enough removed from them to avoid conflict over land use. Also, the new capital was located along a stream, soon called the Santa Fe River, which brought water from the Sangre de Cristo Mountains. Furthermore, the seven-thousand-foot-high site offered clear and cool air, with the Sangre de Cristos as a backdrop and a wide-open view to the west that stretched unbroken to the Jemez Mountains. Once it had been built, Santa Fe would remain on its original site and would long be the center of the non-Indian population in New Mexico. Now more than 375 years old, Santa Fe is the oldest capital city in the United States.

The advent of Governor Peralta began the great missionary period in New Mexico history. From 1610 to 1680 New Mexico's story was a narrative of Spanish efforts to Christianize the Indians and, in a larger sense, to remake Indian culture in the Spanish image. Ethnocentric in their world view, the Spaniards expected the Pueblo peoples to live under Spanish law, to work like Spaniards, to dress in the Spanish manner, and to adopt the Spanish faith. This meant that Indian males were required to wear shirts and pants; women, to wear skirts and to clothe their upper bodies;

New Mexico, 1598–1680

Taos
San Gabriel .San Juan
Rio Arriba
Santa Fe (1610)
Rio Abajo
Zuni
Acoma
Socorro

Oñate's Route

Rio Grande

Pecos River

NEW SPAIN

Santa Barbara

0   100   200 Miles

Present New Mexico state boundaries

and Indian couples, to engage in monogamous marriages sanctified in formal church ceremonies. In adopting these attitudes, the Spaniards disregarded the fact that the Pueblos already possessed a culture and religion as important to them as Spanish culture and the Catholic faith were to the Spaniards. The Spaniards' neglect of Pueblo culture created Indian resentment that would eventually imperil the colony of New Mexico.

The Indians' main contact with Spanish culture came through the mission, a community of Indians under the authority of a priest whom they were to obey both in religious and worldly matters. Because the Pueblo Indians already lived in towns, the missions were established at the pueblos. In beginning his work, a mission priest first preached the Catholic faith and baptized those children who were brought to him. He then viewed these children and other members of their families as the core of the mission's congregation. Once he possessed a following, the priest supervised the building of a church, which included his own living quarters.

Since each pueblo was already a compact structure with no room in the center of the town for a large building, the church and the priest's quarters at most pueblos were separated from the village by a wall. This made the New Mexico mission community different from most others in North America, where the church was located at the very center of the community. But while New Mexico's mission priests remained physically apart from their

Early Spanish Settlement   45

The mission interior at Isleta Pueblo (c. 1950)

congregation, the imposing size of the churches, as well as the presence of Spanish soldiers at the missions, allowed the priests to dominate most pueblos.

The first duty of the Franciscan priests—for New Mexico was one of the Franciscan missionary fields—was to teach religion. After gaining a few converts, the priest found Indians who could learn enough Spanish to memorize parts of the catechism and teach it to others. In turn, the catechist helped the priest to translate the catechism into the Indian tongue. But the priests' efforts to bridge the language barrier usually ended here, for most Franciscans made little real effort to learn any more of the Indian languages than they needed for their work. After establishing a religious routine for the pueblo that included regular prayer services, Sunday masses, and religious plays, the mission priest intruded into the pueblo's daily life by appointing Indians to care for the church buildings, to make sure other Indians came to mass, to look after the horses and livestock, and to weave, cook, garden, and generally serve the Spaniards.

Although the Pueblo Indians had always been accustomed to hard work, some of the jobs assigned by the priests must have seemed oppressive. Church construction, for example, required many Spanish-style bricks—molded and quite large, measuring ten inches wide, eighteen inches long, and five inches thick and weighing between fifty and sixty pounds. With these adobes the Indians built high walls and then topped these walls with vigas, a roof of adobes, and a bell tower. By the time they had completed their work, the Indians had often spent years in building the mission churches. Still other tasks required by the priests seemed not only hard but also degrading and contrary to Pueblo culture. Among other things, the priests told the Pueblo males to build walls, which was culturally a female task; males who obeyed were ridiculed while those who disobeyed were punished.

Punishment at the New Mexico missions tended to be quite harsh—much harsher than at most Spanish missions located elsewhere in North America. Generally, the Spaniards—either priests or soldiers—carried out assessed punishments such as whipping those who broke the rules. The particularly odious practice of shaving the heads of male Indian transgressors was ordered stopped by the viceroy in 1620. For the Pueblos, loss of hair meant loss of self-respect, and until this practice came to an end, some victims of this punishment ran away from their homes.

Over the long haul, however, the priests reserved their harshest punishment for Pueblo religious leaders, who fully intended to continue the practice of their own religion even while outwardly accepting much of the Catholic religion and rituals. Indeed, Pueblo religion was part of everything the Pueblo Indians were and did; and had the Franciscans permitted the Pueblos to practice their religion, New Mexico's history might have turned out differently. Instead, the Franciscans attempted to extinguish native beliefs by outlawing all Pueblo religious rites, singing, dancing, and even symbols such as prayer sticks and kachina masks. In regarding the native rites as devil worship, the priests attacked the very

Acoma Mission, built with Indian labor

A Pueblo Rain Dance with Clowns, 1899

heart of Pueblo religion, destroying or desecrating the native kivas. Yet in desperately trying to wipe out the Pueblo religion, they succeeded only in driving it into hiding.

The attacks on the Pueblo religion may have been harsh and heavy-handed, but the Franciscans acted in the name of both Christianity and Spanish culture. Between 1610 and 1680—the so-called great missionary period of Spanish colonial New Mexico—a total of about 250 Franciscans served in New Mexico. They began their work in the northern Rio Grande pueblos and eventually extended their mission field southward along the river, eastward to the Humanas beyond the Manzano Mountains, and westward to include the Zuni and Hopi. Managing the work of this large missionary field was the responsibility of an official, the *custodio,* whose office was at Santo Domingo and who supervised, in effect, church government in New Mexico.

During this same period the royal governor, who lived in Santa Fe, managed the civil government of the colony. Appointed by either the king or viceroy, the governor directed the government of Spanish citizens outside the missions and assumed responsibility for the defense of New Mexico. Because of Santa Fe's remoteness from Mexico City, a strong governor could become quite powerful. Assisting the governor was a secretary and, after 1660, a lieutenant governor responsible for the region south of Santa Fe. At the local level *alcaldes mayores* enforced the laws, handled problems between Indians and colonists, and acted as local judges by hearing and settling the cases brought before them.

In Santa Fe the people elected four members to the *cabildo,* or town council, which advised the governor on matters of public concern. Also under authority from the crown, each pueblo was ordered to elect a governor and other officials to manage some of their local affairs and to speak for the pueblos in dealing with the Spanish governor. Once selected, each pueblo governor received a symbol of office from Spanish officials, namely, a cane topped by metal in which was carved the Spanish cross. Through the years the governors received two more symbolic canes—a Mexican cane with a silver top and a United States cane with a silver top engraved with the name "A. Lincoln." Today most governors have only two of the three canes—the Spanish and the Lincoln. The Mexican canes were apparently either given to lieutenant governors or were simply lost.

The Spaniards, then, established two types of government in New Mexico—civil government, which was concerned with governing Spanish settlers, and religious government, which managed church affairs. Inevitably, the two jurisdictions clashed, most dramatically over the issue concerning who should have ultimate control of Indian affairs. Although the Franciscans exercised extensive day-to-day authority in the pueblo, the Indians were still subject to Spanish law as part of the *encomienda* system. Under this system Spanish soldiers received *encomiendas,* which empowered them to collect tribute from the Indians in return for military service and in lieu of pay from the king. Eventually, this tribute amounted to an annual levy of one bushel of corn and one other item such as a blanket. During good years the Indians had little problem in paying this tax, but in hard times it became a hardship. Hardest hit were the Indians along the Rio Grande, who were required to pay annual tribute after they had lived for ten years under Spanish rule. Affected least were the Indians on the frontier to the west—the Zuni and Hopi—who were exempt.

In addition to the *encomienda* system, the Spaniards also required Indians to work on the land of their Spanish overseer. Strictly speaking, the Spaniards were to pay for this labor and the work was to last only a limited time. In practice, however, many Spaniards paid little or nothing to the Indians, demanded too much time, or wanted the work done when the Indians needed to be working on their own land. On the whole, the Franciscans accepted the *encomienda* and Indian labor systems, but they became angry when these demands abused their congregations. They also resented attempts by the governor to influence internal pueblo affairs, including the elections for pueblo governor. The Franciscans desired total control of the pueblos, and they viewed such actions by civil officers as direct interference with their mission. As a result of this ongoing power struggle, both sides ignored a 1620 viceregal order banning any outside interference in pueblo elections.

Open conflict between church and state officials was apparent even during the tenure of New Mexico's first royal governor, Pedro de Peralta. In May 1613 Fray Isidro Ordoñez prevented Peralta's soldiers from collecting tribute from Taos Pueblo; when the governor insisted that the levy be collected, Fray Isidro excommunicated Peralta. The priest also ordered that Peralta no longer use levied Indian labor in building the Palace of the Governors in Santa Fe. Outraged, the governor fired a pistol at Fray Isidro when they met during the summer, and in turn, Isidro's agents captured and imprisoned Peralta while he was visiting Isleta. With the arrival of a new governor in 1614, Peralta journeyed southward only to have the documents bolstering his position stolen by the friar's supporters. Later that same year the viceroy relieved Fray Isidro and ordered him to Mexico City to face the inquisition.

From these inauspicious beginnings the conflict between governors and churchmen escalated. For example, during the tenure of Governor Luís de Rosas (1637–41), the quarrel became quite heated. The friars accused the governor of, among other things, forcing both Christian and non-Christian Indians to slave long hours at weaving cloth in a Santa Fe sweatshop; of demanding that the Pecos Indians trade on his behalf with the Apache for buffalo hides and meat; and of allowing cooperative Indians to practice some of their native religious rites in exchange for goods for the governor's private trade.

To the friars, Rosas seemed to be single-mindedly undercutting the authority of the New Mexico clerics in handling Indian affairs. When he was once lectured on the subject by a priest during mass, Rosas responded, "Shut up, Father, what you say is a lie." As the situation worsened, charges spawned countercharges, and the Spaniards of New Mexico were forced to take sides. In January 1640 the governor expelled all churchmen from Santa Fe, and when two priests returned to the capital in April, Rosas attacked them with a stick, leaving them both badly bloodied. When he was finally relieved as governor in 1641, Rosas had been excommunicated; a few months later, he was murdered. In the end such conflicts between governors and clergy only served to weaken Spanish authority in the eyes of the Pueblos. Could a priest called a liar be respected? Should an excommunicated governor be obeyed? Was not such disunity a sign of weakness?

But the Pueblos had little time to dwell on such questions. In addition to the burdens of labor, tribute, and religious intolerance that came with Spanish rule, the Pueblos regularly faced life-threatening problems. Spanish priests and settlers brought to New Mexico diseases for which the Indians lacked any immunity. As a result, smallpox, measles, and whooping cough took a terrible toll. In 1640 alone, about three thousand Pueblo Indians died from smallpox, representing more than 10 percent of the total

The walls of two missions at Gran Quivira, a Humanas Pueblo
(Salinas National Monument)

Pueblo population. Compounding the disease was a change in climate, for after 1650 New Mexico became much drier, with conditions worsening as the years passed. From 1667 to 1672 an extended period of drought made crop failures and starvation commonplace. Yet under the watchful eyes of the Franciscans, the Pueblos could not perform their rain dances, rites which were basic to their religion. At Humanas Pueblo 450 Indians died of starvation, and the pueblo had to be abandoned. Increased attacks by nomadic groups such as the Apache made life more dangerous, and the Spaniards were unable to protect the pueblos.

Even faced with all these hardships, the Pueblo Indians at first made little effort to regain control of their lives, for to act effectively they would need to unite. And unity of purpose would prove difficult to achieve because of the independence of one pueblo from another. What finally provided the catalyst for united action was a renewed crackdown on Pueblo religion by the Spaniards in the 1670s. Ironically, an easing of tension between the civil and religious authorities during that decade paved the way for a joint effort to destroy the native religion once and for all.

In 1675 the governor, at the request of the priests, arrested forty-seven Pueblo medicine men whom the Spaniards regarded as little more than devil worshippers and sorcerers. Spanish soldiers brought the captives to Santa Fe and dealt with them harshly, hanging three, with one hanging himself, and whipping and jailing the remainder. In response Tewa Indians from the pueblos along the Rio Grande came to Santa Fe and confronted the governor in demanding the release of the religious leaders. Faced with po-

La Bajada, dividing the Rio Arriba and the Rio Abajo

tentially disastrous consequences, the governor released the prisoners, including a San Juan Indian named Popé.

In addition to winning the release of the jailed medicine men, the confrontation at Santa Fe provided a valuable lesson to the Pueblo Indians. United they could likely defeat the Spaniards. Yet in addition to overcoming traditional pueblo independence, united action would take careful planning and require the utmost secrecy. Popé, who moved to Taos after being freed, joined other leaders in planning a Pueblo war against the Spaniards.

The Pueblo leaders chose 11 August 1680 as the date for a general uprising against the Spaniards. To let each village know the date, runners carried knotted yucca cords among the pueblos. Each day one of the knots was untied, and the number of knots left told how many days remained until the Pueblo revolt would begin. Since secrecy was vital, leaders of the planned revolt had to neutralize Indians with pro-Spanish sympathies. To this end, Popé even killed his own son-in-law when the young man's loyalty to the cause became questionable.

Pueblo people as far south as Isleta received the message, but so, too, did the Spaniards. Two young Tesuque runners, Nicholas Catua and Pedro Omtua, along with their knotted cords fell into Spanish hands on 9 August. Learning that the Spaniards had uncovered their plans, the Pueblos rose the next day, 10 August, and everywhere they struck the outcome was the same. At Tesuque thirty Spanish settlers lost their lives, while seventy Spanish settlers and priests died in the Taos Valley. Those who survived the attack in the north headed for the only safe haven available, the villa at Santa Fe. In the Rio Arriba area, the area "up the river" from Santa Fe, the Spaniards suffered the greatest losses. Those "down the river," in the Rio Abajo, an area below the lava cliff named La Bajada—meaning "the descent"—also suffered losses, but not in the same proportion. Here, too, the survivors sought a safe place, with more than one thousand Rio Abajo refugees gathering at Isleta Pueblo. Upon hearing that the people to the north had been slaughtered, the Spaniards at Isleta retreated south under Alonso García, the lieutenant governor of New Mexico.

In the meantime, Governor Antonio de Otermín centered the defense of the Rio Arriba at Santa Fe. By 16 August, just six days after the outbreak of the revolt, over 2,500 determined Indians surrounded the capital and threatened its water supply. Although sorties against the besiegers brought the Spaniards some consolation, Otermín received only discouraging news from the Rio Abajo, and his appeals for aid from there went unanswered. With no help in sight, Otermín determined that his position was hopeless, and on 22 August 1680 he surrendered Santa Fe. As the train of battered, frightened Spaniards departed the villa heading south, the Indians simply let them go. After all, the Pueblo peoples had accomplished their purpose—the Spaniards were leaving New Mexico.

As he traveled down the river, Otermín learned the fate of the Rio Abajo survivors and their retreat southward and sent orders for the García party to wait. Below Socorro the two groups of refugees joined forces and marched together to El Paso and out of present-day New Mexico. Otermín briefly placed García under arrest for too quickly vacating the Rio Abajo, but later he

Isleta Pueblo (c. 1890)

reversed himself, deciding that under the circumstances his lieutenant governor had indeed acted prudently.

The Pueblo Revolt took quite a toll. Almost 400 of the 2,900 Spaniards in New Mexico lost their lives, including 21 of the 33 mission priests in the province. Among the Spaniards who died, more than two-thirds had lived in the Rio Arriba. Had the Indians not allowed a peaceful Spanish withdrawal, the number of dead would have been much higher. In addition to the Spaniards themselves, the mission churches felt the full anger of the Indians, who destroyed almost all of these symbols of an alien faith.

Once in El Paso, Otermín and the colonists settled down to await orders to regain New Mexico. In 1681 the orders came, and the governor headed northward with 146 soldiers. The Spaniards found some abandoned pueblos and otherwise contented themselves with burning kivas and destroying whatever the Indians had left behind. Yet some show of armed resistance convinced Otermín that New Mexico was not ready for renewed Spanish occupation. Withdrawing southward, the Spaniards allowed friendly Isleta and Piro Indians to accompany them to El Paso, where they began new lives for themselves, never to return to New Mexico. One of the four settlements they built was named Isleta del Sur, meaning "Isleta of the South."

After two later expeditions in the 1680s also failed to reconquer New Mexico, it became clear that the return of the Spaniards to the upper Rio Grande would have to await another day. In the meantime, the abandoned province was already being transformed. With the Spaniards gone, the Pueblo peoples lost their need or desire for unity, and each pueblo soon resumed its cherished and time-honored independence. Furthermore, the Indians forever abandoned some pueblos, such as those in the Galisteo Valley hit hard by Apache raids; and some Pueblo peoples in the Rio Grande Valley relocated their villages on mesas for better defense against the possible return of the Spaniards.

For the Spaniards, the Pueblo Revolt represented a shocking defeat. Indeed, nowhere else in the Americas did the Indians succeed in driving out their European conquerors. The hopes of eighty-two years—beginning with Oñate at San Juan—in establishing a lasting colony on the Rio Grande seemed perhaps forever lost. And the efforts of the mission priests to save Indian souls for their faith seemed to be lost as well, for the great missionary period—albeit fraught with church–state controversy—had come to an end. But even though the Spaniards did not attempt an immediate return to New Mexico, forces were already at work which in a few short years would convince Spain that a reconquest of New Mexico was not only desirable but also necessary.

4
New Mexico under Spanish Rule, 1692–1821

As the end of the seventeenth century drew near, Spain was smarting from two unenviable distinctions, one deriving from its distinction as the only European nation ever routed from a New World colony by Indians and the other based on its initial failure to reconquer New Mexico. Indeed, the question that Spain needed to answer was whether a return of New Mexico and its people to Spanish rule was worth the cost in money, time, and possibly lives.

For a number of reasons, Spanish officials at last decided that the reconquest of New Mexico was imperative. First, they recognized the need for a buffer zone to provide an extra layer of protection to settlements in what is today northern Mexico; and New Mexico was ideally situated to fulfill that requirement. Second, they felt compelled to bring New Mexico's Pueblo peoples back into the folds of the Catholic church. Finally, they realized that they must act to reestablish national pride and, at the same time, protect Spain's claims to lands in North America against growing threats from other European countries, France especially. In fact, just two years after the Pueblo Revolt, the French explorer Rene Robert Cavelier, Sieur de la Salle, traveled down the Mississippi River to its mouth, thereby establishing for France a claim to the entire Mississippi River Valley. This French claim effectively divided Spanish Florida from other lands claimed by Spain in the present-day United States, lands that stretched from Texas to California and which, of course, included New Mexico.

Having opted for reconquest, Spanish officials assigned the actual task of reconquering New Mexico to Don Diego de Vargas, who was appointed governor and captain general of New Mexico in 1688. Arriving in El Paso in 1691, Vargas brought to his new office honor, courage, and practical experience, for as the head of one of Spain's leading families, he had fought with Spanish armies in Europe before moving to New Spain, where he held a series of political offices. He began his term as the governor of New Mexico by defeating the Indians who had been making life hazardous for El Paso's one thousand residents. He then turned to his primary goal as governor, the reconquest of New Mexico.

Vargas headed north from El Paso in August 1692, twelve years to the month after the Pueblo Revolt had sent the Spaniards fleeing from New Mexico. Taking with him sixty soldiers and one hundred Indian helpers, Vargas planned to retake the pueblo country by peaceful means, if possible. By intentionally firing no shots as the party approached each pueblo, the Spaniards would announce their presence and ask the Indians to return to Spanish rule and the Catholic church. Once the Indians had consented, the priests accompanying the party would forgive the sins of the Indians and baptize any children born since the Pueblo Revolt. Acquiescence by all the pueblos to the peaceful terms Vargas offered would make the reconquest a bloodless affair, but resistance by the pueblos would mean bloodshed. In bringing two cannons with him, Vargas was clearly prepared to fight.

As the Spaniards pushed up the Rio Grande, they found one abandoned pueblo after another, for the Pueblo peoples in the river valley had moved to more defensible positions in an effort to protect themselves against Indian raiding parties and the possible reappearance of the Spaniards. Traveling on to Santa Fe, the Spaniards arrived there on 12 September, only to find the town occupied by a group of Pueblo people who refused at first to believe that the Spaniards were who they claimed to be. Even after the town's occupants were convinced that it was indeed the Spaniards returning to New Mexico, rather than Apache or Pecos Indians trying to trick their way inside, the Indians shouted their resolution to fight. At dawn Vargas again rode forward, offering peace, a full pardon, and a return to the Catholic faith; but the Indians still showed no inclination to give up. It was only after the Spaniards trained their cannons on the town and lined up to attack that the Indians peacefully surrendered. By nightfall the Spaniards had completed the reconquest of New Mexico's capital.

The next morning Vargas and the priests entered Santa Fe and three times raised the royal banner, the same banner that Oñate had brought into New Mexico in 1598 and that Otermín had carried out in 1680. Each time the Spaniards raised the banner, the Indians repeated after Vargas, "Long live the King." After repledging their loyalty to the Spanish crown, the Indians received absolution for their sins.

In the days that followed, the Spaniards were encouraged by what they believed were signs that the Indians had accepted the reestablishment of Spanish rule. Some of the governors from nearby pueblos arrived in Santa Fe to pledge their loyalty, and in late September Vargas and his soldiers visited all the northern

El Señor D. Diego de Barpas Zapata Lujan, Ponze de León, Marques de la Naba de Barcinas, del Orden de S. tiago, Governador, Conquistador, Pacificador, y Capitan General de el Nuebo Mejico, perdió la Vida en Canpaña Rasa por libertar los Vasallos anuados en el Sitio de Bernalillo año de MDCCIV.

Este cuadro, que el Instituto de Cultura Hispánica ofrece al Museo de Nuebo Mejico, es copia del verdadero retrato de D. Diego Barpas Zapata, de la Casa delos Vargas, cuyo original se conserva en la capilla de Don Isidro sita en el Pueti de Santisteban de Madrid.

Don Diego de Vargas

pueblos, making peace with each in turn. Although the Spaniards encountered token resistance, they completed the reconquest of the Rio Grande Valley by October. Pleased by this apparent success, Vargas sent the main party south to El Paso near the end of October, including in the entourage that traveled down the Rio Grande the cannons, the carts, some of the soldiers, and the Spaniards whom Vargas had freed from the captivity that had begun with the Pueblo Revolt.

Once the main party was gone, Vargas and some of his soldiers headed to the western pueblos, whose people were rumored to be preparing to oppose the Spaniards. The rumors, however, amounted to little, for while the western pueblos more actively resisted the Spaniards' return than the pueblos along the Rio Grande, no major fighting broke out. In displaying great personal courage, Vargas walked among and talked to the Pueblo peoples of western New Mexico and persuaded them to agree to the renewed Spanish presence.

When he had finished his visit to the western pueblos, Vargas headed toward El Paso, only to be delayed by a confrontation with an unfriendly Apache band. In the fighting that ensued, the Spaniards captured and killed two Apaches, one of whom died after first converting to Christianity. Ironically, these two were the only Indian casualties of Vargas's initial effort to reconquer New Mexico. True to his original intent, Vargas regained the allegiance of twenty-three pueblos without firing a shot and without burning a single kiva or storehouse. Vargas also managed to lead his soldiers through their four-month adventure without experiencing the killing of a single soldier. Once he was securely back in El Paso and confident that the reconquest had succeeded, Vargas now planned the resettlement of New Mexico.

Almost ten months after his return to El Paso, on 4 October 1693, Vargas left El Paso with a party that included one hundred soldiers, seventy families, eighteen friars, and a number of friendly Indians. Also in his company were the livestock that the colony would need, including some two thousand horses, one thousand mules, and nine hundred head of cattle. A total of eighteen carts carried the heavy supplies, and this time there were three cannons instead of two. Impressive in appearance, the party was nonetheless something of a disappointment to Vargas, for he believed that he needed at least one hundred soldiers and five hundred settlers to set up an effective presidio (fort) at Santa Fe. Among the more unique personalities accompanying Vargas was a Frenchman, Jean L'Archevêque, who had followed La Salle into Texas and had subsequently helped assassinate the great French explorer. Found in Texas by the Spaniards in 1689 and transported to New Spain for questioning, L'Archevêque remained there rather than face French justice, and in 1693 he joined the reconquest.

As the settlers proceeded northward, Vargas and an advance

party rode on ahead to determine the current mood of the Indians. Vargas soon learned that most of the pueblos in the nearly year-long absence of the Spaniards had become openly defiant of Spanish rule. Returning to the main party with this sobering bit of information, Vargas found more bad news awaiting him. Thirty women and children had died on their trek across the area south of Socorro, a path that the Spaniards named Jornada del Muerto, meaning the "Journey of the Dead Man" or, more simply, the "Journey of Death." Almost ninety miles long, the Jornada, as it is still called, runs from present-day Rincon to present-day San Marcial and is flanked by the San Andres Mountains on the east and the Caballo and Fray Cristobal ranges on the west. The main geographical feature of the Jornada is today, as it was three hundred years ago, its total lack of water. After gathering together the surviving members of the party, Vargas pushed on to Santa Fe, where they arrived on 16 December. Once again the town was occupied by Indians, and once again Vargas entered the capital and officially claimed it for Spain. With the completion of these formalities, the Spaniards camped outside Santa Fe and waited for the Indians to leave.

This time, however, the Indians refused to withdraw, and the Spaniards settled into a cold, snowy camp outside town. During the two hard weeks that followed, twenty-one colonists died. At the same time, the Indians inside Santa Fe prepared to

The Palace of the Governors, reoccupied by Vargas, housed Spanish, Mexican, and U.S. territorial governors

New Mexico under Spanish Rule

Black Mesa near San Ildefonso

defend it; and on 28 December they finally dared the Spaniards to attack. Two days later, the Spaniards accepted the challenge and captured the town in what was typically a one-sided battle, made so by the superiority of Spanish weapons. For their resistance, the Indians paid a heavy price. Besides the eighty-one who died by Spanish arms, seventy were executed under orders from Vargas, and four hundred were taken captive. Although the Spaniards held the capital city, the land and the people beyond its walls remained effectively outside Spanish control.

In the years that followed, the Spaniards found that bringing New Mexico back under their control would be a difficult task. For nine months in 1694 a group of Pueblo people who defied Spanish authority periodically launched raids against Santa Fe from their headquarters on the Black Mesa near San Ildefonso until, at last defeated, most of them repledged their loyalty. Also in 1694 the Jemez people killed their mission priest and then, with help from Zuni and Acoma, actively fought the Spaniards. Once again the Spaniards prevailed, but only because of the aid they received from Zia, Santa Ana, and San Felipe pueblos. Driven from their homes into the mountains, many Jemez people went to live among the Hopi or Navajo, who had sheltered many Pueblo Indians who had moved to Navajo country after the Pueblo Revolt. It was probably during this period of relocation that the Navajo, whose women are the most skilled weavers in the Southwest today, began to practice their art of weaving, mostly likely learning it from the Pueblo peoples who came to live among them.

But even the quelling of the two revolts in 1694 did not end the Spaniards' troubles, for one last uprising occurred in 1696, when Indians from several pueblos openly resisted their conquerors. This fracas claimed the lives of six mission priests—two at San Ildefonso—and twenty-one other Spaniards before the Spaniards and their Pueblo allies again prevailed. After 1696 the inhabitants of the Rio Grande pueblos would never again take up arms against the Spaniards.

The Spaniards' victory over the pueblos was a costly one, for it fundamentally disrupted life along the Rio Grande. For the next twenty years the basic question of loyalty to the Spaniards divided the Pueblo peoples. With most of the pueblos experiencing the strife brought on by the reconquest, people living in the same pueblo were often suspicious of one another, and the people of one pueblo did not trust the peoples of other pueblos.

The reconquest also affected the lives of the Pueblo peoples in less subtle ways. Perhaps most of the four hundred Indians taken captive by Vargas at Santa Fe were given as slaves to Spanish settlers, and several thousand Pueblo Indians abandoned the Rio

Jemez Pueblo (c. 1905)

Navajo weaving, learned from Pueblo apostates

Grande Valley during the 1700s rather than live under Spanish rule. Designated apostates by the Spaniards, these Pueblo refugees continued to pose a threat to the Spanish control of New Mexico, largely because of their influence on the people they joined, the Hopi in particular. In 1716 the Spaniards moved some of the apostates back to the Rio Grande, but fifty years would pass before other apostates returned to their homeland. The Hopi, however, were never reconquered by the Spaniards.

Eventually, most of the Pueblo peoples readjusted to Spanish rule and all that it entailed. After resurrecting their missionary work among the Indians, the Spaniards sent additional priests to New Mexico, and by 1740 forty mission priests were living and working among the Pueblo peoples. In addition to supervising the building of new churches and conducting church services, the mission priests tried to restore Pueblo life—insofar as they could—to what it had been during the great missionary period. Still, the priests clearly learned some lessons from the Pueblo Revolt, for they made no further raids on the kivas and no longer attempted to destroy the objects of Pueblo religion. Nor did they punish as harshly those Indians who refused to attend Catholic services or who failed to carry out work that was contrary to Pueblo customs. The Pueblos outwardly embraced Christianity, although they continued to practice their own religious rites while taking care to conceal this fact from the Spaniards.

Despite the new mood of peaceful coexistence between the Indians and their conquerors, life was as hard for the Pueblo peoples during the 1700s as it had been during the 1600s. At the end of the 1700s the Pueblo population was only half of what it had been a hundred years before and only one-fourth of what it had been when the Spaniards first arrived in New Mexico; and by the end of the century the number of pueblos had also drastically declined. Of the more than sixty pueblos located in the drainage area of the Rio Grande during the middle of the 1500s, only nineteen survived, and only four—Isleta, Acoma, Taos, and Picuris—stood on the same spots that they had occupied some two hundred years earlier. The pueblos had also undergone a shift in population, with some of the Pueblo peoples, such as those at Humanas, abandoning their homelands altogether, while one group from Santo Domingo built the new pueblo of Laguna near Acoma in 1699.

Not all of the pueblos experienced these changes to the same degree, but even those pueblos least affected were smaller by the end of the 1700s than they had been during the 1500s. The two main reasons for the decline in Pueblo population were apparent even before 1680. The first was disease, especially the outbreaks of smallpox that hit New Mexico on an average of once every ten years. The second was the devastation of the pueblos by groups

Laguna, the last pueblo founded

of Indian raiders who exacted a toll in both Pueblo lives and property. Contributing in a lesser degree to the decline in Pueblo population were the movements of the apostates to areas outside Spanish control.

The story of the Spaniards in New Mexico after the reconquest was, on the other hand, quite different. From the time of the Spaniards' return under Vargas in 1693 to the end of Spanish rule in 1821, both the number of Spanish settlements and the Spanish population grew. In April 1695 the forty-four families from Santa Fe whom Vargas led into the Española Valley established the villa of Santa Cruz de la Cañada, thereafter commonly called La Cañada. Eleven years later, in 1706, thirty-five other Spanish families established yet another villa, choosing as its site land south of Santa Fe on the banks of the Rio Grande. Erected on land made attractive by a steady water supply, good soil, grasslands, and timber, the Villa de Albuquerque became—with Santa Fe, El Paso, and La Cañada—one of Spanish New Mexico's official villas. Founded under specific grants from the government, these four villas were in fact the only ones authorized while New Mexico was a Spanish colony. With New Mexico's Spanish population centered in the villas during the 1700s, the number of settlers both in and around the villas steadily increased. From the base of 100 soldiers and 70 families that had accompanied Vargas in 1693, New Mexico—not including El Paso—had grown by 1752 to a total of 3,402 settlers. After growing steadily over the next twenty-five years, the number of settlers then more than doubled between 1776 and 1789. The 1790s witnessed such additional growth that the number of Spanish settlers in New Mexico totaled more than 10,000 by the end of the decade. By 1800 New Mexico had become one of New Spain's most populous outer provinces, and in 1817 there were more people living in New Mexico than in all of what is today California, Baja California, Arizona, and Texas.

The population growth of the buffer province of New Mexico must have heartened officials in New Spain, for it occurred at a time of increasing external pressure on the Spanish empire. However, New Mexico was too far from the Mississippi Valley to counter the growing French presence there, a reality that forced Spanish officials to build a defensive perimeter of missions and forts in eastern Texas. In 1718, the year France founded New Orleans at the mouth of the Mississippi, the Spaniards established San Antonio in Texas as a rest stop on the supply route to the outposts facing the French, and by 1740 San Antonio was the most important settlement in this new buffer colony. However, distant New Mexico still held a key position in the defense of New Spain. Besides providing some protection for the mining areas of present-day northern Mexico, New Mexico now had the added responsibility of blunting all foreign penetration across the Great Plains.

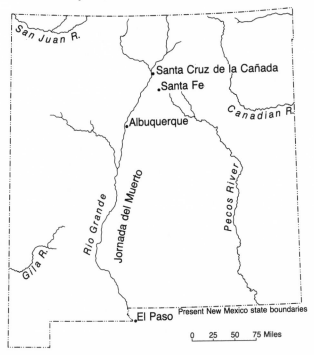

Spanish Villas in the 1700s

San Juan R.

Santa Cruz de la Cañada

.Santa Fe

.Albuquerque

Canadian R.

Rio Grande

Jornada del Muerto

Pecos River

Gila R.

.El Paso

Present New Mexico state boundaries

0   25   50   75 Miles

In the short run, this new responsibility proved the more difficult to carry out, for Spanish officials had a hard time keeping outsiders, especially French traders, from entering their territory. After trading with many of the Indians who lived in the interior of North America, French traders eventually began to trade with the Plains Indians, some of whom moved along the outer border of New Mexico. Such trade threatened New Mexico directly, for, as Spanish officials reasoned, French traders might soon take the additional step of trying to trade with the people who lived inside New Mexico's borders.

In response to the growing French threat, Spanish officials warned New Mexico's governor to look out for any French activity on the outer borders of Spanish territory. They also reminded the governor of Spain's long-standing colonial trade policy, which forbade colonists from trading with foreigners, a policy that applied as much to trade-hungry settlers along the Rio Grande as to anyone else. The heightened awareness of the French menace led New Mexico's governor to send out a small armed force to discover if the French were trading with the Pawnee Indians, a tribe so strong that it dominated the central plains area. If French traders had indeed made contact with the Pawnee, it would mean that French activity had spread considerably west of the Mississippi and posed a potential threat to New Mexico.

The governor gave command of the reconnaissance force to Pedro de Villasur, a young lieutenant from the Santa Fe presidio.

New Mexico under Spanish Rule

Leading forty-two Spanish soldiers, some Pueblo militia, and a few nonsoldiers, Villasur left Santa Fe and headed for the Platte River in present-day Nebraska. Jean L'Archevêque, the selfsame Frenchman who had been with La Salle in Texas and with Vargas during the reconquest, accompanied Villasur to act as translator in the event that French traders were found there. When the New Mexicans reached the Platte, they encountered Pawnees armed with French weapons as well as with their own bows and arrows. The Pawnees fell upon Villasur's party, and when the fighting ended, more than thirty New Mexicans, including Villasur and L'Archevêque, lay dead. The survivors, some of them wounded, could only return to Santa Fe with news of their disastrous defeat.

The Villasur expedition confirmed that the French were trading with the Pawnee, and before long the French extended their trade to the nomadic Indians who lived on the plains of eastern New Mexico. Then, in 1739, the first French traders arrived in Santa Fe, where they discovered a people so starved for goods from outside the Spanish empire that they eagerly bought the traders' wares. Having witnessed the violations of Spanish trade law firsthand and being powerless to stop them, New Mexico's governor wrote to the viceroy of New Spain, asking not for help in enforcing the law, but rather for a relaxation of the law so that trade could legally flow between the Spaniards in New Mexico and the French in the Mississippi River Valley. In a brief reply to the governor's request, the viceroy restated the ban on trade with foreigners; but he, too, was powerless to forestall what quickly became a regular stream of French traders into New Mexico. While knowing that they could be arrested, French traders came anyway because their trade with New Mexicans was extremely profitable.

The inability of Spanish officials to stop the illegal trade stemmed in large part from the fact that there were never enough soldiers in New Mexico to patrol its borders. This lack of adequate troop strength also contributed to another problem experienced by Spanish colonial New Mexico, the continuous raiding of Spanish and Pueblo settlements by the nomadic Indians. Those who first jeopardized these settlements were the Apache and the Navajo, both of whom were probably in New Mexico when the Spaniards began to explore the area. However, the Spaniards had not begun to take notice of these Indian groups until twenty-five years after the establishment of Spain's first New Mexican settlement.

By the 1620s the settlers had begun to record the fact that there were Indians in New Mexico who did not live in villages and who spoke languages and practiced ways of living that differed from those of the Pueblo peoples. While initially failing to differentiate among the nomadic Indians and referring to all of them as "Apache," the Spaniards eventually recorded a special name for each separate Apache band, even at first calling the Navajo an

Latter day Apache warriors, 1873

Apachean band. The Apache and Navajo became a genuine threat to life along the Rio Grande when they acquired horses, which were introduced into New Mexico by the Spaniards. Once mounted, these Indians, as well as such latecomers as the Comanche, posed a constant danger to the settled areas.

From the beginning the Spaniards in New Mexico hoped to bring all of the Indians in the area under peaceful control, and so they tried to group the nomadic Indians together and to Christianize them. Both efforts failed. So it was that the nomadic Indians in New Mexico during the 1600s lived outside Spanish control. The Navajo roamed the mountains and mesas on the west, while the ancestors of the Jicarilla Apache lived in the northeast; the forefathers of the Mescalero Apache lived in the southeast; and the ancestors of the Chiricahua Apache lived to the south and west.

In their raids on settlements during the 1600s, the Navajo and the Apache disrupted life both in New Spain's provinces in present-day northern Mexico and in New Spain's outer province of New Mexico. In the 1670s, for example, the ancestors of the Mescalero forced the inhabitants to abandon the pueblos east of the Manzano Mountains; and at the end of the 1600s, Indians whom the Spaniards simply called Apache had taken control of a large area of the west. By the early 1700s Spanish records stated that the Apache controlled the entire area from present-day northern Mexico all the way northward to Zuni.

Adding to New Mexico's woes following the reconquest was yet another group of nomadic Indians—the Comanche—who entered the area from the northern plains. After raiding the Jicarilla in 1706, the Comanche found the plains northeast of Taos and moved into the area. For a time thereafter, the Comanche camped in the San Luis Valley, at the headwaters of the Rio Grande, alongside the Ute Indians, a people who had traditionally lived in the mountains to the north. Together the Comanche and the Ute launched raids on the Jicarilla and at times on the Pueblo and Spanish settlements, with their joint ventures ending only when the Comanche took control of much of New Mexico's eastern plains during the 1730s and 1740s. While pressing hard upon the Apache in that region, the Comanche also kept up their raids upon the people of New Mexico for the next fifty years.

During the 1700s, then, the Comanche, Ute, Apache, and Navajo disrupted the lives of the people who lived in the Pueblo and Spanish settlements in the Rio Grande Valley. These nomadic Indians took horses, sheep, and other livestock as well as food and other goods, but even more terrifying than the ravaging of property were the attacks on the people themselves. In 1760, for example, the Comanche raided Taos and carried off fifty Spanish women and children, a few of whom were ransomed while others later turned up in St. Louis and New Orleans. In fact, so threatening did the Indian raids become to the people of New Mexico that the Pueblo and Spanish peoples joined forces, with the Indians actively serving in the Pueblo militias formed by the Spaniards. Faced with raiders who preferred hit-and-run tactics to remaining in one place to fight, the Spaniards and their Pueblo allies fought few formal battles, but concentrated instead on defending the settlements and giving occasional chase to raiding bands.

Yet despite having their lives turned upside down by these frequent raids, the Spaniards still found time to trade with the very people who raided their settlements. Once a year Spaniards traveled up the Rio Grande to a trade fair held in Taos, where they were joined by different Indian groups—Comanche, some Apache, and perhaps some Navajo—and by an occasional French trader. A Catholic church official who attended one of these fairs in 1760 described the trade in this way:

> They [the Indians] bring captives to sell, buckskins, many
> buffalo hides, and booty they have taken in other parts—
> horses, guns, muskets, ammunition, knives, meat, and
> various other things. No money circulates in these fairs,
> but articles are traded for each other and in this way
> those people provide themselves.

Nomadic Indian Groups in the 1700s

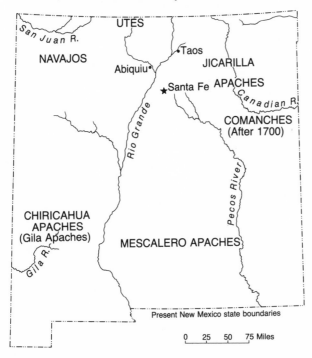

Some of the goods the Indians bought at Taos initially came from French traders by way of the Indians of the Great Plains and, in turn, through the Comanche, who, having traded with the Plains Indians, traveled to the Taos fair. By the 1770s a second fair—this one held in the fall at Abiquiu—had come into being primarily for trade with the Ute Indians. At the trade fairs in both Taos and Abiquiu, the Comanche, the Ute, and other Indians bartered for such goods as horses, knives, bridles, saddle blankets, clothing, and corn. Also actively traded, especially at Taos, were prisoners, usually non-Christian Plains Indians whom the Spaniards ransomed from the Comanche. The Spaniards considered it their duty to acquire the hostages for conversion to Christianity, and they considered it their privilege to use them as servants. Whatever the more compelling motive for their actions, the Spaniards inadvertently inspired the Comanche to seize even more hostages for trade.

The trade fairs brought moments of peace to the people of New Mexico, but the Indian raids almost immediately resumed, with the Indians reacquiring, in some instances, what they had just traded away. In the 1770s these raids became so devastating that they threatened the very survival of New Mexico as a Spanish colony, causing many settlers along the Rio Grande to leave their homes in the country and move into the villas and even into the pueblos. Both the Spanish and the Pueblo peoples lost lives as well as property, and they entertained no hope of better conditions

New Mexico under Spanish Rule

until 1776, when the Spanish king at last responded to the crisis in New Mexico. In setting up a new military region for northern New Spain during that year, the king appointed General Teodoro de Croix, an able military leader, to head the region. General Croix examined the situation and concluded that New Mexico had to be saved as a buffer zone if Indian raiders were to be stopped from controlling the northern border of present-day Mexico.

Chosen to save New Mexico was Juan Bautista de Anza, who had already demonstrated his worth to the Spanish government on more than one occasion. Having fought Indians in New Spain's northern province of Sonora, Anza opened the westward land route from Sonora to Upper California in the 1770s, witnessing the founding of San Francisco by some of his men in 1776. Then, in 1778, Anza made his way to Santa Fe to assume the office of governor of New Mexico. His instructions were to bring the Comanche under control, a task that could be accomplished only by defeating them in pitched battle on their home ground, on the plains that stretch across Colorado and eastern New Mexico. Making the task more difficult was the famous Comanche chief whom the Spaniards called Cuerno Verde, meaning "Green Horn," because the chief wore a distinctive headdress with a buffalo horn painted green. After he defeated the Comanche, Anza was supposed to convince them to join the Spaniards in a war against the Apache.

To fight Cuerno Verde and the Comanche, Anza gathered a six-hundred-member force of some regular soldiers, but mostly Spanish and Pueblo volunteers, and headed northward into Colorado in the late summer of 1779. Following a route different from that used by earlier groups going to fight the Comanche, Anza avoided the pass east of Taos, traveling instead up the western side of the Rocky Mountains. Hidden from the Comanche by the mountains, the New Mexican force once across the Rockies was able to surprise and defeat one Comanche group. Anza learned from his captives that Cuerno Verde was on his way back from a raid into New Mexico and would soon return to his camp west of the Arkansas River. Moving to the south, Anza's force arrived below the Arkansas in time to ambush the returning party. Surrounded and outnumbered by the Spaniards and their Pueblo allies, Cuerno Verde and his followers made their last stand by fighting from behind the bodies of the horses they had killed in desperation. The Comanche fought bravely but ultimately lost, and Cuerno Verde and several other Comanche chiefs died in the fighting.

While Anza's great victory brought no immediate peace with the Comanche, it nonetheless lessened the number of Comanche raids, which had troubled New Mexico for a half-century. In addition, Anza's victory laid the groundwork for a permanent

Juan Bautista de Anza

peace with the Comanche. After years of skilled and patient talks, Anza finally realized his goal when Spanish and Comanche leaders agreed to peace at Pecos Pueblo in February 1786. Thereafter, the Comanche left the people of New Mexico alone. The Spaniards and the Comanche now traded with one another regularly rather than only at yearly trade fairs, and in fulfillment of another of Anza's goals, the Comanche joined the Spaniards in their fight against the Apache.

Fortunately for Spanish America, its protracted Indian wars occurred at a time when no other nation greatly threatened the area. The French threat had ended when France lost its territory in North America as a result of the French and Indian War in North America and the Seven Years War in Europe. In 1762 France transferred New Orleans and the Louisiana area west of the Mississippi to its ally, Spain, and the next year France surrendered to victorious Great Britain the control of Canada and of Louisiana east of the Mississippi. The British also received Florida from Spain because of Spain's friendship with France. Even after its great victory and its territorial gains in North America, Britain posed no real threat to Spanish America because it was soon preoccupied with what would prove to be a losing struggle to retain its own colonies located along the Atlantic Coast.

In 1776 this struggle between Great Britain and its colonies formally became the War for American Independence, won by the colonists with the critically important aid of the French. The Treaty of Paris of 1783 not only recognized the independence of the United States, but also recognized the territory of the United States as extending westward to the Mississippi River. By additional terms of the treaty, Britain returned Florida to Spain. Spain's

New Mexico under Spanish Rule

Spanish settlements in the Rio Grande Valley, 1779
(From Marc Simmons, *Albuquerque,* UNM Press, 1982)

Zebulon Pike

position in the Americas now seemed secure, if for no other reason than the fact that it shared North America with a young nation mainly concerned with its own domestic problems and little interested in expanding beyond its own territory. In 1800, however, Spain under pressure from France gave Louisiana, including New Orleans, back to the French. Three years later, with his dreams of reestablishing a French empire in North America dashed, Napoleon reneged on his promise to Spanish leaders that he would never transfer Louisiana to a third party and sold all of Louisiana to the United States.

For Spain the first question raised by the Louisiana Purchase of 1803 was the problem of what boundaries the United States would claim for its new territory. The Spaniards soon discovered that President Thomas Jefferson's claim that the Louisiana territory extended all the way across Texas to the Rio Grande directly challenged Spain's own land claims in North America. While neither the United States nor Spain was prepared to fight over boundaries, Spanish officials began to worry about United States presence west of the Mississippi and about reports that the Anglo-Americans were trying to turn the Plains Indians against the Spaniards. Of concern as well were the expeditions that the United States sent out to explore the Louisiana territory.

The first of these expeditions, conducted by Meriwether Lewis and William Clark, traveled all the way to the Pacific Ocean and back to St. Louis without coming near Spanish America. However, the Anglo-Americans made alliances with some of the central Plains Indians, as was soon discovered by a Spanish party sent out to learn more about the Lewis and Clark expedition. A second expedition, headed by Zebulon Pike, got underway in 1806. Under orders to look for the headwaters of the Arkansas and Red rivers and to explore the southwestern part of the Louisiana territory, Pike posed a more immediate danger to Spanish America because of his destination.

Word of Pike's line of march soon reached Santa Fe, and the Spaniards quickly responded. They mounted a search eastward to what Spain claimed was the true western boundary of Louisiana, ordering the search party to make friends with the Plains Indians and to form alliances against the United States. Included in the party that left Santa Fe in June 1806 were one hundred Spanish soldiers, three hundred militia, and enough supplies for a six-month journey. In October, however, the party was back in Santa Fe, having missed the Pike expedition, which had already traveled across the Colorado plains to the base of the Rocky Mountains. The name Pikes Peak is a reminder of the hard winter that the Anglo-Americans spent there before entering the Rockies and building a stockade on what they would later say they believed was the Red River. In actuality, the stockade was in Spanish territory, a fact that Pike may or may not have known.

When Spanish troops happened upon the stockade in February 1807, they arrested Pike and company and escorted them to Santa Fe, giving them an opportunity to view a settlement long closed to the eyes of the outside world. With Pike in their custody, the Spaniards confiscated his notes and maps, but otherwise they treated him well, taking him some time later in 1807 to Chihuahua and then to the Louisiana border, where they released him.

Once back in the United States, Pike discovered that Anglo-Americans were anxious to learn about his adventures and about what he had seen during his visit in New Mexico. Writing from memory, Pike provided the outside world with its first detailed account of life in Spanish settlements along the upper Rio Grande. Published in 1810, Pike's account especially caught the attention of Anglo-American traders, who began to ponder how they, too, could find a way to penetrate Spanish New Mexico.

5

Life in New Mexico's Spanish Communities

Zebulon Pike's account of what he had seen in Spanish New Mexico, while informative and provocative, did not really tell the entire story of life in New Mexico's Hispanic communities, for over the span of a hundred years New Mexicans had developed a society unlike any to be found elsewhere. When Spaniards returned to New Mexico with its reconquest in the 1690s, the settlers who accompanied Vargas brought with them their culture. But the life-styles then developed by New Mexicans became divergent because of several factors, including the manner of New Mexico's population growth, New Mexico's isolation from the outside world, and the very nature of the land and its resources.

Among those who came with Vargas were both full-blooded Spaniards and individuals of mixed blood called *mestizos.* As the province's population grew, New Mexico's Hispanic population increasingly became a mixed population as well as one comprised of people born in New Mexico. The 1790 census for the colony, not including Indians, listed only forty-nine people not born inside New Mexico; and among these, twenty-two were natives of El Paso, twenty-five were born in one of New Spain's other provinces, and only two had been born outside the Viceroyalty of New Spain. It can be said, then, that New Mexico's Spanish-speaking settlers had truly become New Mexicans by the late 1700s.

Perhaps the main factor in the development of this native population was New Mexico's isolation from the population centers of New Spain. Another factor was the control that Spanish law imposed upon the movements of its citizens, requiring special travel permits for people who wished to move from one settlement to another. The Spanish government allowed groups of settlers to go to New Mexico in the years immediately following the reconquest, but thereafter the arrival of new settlers largely stopped.

San Miguel del Vado, a later Spanish settlement (c. 1911)

Left to themselves, the settlers in New Mexico intermarried with other groups and had children; and as the population grew, it became more native in its origins and character.

Along with the population of New Mexico, the number of settlements also increased. After founding the villas of Santa Cruz de la Cañada and Albuquerque, settlers scattered over the Rio Grande Valley and then began to move away from the river to settle in other places. Some moved to what later became Abiquiu, Laguna, and San Miguel del Vado, while others formed communities in the Sangre de Cristo Mountains. Isolated from the outside world, the people who lived in these settlements adjusted to the land and to what it offered, developing a society that could be deemed uniquely New Mexican.

One way in which New Mexican society was unique in New Spain was the level of acceptance its people shared. As a frequently dangerous frontier area marking the northernmost advance of Spanish settlement, New Mexico offered its people a degree of social mobility that was unknown in the rigidly class-structured society found in the other population centers of New Spain, especially Mexico City. In New Mexico Spaniards and people of mixed blood alike could become officeholders, rise to high military rank, and become landowners. Indeed, census figures for New Mexico's Spanish communities during the late 1700s listed only two groups of people: "Spaniards and castes"—the castes were people of mixed blood—and "Indians."

The term *Indians* included the Pueblo, Navajo, Comanche, and Ute peoples as well as people the Spaniards called *genizaros*. The *genizaros* were Indians who usually did not live in New Mexico but were in the province because Hispanic New Mexicans had either captured them or had freed them from captivity somewhere else. Those who took charge of the *genizaros* either employed them or allowed them to settle in one of New Mexico's communities. Thus, New Mexican society was remarkable not only because of its many castes and the social mobility that allowed people of mixed blood to become influential members of society, but also because of the way in which some Indians lived within the Spanish communities. While the Indians who lived in these communities often earned their living by working for the Spanish settlers, some of them intermarried with the Spaniards and the castes. Also accepted into the Hispanic communities, to some degree, were blacks and mulattoes.

The initial attraction for many frontier New Mexico settlers was the promise of land, and landownership almost always derived from a grant of land given by a Spanish official to an individual or to a community of people. Originally, the land belonged to the Spanish monarchs, who either gave it away themselves or, more frequently, authorized others to issue land grants for them. Among those empowered to make land grants at various times were the viceroys, the governors of provinces, and persons who were given the responsibility of starting new settlements. In addition to the possibility of owning land, settlers also found that by moving to new settlements they could receive government aid in the form of seed, livestock, tools, and even some financial support. Much like the Homestead Act passed in 1862 by the U.S. Congress, Spanish law in the 1700s required only that the settlers live on the land and farm it for a period of time (four years) before the land became theirs officially. The law also forbade settlers to farm or graze livestock on land which Spanish law recognized as belonging to the Indians. Unfortunately, Spanish settlers frequently violated the law by trespassing on Indian lands both north and west of Santa Fe.

Landownership did not ensure an easy life for those who moved to the frontier, but owning land was critical in Spanish colonial New Mexico quite simply because farming was the province's main occupation. The *encomienda* system that had existed before the Pueblo Revolt was absent from eighteenth-century New Mexico; and while there were some large landowners who employed others to do the work, most New Mexicans were subsistence farmers. They grew primarily corn, wheat, beans, chili, other vegetables, and some fruits, while cultivating some cotton to use with the wool from their sheep to make blankets and clothes. Because the farmers possessed little metal, they relied on wooden tools, including a wooden plow with perhaps a metal tip. Using

The *Acequia Madre* in Albuquerque, 1881

two oxen to pull the plow, they adjusted the angle of the plow to produce furrows of different depths.

Men, women, and children shared the farmwork, planting the seeds, weeding the fields, and harvesting the crops. However, men alone plowed the fields and completed the tasks connected with irrigation, which was as important to Spanish farmers as it was to Pueblo farmers. The men dug and cleaned the irrigation ditches called *acequias,* which carried water from New Mexico's rivers to nearby communities. Around Albuquerque *acequias* carrying water from the Rio Grande to the fields were so wide that small bridges were built across them. In addition to building such bridges, the men also did the actual irrigating of the crops.

The men were the toolmakers as well, constructing wooden plows, hoes, and shovels. They also did all of the wood work, which included making furniture, the wooden parts of houses, and kitchen utensils. They constructed the only vehicles in use in New Mexico during the 1700s and the early 1800s, the two-wheeled carts called *carretas*. After attaching cottonwood wheels four feet in diameter to floor beds made of cottonwood slabs or pine planks and held together by leather, the men finished the *carretas* with sides of lightweight poles. Pulled by oxen hitched to wooden tongues, the *carretas* jolted, lurched, and screeched along the narrow and rough New Mexico trails from the time of Oñate's arrival in 1598 to the advent of Anglo-American wagons on metal-rimmed wheels in the 1820s.

Both men and women built the houses, although only men performed the heavy work. The men began their work by making adobe bricks that commonly measured ten inches wide, eighteen inches long, and five inches thick, with each weighing fifty pounds. After blending with their feet the desired adobe mixture of clay, sand, and straw, the men scooped this mixture into wooden molds. Once the adobes had dried for several days, they were laid on a foundation of stones to form the walls. To hold the walls in place, thick mud was used between the adobes and between each layer of adobes, and at the corners the adobes were alternated, laid first one way and then the other. When the walls were finished, the men laid wooden beams, called vigas, across the width of the house; in some places vigas protruded beyond both the front and the back of the house. Finally, men made the ceilings

A *carreta* at Laguna Pueblo (c. 1882)

Plastering an adobe wall

by placing short, flat boards across the beams and building up the roofs by topping the ceiling boards with brush, a layer of adobe, and eight or more inches of dirt. Although they were flat, these roofs provided some drainage if the vigas used in building the houses varied slightly in size and were arranged in order from the smallest to the largest.

Women put the finishing touches on the houses, both outside and inside, plastering the exterior walls with clay—which, depending upon what was available, might be red, a distinctive shade of brown, or white—and using sheepskin pads to cover the interior walls with a white or earth-colored clay mixture. Typical New Mexican houses in the 1700s were small and built either around a patio or in an "L" shape. While seldom connecting with other rooms, each room in most houses opened to the outside through doorways measuring only five feet in height. The doors themselves were made of wooden planks fastened together with wooden pegs and goathide glue and connected to the door frames with all-wood hinges. Houses had few windows, and what windows there were tended to be quite small. In the houses of early settlers, the windows were likely to be covered by animal skins hung to keep out rain, snow, and wind-blown dust. In later homes settlers stretched animal hides across the windows or used a crude type of glass made from layers of mica.

Inside the houses the light was dim, and interiors were plain.

Spanish colonial furnishings

Although some houses had brick floors by the 1800s, the floors were typically earthen, often soaked with animal blood for hardness, and usually covered with animal hides and hand-woven carpets. Wood-burning, bell-shaped corner fireplaces provided the heat, with house walls forming two walls for the fireplace and chimney. Often built initially with a single room, houses grew as rooms were added to meet new needs and to accommodate new family members. When a son married, he and his bride lived in a room added to his family's house, and certain rooms became storage areas when a family stopped living in them.

The settlers' houses were simply furnished. Most common was the benchlike seat that ran along a wall. Most of these seats were actually rolled-up bedding pushed up against the wall; some seats, however, were made of split logs or adobe and became a permanent part of the wall, while others were made of wooden planks and were movable. Eventually, New Mexicans began to add backs to the seats and to decorate them with carvings. The beds of the early settlers were usually sheepskin or buffalo hides which were rolled up for use as seats during the day. Since individual chairs were scarce, family members sat on the floor to

Life in New Mexico's Spanish Communities

eat their meals. The tables, also few in number, were small and had wooden aprons that hung down, making it difficult for people to sit with their legs under them. The little light that was used at night came from candles set on shelves along with a few other items. Furniture was scarce partly because the settlers used each room, including the kitchen, for both living and sleeping. Furniture makers therefore tried to design functional furniture, using pine from the mountains of New Mexico; and because pine is a soft wood that splinters easily, they made heavy, straight-lined furniture.

Just as the building materials for houses and furniture were suited to New Mexico, so was the food. Corn ground into meal was the main staple, used by the women to make the tortillas often served with another important food source, beans. Because they had few if any plates or eating utensils, people used the tortillas as a sort of spoon to dip the beans out of a common pot. Red chili peppers, a foodstuff originating in the Americas, added flavor and spice to their meals. To cook the meals, the women relied on the corner fireplaces, or they built outside fires when the weather was pleasant. Because metal was scarce, the women might have only a single sheet of metal on which to cook their tortillas. They used Pueblo pottery for their other cooking needs, for carrying water, and for storing food. They did their baking in outdoor, dome-shaped ovens called *hornos*. To conserve fuel, some women built as many as three ovens, each one of a different size to serve different baking needs. Sometimes simply called the "bee-

Ovens outside an adobe home

hive oven," the *horno* soon appeared in the pueblos, for Indians learned from the Spaniards how to make this oven.

Like other items found in New Mexican society, clothes were functional, but they were also colorful. Most settlers, however, had only one change of clothing. The men commonly wore cotton or woolen shirts and pants, wearing the trousers tight around their hips and often open from the knees down. Over their outfits they wore brightly colored woolen blankets that slipped over their heads and rested on their shoulders in the style of ponchos. The men wore sombreros made of straw and leather boots with hard soles and pointed toes. Their long hair was fastened in a single braid, and beards and moustaches were fashionable.

Women's clothing consisted of two basic pieces. One piece was made of cotton, had a low neckline and short sleeves, and hung down to the knees, thus serving as both a blouse and a slip. The other piece, made of heavy woven cloth, was a very full ankle-length skirt that tied at the waist and was often red in color. Women wrapped themselves in shawls that were either oval or triangular in shape, with the latter folded from a square of colored cloth so that it covered both the head and the shoulders. In public women who wore this type of shawl often shielded their faces by placing the right corner of the shawl across their left shoulders. Women wore moccasins in the style of the Pueblo Indians, Spanish-style cotton slippers without heels, or no shoes at all. Most typically, they braided their long hair, painted their cheeks with red juice from *alegría* (coxcomb), and adorned their outfits with whatever jewelry they possessed.

The children, by contrast, wore little or no clothing until about age eight, when they began to wear garments similar to those worn by their parents. The boys had to wait years before they could wear either hats or shoes, for both items were regarded as signs of manhood that had to be earned.

While many life-styles were common to Spanish colonial New Mexico, including the fact that most people were subsistence farmers, some New Mexicans earned a living through nonfarming occupations, while others were wealthy. Next to farming, the second most commonly held job among New Mexican villagers in the 1700s was that of day laborer, with about one person in eight earning a living by working on a daily basis for others. One person in eight worked at a job connected with weaving, including those who carded (combed), spun, and wove the wool. Fewer people—about one in sixteen—raised livestock, while approximately the same number earned a living as skilled carpenters, shoemakers, blacksmiths, tailors, masons, and silversmiths. Even fewer New Mexicans were servants, household servants most commonly, with female servants more numerous than their male counterparts. Among those who worked in the service of others, more than half were Indians, another one-third were castes, and only one in ten was a Spaniard. Some Indian servants included captured Navajos and Apaches, who lived in virtual slavery. This accepted New Mexico practice lasted until 1867, when it was specifically outlawed by the U.S. Congress.

The wealthiest New Mexicans, who were also few in number, often owned large farms on which they raised both crops and livestock. Unlike subsistence farmers who did their own work, large landowners hired others to care for their farming and livestock-raising enterprises. Historians disagree about whether there were true *haciendas* in Spanish colonial New Mexico; but in their correspondence and family papers, the large landowners frequently referred to themselves as *hacendados* and to their landholdings as *haciendas*. Other wealthy New Mexicans pursued careers in government and military service. Whatever the source of their wealth, affluent New Mexicans delighted in trying to copy the affectations of the upper classes living in Mexico City. Their adobe homes, which were larger and grander than the homes of most New Mexicans, were furnished with finely carved tables, chairs, tall cupboards, and chests of different sizes.

The implements of their daily lives included silver knives, forks, and sometimes plates; separate dishes and glasses for their dinner guests; and copper kettles and iron pots. The food they served was native to New Mexico, but their diet was more varied than that of most settlers. Their clothes, also more varied, served as a visual reminder of their affluence. Wealthy men trimmed their fine clothes with silver buttons, silk sashes, and silver buckles and completed their outfits with expensive blankets and felt hats or beaver sombreros. The richer they were, the more silver adorned their saddles; and while riding horseback, they wore yellow buckskin leggings. Wealthy women trimmed their clothing with ribbons, lace, silk, and velvet and wore skirts that were even more colorful than those worn by most New Mexican women. Their wardrobes were larger and contained both cotton prints imported from other areas in New Spain and more and finer jewelry.

While wealthy New Mexicans had demonstrably more exquisite life-styles than most settlers, no one in New Mexico lived a truly comfortable life. New Mexico's isolation and its location on the frontier ensured that life would not be too easy for any of its residents. While New Mexico's Spanish communities lay long distances from the other population centers of New Spain, its isolation was also created by the poor and too few roads running across sandy or packed soil as well as inadequate methods of transportation limited to horses, mules, and oxen-drawn *carretas*. Still other factors contributing to the province's isolation were a shortage of trade and an unreliable communication system dependent upon trade caravans, mule trains, and special mail riders. A trade fair was held each January in the city of Chihuahua, which lay forty days away from Santa Fe, which meant that car-

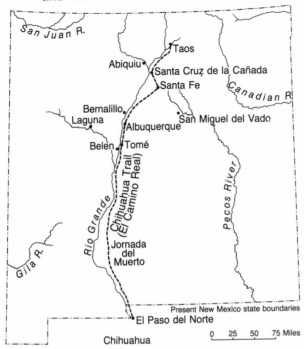

**The Chihuahua Trail
and Areas of Settlement about 1800**

San Juan R.

Taos

Abiquiu

Santa Cruz de la Cañada

Santa Fe

Canadian R.

Bernalillo

Laguna

San Miguel del Vado

Albuquerque

Belen Tomé

Rio Grande

Chihuahua Trail
(El Camino Real)

Pecos River

Gila R.

Jornada
del
Muerto

Present New Mexico state boundaries

El Paso del Norte

0   25   50   75 Miles

Chihuahua

avans, including pack mules and *carretas,* had to leave New Mexico in November in order to reach the fair on time. At the fair trade was somewhat limited because New Mexicans had so little money that they relied mostly on a system of barter. Bringing with them Indian blankets, sheep, hides, piñon nuts, and El Paso wine, New Mexicans traded their wares for iron tools, clothes, shoes, chocolate, sugar, tobacco, liquor, paper, and perhaps a few books.

Isolated from the outside world, New Mexicans not only spawned their own native population and their own ways of living, but developed their own culture as well. The culture that became uniquely New Mexican evolved over a period of time, blending the Spanish culture, which the early settlers brought with them to New Mexico, with the land itself. One example of the way in which this blending process occurred can be seen in the New Mexican celebration of special occasions. New Mexicans borrowed from Spanish culture the tradition of celebrating religious events as well as the birth or marriage of a member of the Spanish royal family, but at the same time, they developed local celebrations that also became a part of New Mexico's cultural heritage. One of the more famous local celebrations marked the reconquest of New Mexico by Don Diego de Vargas.

When Vargas reentered New Mexico in 1693, he brought with him a statue of Our Lady of the Rosary, whom he vowed to honor in an annual procession once he had retaken Santa Fe. He also vowed to build a special chapel to house the statue during

Life in New Mexico's Spanish Communities

La Conquistadora

the remainder of the year. Some years after Vargas's successful return to Santa Fe, the tradition of a yearly celebration to mark the reconquest began, becoming even more formalized on 14 September 1712, when the Santa Fe town council announced that the celebration would thereafter follow a specific pattern. Included would be a Catholic mass and sermon and a procession through the plaza carrying Our Lady of the Rosary—called by some *La Conquistadora*—as well as a reaffirmation of loyalty to the Spanish ruler by the citizens of Santa Fe and, finally, a fiesta. To this day the Santa Fe Fiesta reenacts one of the first uniquely New Mexican celebrations.

Another Spanish cultural tradition brought to New Mexico was the practice of displaying images of saints, known as *santos,* a practice common to churches and homes in both Spain and New Spain. Some time after 1750, New Mexican religious image-makers, people called *santeros,* began to create images of saints that were distinctively local in appearance. Some New Mexican *santeros* fashioned *retablos*—paintings or carvings made on flat surfaces such as rectangular tablets or boards—while others carved wooden representations of saints, called *bultos,* from round cottonwood or pine limbs. The crucifix was perhaps the most vivid of all New Mexican *santos,* for the *santeros* revealed through Christ's suffering on the cross the feelings of both pain and forgiveness. The displays of New Mexican *santos* in churches, homes, museums, and fine arts centers continue to reflect the contributions of local *santeros* to the Spanish tradition of displaying holy images.

Many of the other Spanish cultural traditions brought to New Mexico also blended into what became a distinctively New Mexican cultural heritage. During its Spanish colonial period, New Mexico produced unique forms of drama, dance, folk tales, and music. Unsurprisingly, many of the local traditions possessed a religious focus because just as Spanish culture and the Catholic faith went together, so did religion and the lives of the people in New Mexico's Spanish communities. As long as New Mexico's missions received support from the Spanish government and the Franciscans, the Franciscan priests remained the province's religious leaders. In the late 1700s, however, the government withdrew its support from the missions, which had always been costly,

A *retablo* of San Rafael

A carving of the Crucifixion (c. 1825)

and shortly thereafter, the Franciscans decided that they alone could not bear the cost of New Mexico's churches. In the absence of support from either the government or organized religion, New Mexicans developed their own religious practices, as they had developed their own life-styles so many other times when they were left to their own devices.

Thus, in some northern New Mexican mountain communities, a brotherhood of villagers began to emerge in the late 1700s to carry out the religious offices vacated by Franciscan priests. Known as the *Penitentes,* this brotherhood may have been patterned after a group that had enjoyed great popularity in Europe during the 1400s and 1500s. The rites themselves may have been brought to New Mexico by settlers, or New Mexicans may have learned of some of the ideas for both the brotherhood and its rites through books. Whatever the origin of New Mexico's *Penitentes,* the people who lived in the northern mountain communities accepted their rituals. The men who joined the brotherhood sought forgiveness for their own sins as well as forgiveness for the death of Christ upon the cross.

In seeking forgiveness, the *Penitentes* experienced both spiritual pain, which was the focal point of their meetings, and physical pain, which was a part of each member's initiation into the brotherhood. Physical pain was also very much a part of *Semana Santa* (Holy Week) activities, when the members beat themselves with whips of cactus or yucca. On Good Friday, after closeting themselves inside their private *moradas* (chapels), they chose one of their members to play the role of Christ. Next, they reenacted

Penitente rites, 1928

the trial of Jesus according to the gospels, and after the trial they held a procession to a hill marked as *Calvario* (Calvary). The person playing the role of Christ carried a large, man-sized cross on his back. At one time the *Penitentes* tied this person to the cross and stood the cross on end, leaving him until he was nearly dead. Because some *Penitentes* died in this manner, the brotherhood eventually began to tie a large sculpture of Christ rather than a man to the cross. The *Penitente* practices met the needs of a deeply religious people isolated from others and from a formal church. Another important function of the *Penitentes* was community service. Indeed, the services that they provided might be considered as an early form of welfare services, for they aided the sick and the poor, comforted the bereaved, and counseled the troubled. A politically active group as well, the *Penitentes* contributed to a stronger and more unified community.

While New Mexico's isolation led New Mexicans to develop local traditions and a distinctive culture, this isolation also kept New Mexicans from sharing the thoughts and practices of the rest of the world. During the time that New Mexico was a Spanish colony, there were no public schools or colleges, no newspapers, and no locally printed books. Although educated New Mexicans exchanged books and ideas and some formal schooling was available in the few private schools that had been founded, the norm was a colony whose people were simply removed from the thoughts shared by educated people living elsewhere. New Mexico's isolation even affected its medical practices, for there were few doctors and little formal medicine in the province. Local remedies

Life in New Mexico's Spanish Communities   89

and medicines extracted from plants and administered by herbalists were the order of the day, and while such treatment might be effective at times, it left New Mexicans vulnerable to outbreaks of devastating diseases. Smallpox epidemics took a particularly heavy toll, killing, for example, 142 Santa Fe residents in just a two-month period during 1781. When New Mexicans could share in outside medical practices, they benefited greatly. In 1805, six years after the development of the cowpox vaccination method against smallpox, the first vaccine reached New Mexico, initiating a ten-year vaccination program. The program's results were impressive, with the vaccinations reducing the outbreaks of smallpox, increasing the life expectancy of New Mexicans, and contributing to the growth of New Mexico's population during the early 1800s.

Continuously settled and under Spanish rule for nearly 130 years, New Mexico remained a Spanish colony until 1821. From 1693—when Spanish colonists began to resettle in New Mexico as part of the effort to reconquer the area—to 1821—when Spain lost control over New Spain—New Mexicans found themselves largely left alone, and while they were influenced by the larger Spanish culture of which they were most certainly a part, they nonetheless developed their own life-styles and their own cultural traditions. Their isolation, their location on the frontier, and the nature of the land in which they lived perhaps dictated that they could not have done otherwise.

6
New Mexico under Mexican Rule, 1821–1848

For three hundred years Spain, the first European nation to expand into the Americas, controlled a huge empire that extended across the Caribbean islands, Central and South America, and parts of North America. Then, in the 1810s, people in various parts of Spanish America began the fight to throw off Spanish rule. As a province of New Spain, New Mexico was inevitably affected by the struggle for independence, and on 21 September 1821 Mexico, formerly New Spain, became an independent country. Word of Mexican independence did not reach Santa Fe until several weeks later, and while New Mexicans had taken no direct part in the revolution against Spain, they nevertheless welcomed the news. They envisioned an end to the prohibition on trade with outsiders, and in fact, with the demise of Spanish rule, Mexican officials removed the unpopular restrictions on commerce.

The first person to profit under this free trade policy was Captain William Becknell of Franklin, Missouri, who traveled to the Great Plains in 1821 to trade with the Plains Indians for horses, mules, and other items. There he had a chance encounter with a group from Santa Fe who invited him to enter New Mexico. When Becknell arrived in Santa Fe, New Mexicans eagerly bought his trade goods with their precious silver coins. Hurrying back to Missouri with news of his trading venture, Becknell carried the important message to Anglo-American traders that they could now conduct business with Mexico. Within a year these traders made clear their intentions to take advantage of Mexico's new policy by sending the first of what were to become annual trade caravans from the United States into New Mexico.

At first, the trade caravans were made up of pack animals only, but by 1824 traders were using wagons as well as animals to carry their goods. Mostly from Missouri, the traders traveled across plains and mountains to reach New Mexico, heading initially for the village of Taos, which served as New Mexico's first port of entry. From Taos they moved on to Santa Fe, which soon became the region's main port of entry and primary trading center. Beyond Santa Fe lay still other markets, most of them in present-day northern Mexico, and some of the traders carried their goods south along the Chihuahua Trail, which was also known as the Camino Real. Everywhere they went the Missourians found a people starved for goods from the United States. By the 1840s the annual caravans heading for Santa Fe included many wagons, each of which carried as much as five thousand pounds of valuable goods. In 1843 alone, goods brought into Santa Fe had a value of about a half-million dollars.

The wagons bound for Santa Fe traveled over what came to be known as the Santa Fe Trail, which actually followed two routes into New Mexico. The so-called mountain branch crossed the plains to Bent's Fort, near present-day La Junta, Colorado, before entering New Mexico over Raton Pass. The other route, the so-called Cimarron Cutoff, crossed the plains into New Mexico through the present-day Oklahoma panhandle. Once inside New Mexico, both branches of the trail ran to the east side of the Sangre de Cristos, coming together just before the trail cut around the southern prow of the mountains. The trail's route finally passed through San Miguel del Vado, entering Santa Fe from the southeast.

When Mexican officials lifted the Spanish ban on foreign trade, they had no way of knowing how great the trade with the outside world would become. Within a short time, however, they realized that the trade would be extensive and that traders from the United States would control the bulk of this extremely profitable commerce. They also realized that once the trade had begun,

Aerial view of the Santa Fe Trail near Fort Union

New Mexico

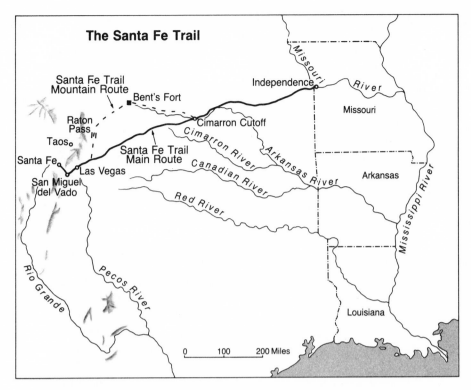

The Santa Fe Trail

they were powerless to stop it. Mexican officials could only require traders to obey certain regulations, to fill out detailed papers, and to pay taxes on the goods they brought into Mexican territory. As the volume of trade grew and as New Mexicans became more and more dependent upon it, both the society and the economy of New Mexico underwent changes.

First and foremost, the trade reshaped the needs and wants of the residents of Santa Fe and other Mexican towns. Now, the people could buy different kinds of cloth and clothing, including hats, gloves, handkerchiefs, and ribbons; building materials, furniture, tools, silverware, glassware, dishes, candles, paints, paper, and ink; foods, spices, medicines, and tobacco; books and almanacs; and wagons with metal-rimmed wheels that the traders sometimes sold before returning to their home bases. In addition, the traders brought New Mexicans their first printing press.

Besides providing New Mexicans with a greater variety of goods than they had previously known, the trade allowed Anglo-Americans to move into New Mexico and to establish their control over much of its economy. Indeed, the U.S. government—in recognizing the value of the Mexican trade—went so far as to spend money on improving the Santa Fe Trail. And while Anglo-American traders made the largest profits from this trade, Mexican citizens, who were sometimes members of New Mexico's most prominent families, also realized profits. By 1839 New Mexican traders, including José Chávez y Castillo and Antonio José Chávez, were sending their wagons into the United States for goods that

Covered wagons in Santa Fe plaza, 1861

found a ready market in Santa Fe. Other New Mexicans carried the American goods south from Santa Fe to Chihuahua, Durango, and other towns in present-day northern Mexico. Among these traders were José and Juan Perea, Ambrosio Armijo, Antonio J. Ortiz, Antonio José Otero, Santiago Flores, and Manuel Armijo, a governor of New Mexico during the Mexican period.

Occurring at the same time was another kind of involvement of outsiders in New Mexico, namely, the arrival of trappers who viewed the area as a source of animal furs. Trappers had shown interest in New Mexico as early as 1805, but it was not until the 1820s that this interest peaked, for during this decade hatmakers in such places as Paris, London, and New York constantly demanded beaver pelts. In response to this increasing demand, a special group of mostly French-Canadian and Anglo-American fur trappers known as mountain men moved into northern New Mexico. In most cases they were in New Mexico in violation of an 1824 law that allowed only permanent residents of Mexico to trap beaver. Rather than obey this law, the mountain men illegally bought licenses from New Mexicans who had existing licenses, illegally operated as the silent partners of New Mexicans, or simply ignored the question of licenses altogether.

Because Taos was the village nearest the mountain waters where the beaver lived, it became the headquarters for the fur trade. There the mountain men could buy the supplies they needed to supplement the beaver-trapping equipment they brought with them from St. Louis; then, in the fall they would leave the town for the mountain streams nearby. Their ventures during the winter months held both dangerous and profitable possibilities. The dangers were posed by the Indians who fought to keep their ancestral hunting grounds, grizzly bears who roamed the forests in large numbers, and thieves who would rather steal than trap their own pelts. However, the possible profits were equally great, for a single trapper could take out of the mountains as much as four hundred pounds of beaver pelts during a single season.

With the end of the trapping season, the mountain men moved back into Taos only to face a new danger—the Mexican government. The government had built its northernmost customs house in Taos, and Mexican officials were of course much more interested in the mountain men after the trapping season than before it began. Some of the mountain men were arrested, and their entire catch was confiscated. Other mountain men escaped prosecution under the law because they produced illegally obtained licenses, bribed government officials, or successfully eluded official attention.

Because of the burgeoning fur trade of the 1820s, Taos became home to many mountain men, who soon constituted the largest single group of outsiders living in the town. Some of the better-known trappers were the Robidoux brothers, François Le Compte, Antoine Le Roux, Bill Williams, and Thomas Fitzpatrick; and the best known was Christopher (Kit) Carson. Arriving in New Mexico with a wagon train in 1826, Carson remained to become a trapper, hunter, and scout. In 1843 he married Josefa Jaramillo, thereby becoming a member of one of Taos's most prominent families and a highly respected member of the community.

Following hard upon the heels of the mountain men were businessmen who also stood to gain from the trade in furs. Chief among these newcomers were Charles Bent, William Bent, Cerán St. Vrain, and Marcellin St. Vrain. Together these four men formed their own company—Bent, St. Vrain and Company—and began work on a fort near present-day La Junta, Colorado, which was completed in 1832. Built of adobe bricks made by New Mexican workers from Taos, Bent's Fort was secure against possible attack. It was also a money-making enterprise for its investors, and by the end of the 1840s, the fort was the economic center of the fur trade. Trappers purchased their supplies at the fort, and both trappers and Indians brought their furs there. As it expanded its operations, Bent, St. Vrain and Company traded Mexican blankets to the Plains Indians, shipped buffalo hides to St. Louis, and

Kit Carson

Cerán St. Vrain

caught and sold wild horses. In addition, the company owned a store and a flour mill in Taos and a branch store in Santa Fe. And after expanding its operations into present-day northern Mexico, company agents operated in both Chihuahua and Sonora.

Thus, newcomers in the guise of traders, trappers, and entrepreneurs began to penetrate New Mexico and to alter its economy in the years following Mexican independence. Their arrival also began to break down the isolation that had separated New Mexico from the outside world. At the same time, the changes that occurred following Mexican independence did not alter the basic fact that New Mexico was still a frontier area and that frontier life remained dangerous. Indian, notably Navajo, raids disrupted life during the 1820s, for example; and as always, there were too few soldiers in New Mexico to protect its people. Even an 1826 Mexican law increasing the number of cavalry companies assigned to New Mexico from one to three brought no immediate relief because the two new companies did not arrive at once.

Also unchanged by the fact of Mexican independence was New Mexico's separation in time and distance from Mexico City and other important Mexican cities. This separation meant that the central government of Mexico only loosely controlled affairs in New Mexico and had little control over local officials. It also meant that Catholic church officials in Mexico failed to support the church in New Mexico, essentially leaving the northern church leaders on their own. As a result, many New Mexicans did not really think of themselves as Mexicans, and left alone by Mexican state and church officials, New Mexicans developed no deep sense of loyalty toward Mexico.

Still, New Mexico remained a part of Mexico for twenty-five

years, and under Mexican rule its government did not change much in its formal outline. After its status was changed three times between 1821 and 1824, New Mexico in 1824 became a separate territory and remained a territory until 1837. New Mexico's main official during its territorial period was the *jefe político,* who headed the civil government and was the equivalent of a governor in authority and function. Indeed, historians have often referred to the *jefe políticos* simply as governors. These officials were responsible for enforcing the laws of the country and for acting as a court of appeals for cases that had been decided earlier at the local level. Locally, New Mexicans still had their *alcaldes,* who served as justices of the peace and sometimes as mayors. In addition, the territory had a small advisory body, which possessed no lawmaking power and usually consisted of the *jefe político's* close friends.

New Mexico's government sometimes worked well, but at other times it broke down. Under Mexican law, for example, the fact that there was no trial by jury meant that justice depended initially upon the judgment of *alcaldes* and ultimately upon the fairness of the *jefe político,* in the event that a local decision was appealed to him. Similarly, the government's effectiveness in its other functions depended upon the ability of all officials, but especially upon that of the powerful *jefe políticos.* Among those who served as *jefe políticos* during the Mexican period, some were able and equitable in their decisions, while others were incompetent and capricious. Most were native New Mexicans, a factor that allowed them to draw upon the people's support in their efforts to control territorial affairs.

Church affairs were almost always in greater disarray than the affairs of state, for no one very effectively controlled New Mexico's Catholic church. Several factors accounted for such ineffectual control. Beginning in the late 1700s, the churches in New Mexico had been turned over to the local parishes, and by the beginning of the Mexican period only a few Franciscans were still present in New Mexico. Until the 1830s no high-ranking church official had visited New Mexico's churches for more than seventy years. Then, in 1833, a bishop arrived from Durango, a town located more than five hundred miles south of El Paso. After his visit New Mexico's churches officially came under the direction of the church hierarchy, and the Franciscan priests were gone from New Mexico forever.

However, the changes created by the bishop's visit did not work out as planned. With the removal of the last Franciscans from the territory, churches in New Mexico were supposed to have received priests sent from Durango to take over the village churches. But too few priests came, and those who did arrive were helpless to stop the dissolution of New Mexico's churches. The missions, for example, became the property of the Pueblo

New Mexico under Mexican Rule

Indians, and among all of the missions, only five had priests. For the most part, the new caretakers allowed the missions to fall into ruin. Village churches were not much better off, partly because the parish priests who did move into the villages had to depend upon the people of the parish to support the church financially. With only meager support given in most parishes, the priests led hard lives, and their churches fell into disrepair. Still other churches went without parish priests altogether, and as a result, whole areas had no regular Sunday mass and no one to administer the Catholic sacraments.

New Mexicans were also deprived in other ways. While the first public schools appeared in New Mexico during the Mexican period, the number of both public and private schools was small, and most of the teachers were not well trained. Furthermore, the few public schools in operation were closed in 1834 for lack of funds. And while New Mexicans in that same year got both their first printing press and their first newspaper, a weekly named *El Crepúsculo*—meaning "The Dawn"—it lasted only a month. Then, in 1837, Mexico adopted a new constitution that placed even more power in the hands of the Mexican central government. The effect on New Mexico was a change in status, for it lost its identity as a territory and became, instead, a department divided into large government units called prefects. Heading each of the two and later three prefects was an official directly responsible to New Mexico's governor, who was, in turn, directly responsible to the central government in Mexico. Through this reorganization New Mexicans lost some control over their own affairs.

The timing for the change in New Mexico's status under Mexican rule, coupled with a shortage of money and growing unrest, proved to be ominous, for important events were taking place both outside and inside the area. To the east of New Mexico, for example, Anglo-Americans in Texas revolted in 1836 against Mexican rule. After they were allowed by Mexican officials to settle in Texas beginning in the 1820s, the Anglo-Americans had grown in such numbers and strength that by the mid-1830s they felt it possible to oust the very people who had first invited them into Texas. Underlying the revolt was the unwillingness of Anglo-Americans to continue living under the authority of Mexico and to abide by laws that required them to swear loyalty to the Mexican government, to join the Catholic church, and to forego slavery in Texas. Anglo-American Texans fought for and won their independence, quickly establishing the Republic of Texas. In New Mexico, too, more and more Anglo-Americans were making their presence known. Entering the area as traders, they set up businesses, and over a period of time they introduced New Mexicans to ideas about individual freedom and self-government that were different from those they knew as Mexican citizens. New Mexicans had little interest in replacing Mexican rule, but the potential for

CUADERNO

DE ORTOGRAFIA.

DEDICADO A LOS NIÑOS DE LOS SEÑO-

RES MARTINES DE TAOS,

Santa Fe 1834 Imprenta de Ramon
Abreu á Cargo de Jesus Maria Baca

Title page of the first book printed in New Mexico, 1834

unrest nevertheless existed, and eventually it evolved into a full-blown revolt.

What set off the revolt was the appointment in 1835 of a new governor, Colonel Albino Pérez, who was unacceptable to some New Mexicans for a number of reasons. First, Pérez was not a native New Mexican, a major drawback even though it was a characteristic shared by some other top officials during New Mexico's Mexican period. In addition, Pérez was a military officer rather than a civilian, a fact that was also resented by many New Mexicans. Second, as a regular army officer and a strong supporter of the central government in Mexico, Pérez made it clear that he did not approve of the indifferent administration of government affairs in New Mexico and that he alone intended to control local affairs. Third, he announced new taxes under orders from the central government in Mexico; some of these taxes applied directly to Anglo-Americans and other foreigners who traded and ran businesses in New Mexico, while other new taxes affected the

New Mexico under Mexican Rule   99

economic well-being of New Mexico's native population. Included among the latter were taxes on woodcutters, on sheepherders who drove their sheep through Santa Fe on their way to market, and on dances and other public performances. In addition, the governor announced that all those who did not have regular jobs would be arrested. And while Pérez took seemingly positive action by reopening the public schools, his new laws placed so many restrictions on parents of school-age children that even this action was unpopular.

As a result of the measures enacted by the governor, some New Mexicans in the Rio Arriba country formed an underground movement to oppose Pérez. From the northern mountain communities, this movement spread to the Pueblo peoples, who enjoyed both citizenship and land rights during the Mexican period. All those who joined the anti-Pérez movement had a common goal—to protect their respective ways of living. All that was needed to set off a revolt was a single incident, which occurred midway through 1837.

The summer of 1837 found the Pérez government so short of money that it could neither buy the supplies necessary to run the government nor supply the army stationed in Santa Fe. Desperate for help, Pérez appealed for aid to the Anglo-American traders who were in Santa Fe for the summer and who responded by lending money to the government for needed supplies. However, some officials engaged in the crime of graft, using their positions while buying supplies to make money for themselves. Although the governor dismissed officials who were known to be corrupt, his government still lost popularity because it was punishing native New Mexicans. In fact, the punishment of an *alcalde* at Santa Cruz de la Cañada was the incident that sparked an open revolt against Pérez's government.

What happened had a simple beginning. The Pérez government arrested *Alcalde* Juan José Esquibel on charges of accepting a bribe and jailed him in La Cañada, a village twenty-five miles northwest of Santa Fe. Learning of the government's action, rebels opposed to Pérez soon rallied together in La Cañada, with the northern pueblos especially well represented. The first action taken by the rebels was to march on the jail and free Esquibel. Next, they drew up a plan proclaiming that the rebels would accept for New Mexico nothing less than statehood status under Mexico and that the rebels would not submit to taxation or obey the officials who attempted to collect the taxes. After agreeing to this plan on 3 August, the rebels found that their cause attracted new converts once word spread of what they had done. The so-called Chimayo Rebellion had begun.

Pérez was in Santa Fe when he received news of the nascent rebellion. Believing that the rebels could not be very strong, he set out with some soldiers from the presidio in the capital city,

150 militia—most of whom were from Santo Domingo Pueblo—
and one cannon on wheels. Early on the morning of 8 August,
the day following their departure, Pérez and his force found themselves surrounded by the rebels near the Black Mesa of San Ildefonso. After failing to talk the rebels out of a fight, the Pérez
force withered under attack and retreated to Santa Fe, with the
governor accompanied by only twenty-three soldiers. The Santo
Domingo members of his force had deserted, the cannon was left
behind, and six or seven of the Pérez loyalists had died in the
fighting.

On the same night the governor and some of his followers
slipped out of Santa Fe under cover of darkness, heading south
along the river road. They fled for their lives, but the dawn
revealed that any hope of reaching safety was blocked by rebels
who had anticipated their escape attempt. All of those who had
fled from the capital city now acted independently, including
Governor Pérez, who decided to walk back to Santa Fe in the
hope that he would not be noticed. However, his would-be de-
ception fooled no one, for a group of Pueblo Indians followed
him and seized him shortly after he entered a farmhouse at Agua
Fría, located west of Santa Fe. There the governor lost his head
to his captors, a prize that the Indians carried to Santa Fe, where
they joined other rebels who had marched triumphantly into the
city. The rebels celebrated their victory by using Pérez's head as
a football. Other captured Pérez supporters met deaths that were
equally bloody and violent.

On 10 August, two days after the successful conclusion of
their rebellion, the rebels met to choose a governor who was to
be a native New Mexican. They might have selected Albuquerque's
Manuel Armijo, a former governor and a leading figure in the Rio
Abajo, but instead, they picked José Gonzáles, a native of Ranchos
de Taos and a representative of the northern New Mexican rebels.
Although a well-intentioned man, Gonzáles quickly exhibited an
appalling lack of strong leadership and an inability to control his
rebel supporters. Frightened by the general disorder in the Rio
Arriba, the leaders of the Rio Abajo rallied behind the opportun-
istic Manuel Armijo in an attempt to overthrow Gonzáles. On 8
September, a month to the day after the defeat of Pérez, Armijo
and his followers announced both their formal opposition to the
governor and their loyalty to Mexico.

In mid-September 1837 Armijo and an armed force of supporters marched on Santa Fe. This time the Pueblo peoples remained at their homes, having been told by Armijo to stay out
of what he called "Mexican affairs." Reaching Santa Fe, Armijo's
forces peacefully entered a town exhausted from the excesses of
armed rebellion. After consolidating his power over the next few
months, Armijo in early 1838 executed four lesser rebel leaders
as well as Gonzáles himself, who had been captured following a

Governor Manuel
Armijo

battle at Pojoaque between Armijo's men and rebel troops. Armijo had finally crushed the pro-Gonzáles rebels, and in the process, he had made himself a hero in the eyes of the Mexican government. To reward him, the Mexican government allowed him to remain as New Mexico's governor, a position that Armijo had already assumed for himself. In ruling New Mexico with an iron hand, Armijo served as governor for most of the next eight years.

Unsurprisingly, the 1837 revolt in New Mexico troubled the Mexican government. Officials erroneously suspected that Anglo-Americans had aided the anti-Pérez rebels, when, in fact, some Anglo-Americans had provided Pérez with supplies and had later given financial aid to Armijo in his actions against the Gonzáles forces. Clearly, it was in the best interests of the Anglo-Americans to support a stable situation, and they welcomed the return of order to New Mexico by 1838. Nonetheless, Mexican officials remained suspicious of Anglo-Americans, and Armijo found it to his advantage to fan the flames of suspicion by blaming the foreigners for all of New Mexico's problems. He also found that they could help alleviate the area's financial woes, albeit not willingly. The governor simply confiscated some of the property that belonged to foreigners and placed a tax on each Anglo-American wagon that brought goods into New Mexico, an action that adversely affected the Santa Fe trade.

Still another group of Anglo-Americans experienced Armijo's

punitive actions, but for quite different reasons. In the summer of 1841 approximately 270 Texans sent out by the president of the Republic of Texas headed for New Mexico. Texans advertised their expedition as a trading venture well armed against possible Comanche attack. In reality, the caravan may have had a more diabolical purpose, namely, the design of placing New Mexico under the control of Texas. However, the Texans never reached Santa Fe, for after losing their horses to roving bands of Indians, they were left stranded on the plains. Adrift and afoot, the members of the expedition readily surrendered when Armijo's representatives found them and promised them a general pardon.

Promptly breaking his promise, Armijo sent the captives on a two-thousand-mile march southward to Mexico City. Tied together and given little to eat, the Texans suffered every step of the way. Those who lagged behind were shot; those who survived faced varying fates. Some were released almost immediately upon reaching Mexico, while others escaped; but most captives remained prisoners until the following year, when at last they gained their freedom. Armijo's actions, while seemingly harsh in retrospect, only served to consolidate his power as New Mexico's governor. By defending New Mexico against an invading foe, he had reestablished himself as a hero in the eyes of the Mexican government. The Texas–Santa Fe expedition also nurtured feelings of distrust and hatred between New Mexicans and Texans, feelings that were to last for many years.

As popular as Armijo was with the Mexican government, he was at least as unpopular with most of the people of New Mexico, and he eventually became an even more hated figure than Pérez had been. Still, Armijo did have his supporters, including the people whose support he bought with land. As governor, Armijo could make land grants, and while the law limited the size of land grants to be awarded, he ignored both the spirit and the letter of the law. A number of his grants exceeded one hundred thousand acres, and three Armijo land grants were particularly large. Two of these—one a million acres—lay in present-day Colorado, north and east of Taos; and the third land grant, which eventually became the property of Lucien Maxwell, spread across much of present-day northeastern New Mexico. In awarding the grants, Armijo often kept for himself a share of the land, an action that he took, for example, when parceling out land in two of the three largest grants that he made.

Armijo had his supporters, but the support he enjoyed as the representative of the Mexican government in New Mexico was neither strong nor loyal. New Mexicans had participated in a revolt against a Mexican governor in 1837, and while they made no move in the 1840s to overthrow Armijo's government, their discontent with him grew throughout his tenure in office. If either the authority of Armijo or the control of the Mexican government over New Mexico were challenged, the likelihood of New Mexicans coming to their aid was remote.

The challenge to Mexican rule in New Mexico came in 1846, when war broke out between the United States and Mexico. Relations between the two countries had been strained since United States annexation of Texas in 1845. Also complicating relations was the dispute over the location of Texas's southern boundary, with the United States claiming the Rio Grande as the boundary and Mexico, which had never officially recognized Texas independence, claiming that the boundary extended no farther south than the Nueces River. In fact, no settlements of Anglo-Americans had existed south of the Nueces River when Santa Ana agreed to Texas independence following his defeat by the Texans in 1836. Another factor in the dispute was the claim by United States citizens that the Mexican government owed them money for property losses suffered inside Mexico. Still another factor was the mood in the United States that favored westward expansion, at the very least across the entire continent. Known as Manifest Destiny, this expansionist attitude favored the annexation of Texas and the acquisition of all the Oregon country (jointly occupied at that time by the United States and Great Britain) and California (then a possession of Mexico).

The issue of Manifest Destiny came to a head with the election of 1844, for the winner of that presidential election, James K. Polk, ran an expansionist campaign that called for the outright annexation of Texas and the occupation of the entire Oregon country north to latitude 54°40′. Indeed, in supporting Polk, proponents of Manifest Destiny rallied behind the bellicose campaign slogan, "Fifty-four Forty or Fight!" By joint resolution Congress annexed Texas just days before Polk was sworn in as president in March 1845, and in the following year the United States and Great Britain agreed to divide the Oregon country along the forty-ninth parallel.

The question of California, which Polk announced that he also wanted to acquire, was not so easily resolved. Polk initially tried to buy California from Mexico, sending John Slidell to Mexico City in the fall of 1845 to offer the Mexican government 25 million dollars for California. Furthermore, Slidell was to tell Mexican officials that the United States would assume the money claims that U.S. citizens had against Mexico, claims whose total had been fixed at about 2 million dollars in 1840. Slidell's mission, however, came to nothing, for the Mexican government, aware that it would lose popularity and fall from power if it sold California to the United States, refused even to see Slidell. If the United States wanted California, it would have to find some other way to get it.

President Polk, adamant about acquiring California, forced the issue in late March 1846 by ordering General Zachary Taylor to lead approximately three thousand troops across the Nueces River and all the way to the Rio Grande. On 12 April Mexican General Pedro Ampudia sent a message to Taylor asking him to move his U.S. troops back across the Nueces or face war with Mexico. When Taylor did not move out of the area, Ampudia and his force crossed the Rio Grande on 25 April. Mexican troops soon encountered United States soldiers sent out from the fort that Taylor had built, and in the fighting that ensued the Mexican army soundly defeated Taylor's party.

Word of the fighting and the loss of American lives reached Polk on 9 May, providing him with precisely the excuse he was looking for to enter a war against Mexico. In asking Congress for a declaration of war, Polk claimed that the war had already begun through Mexico's act of shedding American blood on American soil. Abraham Lincoln, a young Whig representative from Illinois, demanded to know the exact spot where blood had been shed, but a majority in Congress voted on 13 May to declare war on Mexico.

The war was notable for several reasons. For its part, the Mexican government fully expected to defeat the United States, even though its army had little equipment, the morale of its soldiers was low, and political conditions in Mexico were so unstable that one government after another rose and fell from power. On the other hand, the United States was equally unprepared, and the war itself divided public opinion, for not all United States citizens favored expansion. The antislavery factions particularly opposed the war, for they perceived it as a way of adding new territory and expanding slavery.

United States armies campaigned both in present-day Mexico and in the northern Mexican borderlands of New Mexico, Arizona, and California. Mostly small in numbers, these armies often had to march across vast areas simply to reach their objectives. For example, the Army of the West, commanded by Stephen W. Kearny and totaling only seventeen hundred soldiers, was under orders to march from Fort Leavenworth on the Missouri River to Santa Fe and then, after taking control of New Mexico, to continue all the way to California, where it was also to take charge.

Setting forth on the first leg of its journey in June 1846, Kearny's army followed the mountain branch of the Santa Fe Trail to Bent's Fort, arriving there in early August. Kearny paused at the fort to plan his entry into New Mexico as well as to send a message by two couriers to Manuel Armijo, urging the governor to surrender. Kearny's representatives met privately with Armijo, and they may have paid him thousands of dollars for his cooperation. Whatever transpired at Santa Fe, the Army of the West entered New Mexico by way of Las Vegas, thereby avoiding a possible confrontation with the Indians from Taos Pueblo.

Reaching Las Vegas on 15 August, Kearny claimed New Mex-

General Stephen W. Kearny

ico for the United States, telling the people that they had nothing to fear if they peacefully accepted U.S. rule. From Las Vegas Kearny and his army moved toward Santa Fe, fully expecting to be forced into battle, perhaps in Apache Canyon, which lay to the east of the capital city. In fact, an irresolute Armijo had led New Mexico's defenders into Apache Canyon, only to disband his troops even while denouncing them as undisciplined cowards. When Kearny marched into Santa Fe, Armijo, a few supporters, and pack animals carrying all the riches that Armijo had been able to gather were already on the road to Albuquerque. Armijo blamed his soldiers for his retreat from New Mexico, telling the Mexican government that they and not he were responsible for the loss of the province.

Kearny's conquest of New Mexico was a bloodless affair. He assured the people of Santa Fe, just as he had assured the people of Las Vegas, that they had nothing to fear and that the Anglo-Americans were their friends and protectors. During the more than five weeks that he remained in Santa Fe, Kearny accomplished several things. He received the allegiance of some of the Pueblo leaders, issued a code of laws that recognized the legitimacy of Spanish civil law and institutions, and appointed New Mexico's first Anglo-American governor, Charles Bent of Taos. In addition, Kearny helped to select a site near Santa Fe for what was soon to be Fort Marcy. With his work completed, Kearny left Santa Fe on 25 September, heading for California and the end of his twenty-five-hundred-mile campaign. Remaining behind to defend New Mexico was Colonel Alexander W. Doniphan and his Missouri Volunteers.

Once additional troops arrived in Santa Fe, Doniphan was also free to leave. Heading down the Rio Grande, Doniphan and

Governor Charles Bent

his troops reached Doña Ana, a village located just north of present-day Las Cruces, on 22 December. There they learned that Mexican Colonel Antonio Ponce and two thousand soldiers were prepared to block any farther advance downriver. The meeting between these two armies resulted in the Battle of El Brazito, a half-hour skirmish in which Doniphan's troops beat back the attacking Mexican soldiers. Only seven of Doniphan's men were wounded, while forty-three Mexican soldiers died in the fighting. The Battle of El Brazito was the only armed resistance that Doniphan faced within New Mexico as well as the only actual battle of the Mexican–American War fought inside the territory.

Doniphan now headed for Chihuahua and eventually the Gulf of Mexico, where the march of his Missouri Volunteers ended after covering thirty-five hundred miles. Doniphan left New Mexico believing, just as Kearny had, that the settlements along the Rio Grande were securely under U.S. control. However, neither Doniphan nor Kearny had reckoned with Colonel Diego Archuleta, who had been second in command to Armijo. Archuleta had been led to believe that the United States would claim only the land east of the Rio Grande and that he would then be free to rule that part of New Mexico that lay west of the river. Kearny had indeed officially claimed only the area east of the river, but Kearny's actual claim mattered little, for Anglo-Americans had soon taken control of the land west of the river as well. Angry at this turn of events, Archuleta began to conspire against the newcomers by stirring up some of the northern Pueblo peoples as well as taking other actions.

Learning of the conspiracy, Colonel Sterling Price, Doniphan's replacement, arrested several rebels but failed to apprehend Archuleta and coconspirator Tomás Ortiz, both of whom were already en route to Mexico. Price also failed to head off the rebellion against U.S. rule. On 19 January 1847 a group of Hispanos and Taos Indians attacked the village of Taos, where they killed a Hispanic official, the Anglo-American sheriff, and Governor Bent. Bent nearly escaped when his wife, his sister-in-law Josefa Carson, and a servant woman dug a hole with kitchen tools through an adobe wall and into an adjoining house. Although they successfully completed the escape passage, it came too late to save Bent's life.

Breaking into the Bent house, the rebels spared the lives of the women and children, but they killed the governor and paraded his scalp on a board through the Taos streets. North of Taos, at Turley's Mill in Arroyo Hondo, rebels killed eight other Anglo-Americans. In the following month Colonel Price struck back, defeating the rebels in a battle near La Cañada. The rebels retreated inside Taos Pueblo, and there Price and his men brought the Taos Rebellion of 1847 to an end. In the fighting at the pueblo, 150 rebels lost their lives before 400 others, who had taken cover in the pueblo mission of San Geronimo, surrendered. Six rebels taken captive were later hanged under orders from U.S. officials.

Still other 1847 revolts against U.S. rule occurred at Mora and Las Vegas. At Mora, a village east of the Sangre de Cristo Mountains, rebels killed five Anglo-American businessmen, only to lose fifteen lives among their own number when, in late February, a U.S. army officer, Captain J. R. Hendley, led a counter-

The ruins of San Geronimo Mission, where the Taos Rebellion ended

New Mexico in the War with Mexico, 1846–1847

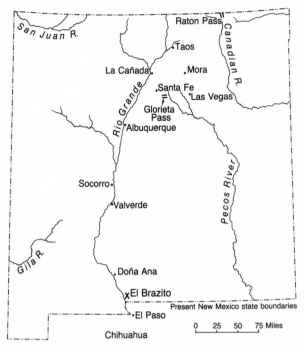

attack on their position. The rebellion at Mora was ended, but both sides paid a heavy price; in addition to the rebels who died, Hendley was also killed and the town itself was nearly destroyed. Four months later, in June, word of the conspiracy in Las Vegas reached U.S. officials, who responded by sending an armed force to Las Vegas, where once again the price for rebellion ran high. The soldiers killed a handful of Las Vegas residents who resisted and took fifty captives back to Santa Fe, thirty of whom were later executed.

By the summer of 1847 U.S. officials had restored control over New Mexico, but only after the initially bloodless conquest of New Mexico had given way to considerable bloodshed. Elsewhere in Mexican territory, United States armies also prevailed, occupying California and winning important victories in northern Mexico, at Buena Vista under Zachary Taylor and at Chihuahua under Alexander W. Doniphan. Finally, in September 1847, an army of ten thousand led by General Winfield Scott captured Mexico City and brought the fighting to a close. The peace talks that soon began finally culminated in the drafting of a treaty that both sides signed on 2 February 1848. Ratification of the treaty by the United States followed on 10 March, and the war was officially over.

By the terms of this treaty, known as the Treaty of Guadalupe Hidalgo, Mexico recognized Texas as part of the United States, and the Rio Grande was designated as the southern boundary of Texas. In addition, the United States gained from Mexico the

New Mexico under Mexican Rule

northern lands occupied by its forces, including California and New Mexico, with the latter encompassing in 1848 most of the present-day American Southwest. In return for this land, the United States gave Mexico 15 million dollars and assumed up to 3.25 million dollars in money claims that U.S. citizens filed against the Mexican government.

The Spanish-speaking people who lived on the land transferred to the United States were given the choice of either moving to Mexico or staying where they were. Most remained and became, under the terms of the treaty, citizens of the United States. The Indians living in New Mexico also stayed, but U.S. citizenship was not accorded them for another seventy-six years. Whatever their citizenship status, all of the people of New Mexico as well as the land itself came under the formal rule of the United States in the year 1848.

7

Troubled Days in Territorial New Mexico

As the people of New Mexico entered a new phase of their history—now as citizens of the United States—they faced an uncertain future. They simply did not know what changes their lives and their land might undergo now. One unforseen change, for example, was a marked increase in population. Numbering 61,547 in 1850, New Mexico's population climbed to 119,565 in 1880 and to 327,301 in 1910. Other unexpected changes included alterations in boundaries and in matters of public concern, both of which were partly related to the intersectional rivalry between the American North and South. At the same time, New Mexicans faced a future made more uncertain by the frontier conditions that rendered life in New Mexico difficult and occasionally dangerous, as Indian warfare, range wars, and acts of lawlessness became commonplace occurrences during the territorial period.

From a practical standpoint, New Mexicans first had to adjust to the new Anglo-American government. Announced by Stephen W. Kearny after his arrival in 1846, the first United States government for New Mexicans was outlined in what is known as the Kearny Code, which combined both Mexican and Anglo-American law and divided power among separate executive, legislative, and judicial branches of government as well as providing for local government. Some offices named in the Kearny Code were new to New Mexico, while others had existed during the Mexican period.

Once Kearny had drawn up and printed his code—using the territory's only printing press—he appointed a governor, judges, and other nonelected officials. The people then elected their remaining officeholders, including the members of the legislature. The idea of electing lawmakers was new to New Mexicans, as were such concepts as trial by jury and freedom of religion.

However, New Mexicans were not governed by the Kearny Code for very long. Unhappy with the very fact of Anglo-American rule, some members of the territory's leading families became even more disturbed by each turn of events. For example, Kearny's appointments to office favored American traders and business-men. Whereas native New Mexicans had been part of the power structure during the Mexican period, only two received appoint-ments to high office in the new government. Also disturbing were rumors about what would happen to New Mexico under a new system of laws. There were predictions that Hispanic and Indian peoples would lose their land, while other prophecies warned that land taxes would be instituted. Still other rumors suggested that church leaders would lose their power and consequently their ability to influence the lives of the people.

In response to the imagined as well as to the real conse-quences of American rule, some New Mexicans rebelled in 1847. This so-called Taos Rebellion not only cost lives among both rebels and Americans, but it also brought down the first U.S. civil gov-ernment in New Mexico. For the next four years New Mexicans were forced to submit to military government and martial law. Army officials were sent to govern the territory, and they ruled over the people with an iron hand. They expected appointed officials to follow orders, and they tolerated insubordination from no one.

On another front American rule created boundary problems for the territory. The Treaty of Guadalupe Hidalgo stated in 1848 what lands the United States would gain from Mexico, but the southern boundary of New Mexico remained at issue. Indeed, an 1849 boundary-line survey failed to satisfy either the United States or Mexico. But of even greater concern was the territory's eastern boundary, for Texas claimed all land west to the Rio Grande, including Santa Fe. The fact that Texas was a slave state further complicated the dispute and immediately involved New Mexico in the national debate over slavery within the territories.

After its own heated debate over the differences separating the North and the South, the U.S. Congress reached a compromise in 1850, which had the long-range effect of postponing the Amer-ican Civil War for a decade as well as the more immediate effect of settling once and for all the Texas–New Mexico boundary issue. Congress fixed New Mexico's eastern boundary on paper at 103° west longitude, although when it was finally drawn, the boundary line was one-half mile west of this longitude. In exchange for Texas relinquishing its claim to eastern New Mexico, the United States gave Texas 10 million dollars, money that an indebted Texas sorely needed.

The Compromise of 1850 also resolved the question of im-mediate statehood for New Mexico, a question that had split New Mexico into two opposing camps as early as 1848. Those favoring

New Mexico Territory, 1850–1863

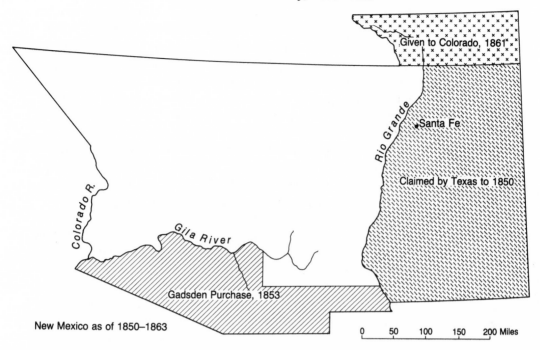

Given to Colorado, 1861

Rio Grande

Santa Fe

Claimed by Texas to 1850

Colorado R.

Gila River

Gadsden Purchase, 1853

New Mexico as of 1850–1863

0   50   100   150   200 Miles

statehood had actually drawn up a constitution in the summer of 1850 and had applied for admission to the Union as a state. However, like many subsequent efforts in the nineteenth century, this effort to secure statehood for New Mexico failed. Congress turned down the request and instead established New Mexico as a territory on 9 September 1850. New Mexico's bid for statehood failed chiefly because many northerners opposed slavery in the western territories and guarded against what they feared was the possibility of New Mexico becoming a slave state.

While denied statehood, New Mexico found that its future with or without slavery was a concern that the members of Congress addressed. The Compromise of 1850 divided the land gained from Mexico, except California, into two territories—the New Mexico Territory and the Utah Territory. Then, it gave the people of these two territories the right to vote either for or against slavery when they applied for statehood. In 1848 New Mexicans had gone on record in opposition to slavery, more because they disliked Texans than because they abhorred slavery. An apparent shift in attitude surfaced in an 1859 law passed by the New Mexico legislature that recognized the rights of slaveowners within the territory. How New Mexicans might have voted on slavery at some later date is simply impossible to know because the American Civil War intervened and determined that slavery would henceforth exist nowhere in the United States. The territory's legislature quickly repealed its two-year-old slave code following the outbreak of war in 1861.

For most Americans the ten years following the Compromise of 1850 were a time of growing conflict as intersectional differences between North and South soon reemerged and became ever more irreconcilable. Yet for New Mexicans the 1850s were primarily a time of development. Now organized as a territory, New Mexico once again possessed a civil government in Santa Fe of appointed and elected officials, which would remain much the same throughout the territorial period. A governor and three judges were appointed by the president, with the judges serving as both supreme court and district judges. The territorial legislature, however, was an elected body whose members represented the people living in different parts of New Mexico. The people also sent a nonvoting delegate to Congress, and they had some say in their local government. In short, New Mexico's government was similar to that of other U.S. territories.

Another aspect of New Mexico's development during the 1850s was the addition of land to the territory. The failure in 1849 to agree on a boundary between the United States and Mexico had left both sides unhappy. In 1853 the U.S. minister to Mexico, James Gadsden, proposed a settlement. In agreeing to the United States proposal, Mexico gave up a large area of desert land—located today in the southern parts of New Mexico and Arizona—in exchange for a payment of 10 million dollars, a sum greater than what the United States had paid for Florida or would pay for Alaska.

Known as the Gadsden Purchase, this agreement accomplished two things. First, it fixed the southern boundary of what was then the New Mexico Territory, and in the process, it added land to Doña Ana County, one of the nine counties into which the territory was divided in 1853. Second, the new land provided a possible transcontinental railroad route, which would eliminate the need for laying tracks across major western mountain ranges. Furthermore, this proposed transcontinental route would cross the southern part of the country, a factor that had initially prompted Secretary of War Jefferson Davis to assist in arranging the Gadsden Purchase.

For New Mexico the 1850s were also a time of population growth and expanded settlements. The discovery of gold in California in 1849 gave new impetus to the westward movement, and it eventually brought some new settlers to New Mexico, whose population was increased not only naturally, through the number of new births, but by the presence of U.S. soldiers as well. The result was a marked increase in the territory's population, which grew between 1850 and 1860 from 61,547 to 93,516.

Among the newcomers from the East were many with backgrounds in business, who helped to change New Mexico's economy. Building stores in New Mexican towns, these new businessmen replaced the traders of the Santa Fe and Chihuahua trails. They

Earliest known photo of Santa Fe, looking west toward the Jemez Mountains, 1859

operated on a much larger scale and offered their customers goods brought from the eastern business centers of the United States. Chief among this new generation of business leaders were German–Jewish merchants, with Jacob Solomon Spiegelberg, who had traveled with Kearny in 1846, first to arrive. Non-Jewish merchants who entered the area included Franz Huning. Born in Germany, Huning settled in Albuquerque in 1857, building business interests there and later expanding them into Los Lunas.

As the population and commercial interests of the territory expanded, so did New Mexico's settled areas. In southern New Mexico the region's first real settlement, the Mesilla Valley, became a farming area. And northern New Mexico, which had long been settled, experienced further growth when New Mexicans moved even farther north in the 1850s, with some settling in the San Luis Valley, while others moved up the Conejos River and into the area where the Spaniards had arrested Zebulon Pike.

Yet these northern settlers and the land they settled did not remain a part of New Mexico for long; they were caught up in the rush to the Colorado Rockies following the discovery of gold there in 1859. Much like the gold rush to California ten years earlier, the arrival of fortune seekers in the Rockies swelled the area's population and commanded the immediate attention of lawmakers in Washington, D.C. Congress, which had responded to California's population explosion by making it a state in 1850, reacted to the burgeoning population in the Rockies—with an eye on the impending breakdown in relations between North and South—by establishing the Colorado Territory. Under the act that

Forts and Stagecoach Routes in New Mexico

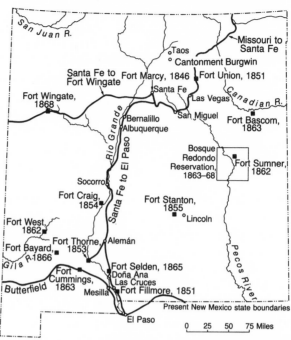

A stagecoach at Hillsboro

organized the new territory, Congress moved New Mexico's northern boundary to 37° north latitude. As a result, New Mexico lost its settlements in the San Luis Valley and along the Conejos River and, at the same time, control of the rich coal deposits near Trinidad.

While the losses to its northern neighbor clearly hurt New Mexico, the territory mostly benefited from the changes caused by the growth of the West. The national government took a new interest in the well-being of westerners. To help protect New Mexicans, for example, the government built a series of forts as defensive positions against Indian raids. Located along the territory's major transportation and communication routes, these forts also facilitated stagecoach travel; and by 1850 the Butterfield Overland Mail Company, the leading stagecoach line, ran stages twice a week from St. Louis, Missouri, to San Francisco, California. The route they followed carried them across southern New Mexico and helped to link this area to the rest of the country. Thus, by providing ties to the outside world, the Butterfield stages played a major role in the development of New Mexico during the 1850s.

In similar fashion New Mexico's churches began to reflect its new identity as a U.S. territory. Among other changes, New Mexicans were given a new leader for the Catholic church, Jean B. Lamy. Born in France, Lamy had served the church in the United States before arriving in New Mexico in 1851. Two years later, New Mexico was removed from the Mexican diocese of Durango, and Lamy became the bishop of Santa Fe. By nature a stern person, Bishop Lamy concluded from his study of New Mexico's Catholic church officials that they were lacking in discipline, and he was greatly disturbed by what he believed to be the carefree way in which they lived and conducted church affairs. For example, Father José Manuel Gallegos of Albuquerque angered Lamy by operating a store, which he kept open even on Sundays, under the supervision of his mistress.

Three bishops (*left to right*): Salpointe of Santa Fe, Lamy of Santa Fe, and Machebeuf of Denver, with two unidentified men at right

Father Antonio José
Martínez of Taos

In response to the situation as he viewed it, Bishop Lamy began a reform program designed to bring New Mexico's clergy into line. However, this effort at reform immediately set Lamy at odds with some leading clergy who felt that the reforms would profoundly alter New Mexico's traditional Hispanic Catholicism. Chief among those who resisted Lamy's proposals were Father Antonio José Martínez in Taos and, as might have been expected, Father Gallegos of Albuquerque; but their resistance came to naught. In the end, Lamy removed both men from the church; but while the bishop won the fight, some historians have defended the position of Father Martínez in his policy disagreements with Lamy, pointing out that the major cause of the break between Lamy and Martínez was the issue of power, of what constituted the rights and responsibilities of New Mexico's priests. Lamy largely disapproved of Martínez because of his involvement in politics and his refusal to follow the bishop's policies to the letter. For example, Bishop Lamy insisted that tithing was a mandatory obligation, while Martínez, ever mindful of the impoverished state of many of his parishioners, held that it was a voluntary practice within the Catholic church.

Throughout his lengthy tenure at the head of New Mexico's Catholic church, Lamy brought many changes, overseeing the building of forty-five new churches, St. Michael's College in Santa Fe, and many parochial schools. In the absence of free public schools in New Mexico, parochial schools were especially critical in educating the area's young people. As a result of his accomplishments, Lamy was elevated in 1875 to archbishop of New Mexico.

During the same period that Lamy was instituting changes

in the Catholic church, New Mexico was also getting its first Protestant churches and schools. Baptist missionaries and ministers began to arrive in New Mexico in 1849, and five years later, Baptists built New Mexico's first Protestant church in Santa Fe. At about the same time, Presbyterians and Methodists arrived, and in 1863 a visiting bishop conducted New Mexico's first Episcopalian church services, although the earliest Episcopalian groups did not form until later. New Mexico's earliest Protestant churches focused on missionary work among the Indians and in building church-related schools. Then, in 1871, Thomas Harwood's arrival at Watrous signaled much new activity among New Mexico's Protestants. A Methodist minister, Harwood was a very active leader until the end of the 1800s. Protestant churches were in New Mexico to stay, with their growth awaiting only the coming of railroads and the arrival of large numbers of American Protestants.

Also in New Mexico to stay was the Church of Jesus Christ of Latter-Day Saints. Led by Brigham Young into Utah during the 1840s, the Mormons had established a prosperous community based on irrigation farming at the Great Salt Lake. From Utah Mormon families spread to other areas, moving into western New Mexico in the 1870s. They settled at Ramah near Gallup and elsewhere, with still greater numbers moving into New Mexico in the years that followed. Today New Mexico has a very active Mormon community.

Like the rest of the nation, New Mexico soon found itself involved in the life-and-death struggle of a country torn apart by civil war. Precipitating the crisis was Abraham Lincoln's election as president in 1860, which was a victory only for northern voters. Before Lincoln even took the presidential oath on 4 March 1861, seven southern states, unwilling to test the new president, seceded from the Union and formed the Confederate States of America. Once they withdrew, a waiting period followed, which ended abruptly on 12 April, when southern troops opened fire on Fort Sumter in Charleston Harbor, South Carolina. The most bitter conflict in U.S. history was underway, with twenty-three northern states arrayed against a final total of eleven southern states, as four additional states seceded after 12 April.

The outbreak of the war had an immediate effect on New Mexico. Many of the army officers in the territory resigned from the U.S. Army to join the Confederate armed forces. The outbreak of the war also brought the struggle to New Mexico because the territory fit into the Confederacy's overall plans. These plans, which called for the conquest of New Mexico, had the support of top Confederate leaders, including Jefferson Davis, the president of the Confederate States of America and a far-sighted individual who had long seen the value of the Southwest.

The Confederacy wanted to conquer New Mexico for a number of reasons. First, if the Confederacy controlled New Mexico, it might then take over California, enabling the South to draw on California for gold, manpower, and seaports. Second, the control of the Southwest would give the Confederacy a pathway into Mexico, allowing the South to move its troops into Chihuahua and Sonora from El Paso and present-day Arizona. Finally, if the South controlled the West from New Mexico to California, European nations might take notice, even recognizing the Confederacy as an independent country and lending financial aid or more direct military support.

New Mexicans themselves also began to contemplate the future of their territory. They, too, tended to divide along sectional lines, in large part because northern and southern New Mexico had grown into two distinct regions. The economic lifeline of northern New Mexico ran along the Santa Fe Trail to Missouri, a border state which did not secede; and this fact, in addition to the distrust of Texans that had lingered from the time of the Texas–Santa Fe expedition, meant that most northern New Mexicans remained loyal to the Union. Many southern New Mexicans, on the other hand, cast their lot with the Confederacy. Southern in their attitudes, they turned Doña Ana County into a center for secessionist activity. Those who favored secession even went so far as to hold an informal convention in Mesilla in March 1861, with delegates passing a resolution declaring the land south of 34° north latitude to be Confederate land and raising the Confederate flag over the town. Fort Fillmore, which was still under Union control, lay less than three miles away.

Military operations in New Mexico began in the summer of 1861. Confederate troops gathered at Fort Bliss, near El Paso, began to advance on Fort Fillmore, which controlled the route westward. Under the command of Colonel John R. Baylor, the southern force of three hundred soldiers captured the fort on 26 July. The troops at the fort attempted to escape to Fort Stanton, but the four hundred fleeing Union soldiers were overtaken at San Agustin Springs and captured.

Although no other fighting took place in New Mexico during 1861, the time was utilized in making plans for the Union defense of the territory. Colonel Edward R. S. Canby, who initially had 2,466 men under his command, received permission to enlist the aid of volunteers, and he soon increased his numbers by organizing two volunteer regiments in August 1861. Commanding these regiments were New Mexicans Kit Carson and Miguel Pino. Canby also planned for the defense of New Mexico by focusing on two points: Fort Craig, located on the west side of the Rio Grande one hundred miles south of Albuquerque, and Fort Union, situated in northeastern New Mexico, near Las Vegas. In addition, Canby strengthened the defenses of Albuquerque and Fort Marcy in Santa Fe.

Meanwhile, Brigadier General Henry H. Sibley was making

Colonel Edward R. S. Canby   Brigadier General Henry H. Sibley

plans for the Confederate invasion of the territory. Sibley, a career soldier who had been an army officer stationed in New Mexico prior to the war, began organizing and training his invasion force in late 1861 at San Antonio, Texas; and while a majority of his troops were under twenty-five years of age, most were also experienced frontier fighters. Sibley's plan of attack was to enter New Mexico by moving up the Rio Grande Valley, a route that offered several advantages, including the possibilities of gaining food and supplies in the valley, military supplies at Albuquerque and Santa Fe, and control of the western end of the Santa Fe Trail.

Sibley's small army left San Antonio for El Paso, where it was joined by some of Baylor's troops. From El Paso Sibley's forces marched northward, reaching Mesilla on 11 January 1862 and then pushing up the Rio Grande Valley during the first week in February. Facing little opposition at first, some of Sibley's forces—Confederate artillery and a wagon train—were only seven miles south of Fort Craig by 12 February. By this time Sibley's army numbered about 2,600 men, while opposing the Confederate force from inside Fort Craig were 3,810 Union Regulars and New Mexico Volunteers under Canby's command. But no battle occurred at Fort Craig because Sibley, on the east side of the river, decided not to assault the fort, but to outflank it and thus force the Union troops into the open for battle. To accomplish his objective, Sibley ordered his army to move northward.

In response to Sibley's movements, some Union troops left the fort and moved upriver. Fighting broke out on the morning of 21 February, when soldiers from each side reached a ford on the Rio Grande six miles north of Fort Craig, at a place called Valverde. The battle started on a small scale, but it soon grew as

The Civil War in New Mexico, 1861–1862

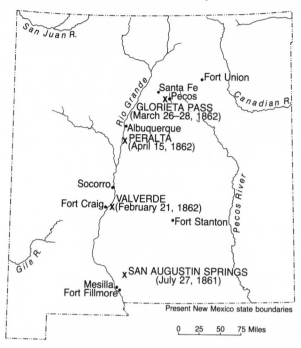

both sides sent in more troops. Fort Craig was all but abandoned as Union soldiers rushed to Valverde. When the battle lines were at last drawn, the Union troops were situated at the ford on the east side of the river, with the Confederates facing their foe. Fighting all day, neither side enjoyed an advantage until 4:30 in the afternoon. At that time, Confederate troops attacked the Union left. After capturing an artillery battery, the Confederate soldiers turned the guns on the retreating Union forces. This rout caused Canby to cross back over the river and into Fort Craig. Union losses at Valverde, including dead and wounded, numbered 306 officers and enlisted men; Confederate losses, 185.

The Confederate soldiers remained at Valverde for a couple of days before breaking camp and advancing toward Albuquerque. In doing so, however, they violated a fundamental rule of warfare, for they left Canby and his men at their rear. As the troops moved up the valley, they met little formal resistance, although they received a cool reception from the people they met, people who did not favor the southern cause and resented the way in which Confederate troops confiscated food and other goods without payment. In Albuquerque only a few residents helped the southerners. Nonetheless, the Confederates captured the city on 2 March and laid claim to it by raising the Confederate flag in the plaza.

Sibley remained in Albuquerque with two companies, while the remainder of the southern army moved northward, capturing Santa Fe and ordering the capital city's residents to swear allegiance to the Confederacy. However, not even the capture of Santa Fe brought New Mexico under southern control. Confederate forces could not control New Mexico unless they defeated its Union troops, including those stationed at Fort Union.

Fully aware of the task that lay ahead of them, the Confederate troops now advanced toward Fort Union. However, they never reached the fort, for Union troops intercepted and engaged them at Glorieta Pass, east of Santa Fe and near the southern end of the Sangre de Cristo range. Several miles long and one-fourth mile wide at its center, Glorieta Pass has steep, rugged walls at either end. It was here that Union troops, including a regiment of Colorado Volunteers, held off the Confederate advance toward Fort Union.

The first clash of arms came on 26 March 1862 at Apache Canyon, at the western end of the pass. On this first day the Union forces held their ground while the Confederates retreated. The next day the opposing armies probed, reconnoitered, and waited. Reinforcements arrived for both sides, and a second battle—the Battle of Glorieta Pass—commenced on 28 March. The fighting

Aerial view of Fort Union

was intense, and it appeared as though the southern forces might carry the day until the Union troops accomplished a clever maneuver. The Colorado Volunteers under Major John M. Chivington sneaked behind the enemy lines and proceeded to destroy the Confederate ammunition and supply train. The Coloradans burned seventy-three wagons and killed between five hundred and six hundred horses and mules. Believing this attack was led by Canby's forces up from the south and seeing no possibility of new supplies, the Confederates retreated toward Santa Fe and from there to Albuquerque. They had lost not only their supply train, but 350 men had been killed, wounded, or captured, compared to the Union's losses of 150.

The Battle of Glorieta Pass was the beginning of the end of the Confederacy's plans for New Mexico and for land farther west. Indeed, historians sometimes refer to Glorieta as the "Gettysburg of the West," because the battle was the turning point of the war in the Far West just as the confrontation at Gettysburg, Pennsylvania, was the turning point in the East.

To compound Sibley's problem, Canby left Fort Craig on 1 April and started moving up the valley toward Albuquerque. On 10 April he began bombarding Confederate positions within the town, and two days later, Sibley ordered a retreat southward out of Albuquerque. Canby intercepted and defeated part of Sibley's forces at Peralta. As the remaining southern troops retreated downriver, Canby's men shadowed them as far as Fort Craig. Realizing that Sibley's intention was to quit New Mexico, Canby did not feel compelled to risk any more troops in battle.

Beyond Fort Craig the Confederate retreat became a disaster. Sibley, seeking to elude possible pursuing Union forces, led his men into the San Mateo Mountains, where exposure, bitter cold, disease, and unfriendly Indians claimed many lives. The Apache even poisoned well water along the route of the retreat. A beaten Confederate army returned to Fort Bliss, Texas, with its dreams of conquest shattered. Elsewhere in the United States the Civil War lasted until April 1865, but in New Mexico the fighting was over by August 1862.

Although the Confederacy had failed in its plans to capture New Mexico, the war nonetheless had several effects on New Mexico even after the fighting ended. One effect of the war came in 1863, when Congress turned the western half of New Mexico into the Arizona Territory. New Mexicans accepted this action because they retained the fertile Mesilla Valley—under another plan Mesilla would have been lost—and because officials in Santa Fe now had less area to govern. Now, the people of New Mexico and the people of Arizona went their separate ways.

The fighting in New Mexico during the Civil War also had the effect of renewing Indian warfare. During the war Indians had observed fighting between Union and Confederate armies, the abandonment of forts, and the withdrawal of Union troops, who were needed for battles in the eastern half of the United States. Reacting to what they had seen and believing that they would face little or no opposition, the non-Pueblo Indians stepped up their raids on the settlements. For New Mexicans and other westerners, such raids meant horror and hardship.

The Apache and the Navajo raided at will until General James Carleton and his California Column arrived to take command of the Department of New Mexico. Although his arrival in September 1862 came after the withdrawal of Confederate forces, Carleton assumed the command formerly held by Canby, and he immediately turned his attention to the Indian problem, reopening existing forts, building additional ones, and announcing an Indian policy.

Consistent with then current U.S. Indian policy, Carleton's plan had three phases when it was finally put into force. First, Carleton issued a warning to all Indian leaders, telling them that those who did not respect the peace would be punished. Second, he sent troops under Colonel Kit Carson and other field commanders to pacify Indian groups who continued to raid. Confronting first the Mescalero Apache and then the Navajo, the commanders were acting under orders to defeat those Indian tribes, not bargain with them. Third, Carleton ordered his troops to remove the Mescalero and the Navajo, once they had been defeated, to reservations. Inherent in Carleton's orders was the understanding that these reservations were to be the permanent homes of the Indians, places where the Indian peoples would learn Christianity and farming and where their lives would be directed by the government.

The Mescalero Apache of southern New Mexico were the first Indians in the territory to experience reservation life. Altogether four hundred Mescalero warriors and their families were removed to the Bosque Redondo Reservation following a campaign waged against them by Colonel Carson and his troops in the summer of 1863. Located on the Pecos River in eastern New Mexico, the reservation was close to one of Carleton's new forts, Fort Sumner.

After relocating the Mescalero, Carson, assisted by Lieutenant Colonel J. Francisco Chaves, commander at Fort Wingate, set out against the Navajo in 1863, leading their troops into western New Mexico, the home of the Navajo. In the two-year campaign that followed, few Navajo died, but they lost because their very livelihood—their crops and their livestock—was destroyed. Faced with starvation, one Navajo band after another agreed to resettlement at the Bosque Redondo. To reach the reservation, thousands of Navajo marched from their homeland in northwestern New Mexico to the Bosque Redondo in southeastern New Mexico. Remembered in Navajo history as the "Long Walk," this journey was so horrible that the Navajo often date events by it, with some events in Navajo history happening before and other events happening after the Long Walk.

The removal of the Navajo people to the Fort Sumner area was not only traumatic for the Navajo; it was disastrous. Although the Navajo and the Mescalero did not get along, the government settled them on the same reservation. More debilitating still was the failure of crops, for the land simply would not support its new population of nine thousand people. As a result, food, fuel, and clothing were in short supply. Finally, the government found it difficult to manage the reservation effectively, largely because it was more costly to operate than officials had anticipated. For all these reasons, the Bosque Redondo Reservation failed.

The first to leave the reservation were the Mescalero, who simply left on their own in November 1865. At first, they broke into small bands, returning eventually to their original homeland near Fort Stanton. Realizing that its relocation of the Mescalero had failed, the federal government recognized the return of the Mescalero to their homeland in 1873 by establishing a permanent reservation for them in the White and Sacramento mountains.

The Navajo remained at the Bosque Redondo until 1868. In May of that year General William Tecumseh Sherman of Civil War fame extended an offer to the Navajo in the name of the U.S. government. If the Navajo promised never again to fight, they could choose one of three places to call their home. They could remain at the Bosque Redondo Reservation, or they could move to a reservation to be set aside for them in the Arkansas River Valley of the Indian Territory. If they chose this option, the Navajo were guaranteed fertile soil and a ready water supply. As a third possibility, they could return to the land of northwestern New Mexico and northeastern Arizona. On 29 May the Navajo tribe unanimously chose this third option, making known in no un-

Navajos at Bosque Redondo

certain terms their desire to return to the land they had called their home before their removal to the Bosque Redondo.

Sherman may or may not have been surprised by this decision, but he certainly felt that the land was no great loss to the government. Indeed, he had advised President Andrew Johnson that the land was of no use whatsoever to the United States. From their perspective, the Navajo saw the land in a different light, for it was their homeland. One Navajo clan leader, Barboncito, explained the Navajo's decision in these words:

> I hope to God you will not ask us to go to any country but our own. When the Navajos were first created, four mountains and four rivers were pointed out to us, inside of which we should live, and that was to be Dinetah. Changing Woman gave us this land. Our God created it specifically for us.

The U.S. government granted the Navajo's request by creating the Navajo Reservation, a smaller area than where the Navajo had once lived and which did not include the four mountains mentioned by Barboncito. Nonetheless, the Navajo were happy to return to their homeland, and they settled down to life on the reservation. They never again raided New Mexico's settlements, but made a lasting peace with the U.S. government in 1868. Following the example of the Mescalero and the Navajo, the Jicarilla Apache also soon agreed to move to a permanent reservation, located in northern New Mexico.

While following a policy of placing non-Pueblo Indians on reservations, the federal government largely ignored the Pueblo peoples and their problems during the territorial period. Other than receiving confirmation of their land grants after 1854 and new governors' canes from President Lincoln as a reward for their neutrality during the Civil War, the Pueblo peoples were left to care for themselves. The U.S. government did not recognize them

Post trader's store at Fort Stanton, near White Mountain

Troubled Days in Territorial New Mexico

as full citizens, even though they had been citizens of Mexico during the Mexican period.

During this period Indians who did not even live in the territory became a part of New Mexico's story. Carrying on raids with impunity in the 1860s, Plains Indians disrupted life on the eastern plains and threatened New Mexico's lifeline to the East by making it hazardous for anyone to travel to or from the territory. The U.S. government finally struck back in 1874 by deploying troops to the eastern plains, including the Ninth and Tenth Cavalry regiments. These regiments were unique because the black soldiers serving in them were issued leftover horses and equipment and housed in run-down forts and yet did their work well. Moving across the plains, they chased the various bands of marauding Indians until the Indians surrendered and were removed to reservations in the Indian Territory, now part of Oklahoma. In the process of subduing the Plains Indians, the black soldiers gained the respect of the very people they fought, receiving from them the epithet "Buffalo Soldiers." To the Indians, the soldiers' curly hair resembled that of the buffalo—"God's cattle." The Buffalo Soldiers also gained the respect of their country, for eleven of them were Medal of Honor winners and their units, the Ninth and Tenth Cavalry regiments, had the lowest desertion rate in the entire army.

The Buffalo Soldiers patrolled, indeed explored, the eastern plains until after the coming of the railroad, and they helped to open the Llano Estacado in eastern New Mexico for settlement. Still, their work of pacifying roving bands of Indians was not finished, for even as peace came to the eastern plains, the Buffalo Soldiers moved to southwestern New Mexico in the 1880s to join others in fighting bands of Apache there and in southeastern Arizona. It was the Apache, then, who wrote the final chapter on Indian wars in New Mexico and who were among the last Indians anywhere in the country to resist U.S. authority. Their story and the story of their leaders—Victorio, Nana, and Geronimo—are well known in fiction and film. The first of these great Apache leaders, Victorio, led his followers off a reservation in 1879, and as his band raided from the Rio Grande into Arizona, it destroyed everything in its path.

The raids came to a temporary halt with the death of Victorio in 1881, but they were soon resumed by a band of Apache under the leadership of Nana, Victorio's son-in-law. Before being confined to the San Carlos Reservation in eastern Arizona, Nana fought and won eight battles against U.S. troops. Then, in 1885, Nana and Geronimo—who headed a small band of Chiricahua Apache—escaped from the reservation and warred against the United States until they surrendered in 1886. In that year the U.S. government sent all 502 Chiricahua Apache to prison in Florida, later relocating them to Fort Sill in Oklahoma. Longing to be

New Mexico

Buffalo Soldiers in camp, 1892

back home, some 187 Chiricahua received permission in 1913 to return in peace to New Mexico, where they lived on the reservation with their cousins, the Mescalero.

It is not surprising that some of the last Indian raids in the United States occurred in New Mexico, for New Mexico was a frontier region of isolated communities beset not only by Indian raids on non-Indian settlements, but also by lawlessness within the communities themselves. The most celebrated case of this breakdown of law and order within territorial New Mexico was the so-called Lincoln County War, which began in 1878, dragged on until 1881, and embroiled both sides in seemingly endless rounds of murder and reprisal. At the time of the conflict, Lincoln was the largest county in the United States, covering one-fifth of the entire New Mexico Territory.

The story of the Lincoln County War exemplifies an important side of life in New Mexico in the period after the Civil War. In fact, the trouble in Lincoln County had its origins in the aftermath of the war, beginning innocently enough with the opening of a store in Lincoln by a man named Lawrence G. Murphy, who had served with the New Mexico Volunteers during the Civil War. Soon, Murphy controlled the county's economic life, not only setting prices for goods as the owner of the county's only store, but also farming and raising cattle as well as arranging for most of the wagon trains that traveled to Lincoln. So powerful was Murphy that he determined who owned land, who could find jobs, and even who could stay in the county. Forced to move to Santa Fe because of poor health, Murphy was not present in Lincoln when most of the trouble there took place, but the men to whom he sold his business interests in Lincoln in 1876 would lead one of the two groups that fought in the Lincoln County

War. These two men, James J. Dolan and John H. Riley, were determined from the very onset to control the economic life of Lincoln just as Murphy had done.

The other group that fought in the war were relative newcomers to the area, and their leader was Alexander A. McSween, a lawyer who moved to Lincoln in 1875. McSween was soon at odds with the power structure because he handled lawsuits brought against Murphy by, among others, famous cattleman John S. Chisum, who believed Murphy to be dishonest. The lawsuits came to nothing, given Murphy's position in the county, but McSween continued to annoy the powerful by investing in a cattle ranch and by securing investment capital that would allow him to open a bank and a new store. McSween's plans surfaced in August 1877, much to the annoyance of Dolan and Riley, who had no intention of tolerating competition. As for McSween's financial backing, some of the money may have come from Chisum, while other money definitely came from John Henry Tunstall, an Englishman from a wealthy family who had arrived in Lincoln in November 1876. In aiming to become a great cattle rancher, Tunstall formed a partnership with McSween that would formally go into effect in May 1878.

Once the battle lines between old-timers and newcomers were drawn, not much was needed to turn economic rivalry into a full-fledged war; and a legal matter ignited it. In December 1877 some of McSween's clients appeared in Judge Warren Henry Bristol's court in Mesilla to present a signed complaint against McSween, charging him with embezzling money from an estate which, according to the plaintiffs, he should have turned over to them. In responding to the complaint—which had the backing of the local district attorney, William L. Rynerson—Judge Bristol issued a warrant for McSween's arrest. In Las Vegas, New Mexico, at the time of the court action, McSween was arrested on 27 December, on the order of the U.S. attorney for the territory, who was none other than Thomas B. Catron, then and for years afterward one of New Mexico's most powerful politicians. Catron, Bristol, and Rynerson were all sympathetic to Dolan and Riley.

Returned to Mesilla to answer the charges against him, McSween in January 1878 pleaded not guilty, but to no avail. Judge Bristol found for the plaintiffs and directed the sheriff of Lincoln County to take eight thousand dollars in property from McSween, which was the amount sought in the complaint. The legal actions against McSween were part of a Dolan–Riley campaign to ruin their competitor, but the days of legal actions were soon at an end; on 18 February a sheriff's posse shot and killed Tunstall on the road to his ranch. Heading the posse was Sheriff William Brady, who had served with Murphy in the New Mexico Volunteers; and in Brady's possession was a new court order directing the sheriff to confiscate property belonging to Tunstall.

As McSween's soon-to-be partner, Tunstall had angered the Dolan–Riley group by backing McSween.

Among those who witnessed the cold-blooded murder of Tunstall was William H. Bonney, alias Billy the Kid, who, having been befriended by Tunstall, vowed to avenge the Englishman's death. However, Bonney was not solely to blame for the bloodbath that followed, for when the territory's legal officers failed to act on Tunstall's murder, vengeance on both sides became commonplace. In the days that followed the death of Tunstall, some of McSween's people shot and killed two Dolan–Riley supporters as they rode toward Lincoln, and on 1 April some of them killed Sheriff Brady and one of his deputies. Bonney himself took part in Brady's murder, and three days later he and others shot down A. L. "Buckshot" Roberts at Blazer's Mill. Yet this revenge did nothing to advance the McSween cause, for a new sheriff sympathetic to Dolan and Riley took Brady's place—a sheriff appointed by the territory's governor, Samuel B. Axtell, who, in turn, had borrowed money from Murphy.

Harassed by additional legal actions following Sheriff Brady's death, McSween rode out to the Chisum ranch to seek Chisum's advice in early July 1878. Together they decided that McSween would return to Lincoln and stand his ground. Accompanied by forty-one men on the return trip, McSween arrived back in Lincoln on 15 July and took ten men into his own house, while the others assumed positions around the town. Ready to oppose McSween was the new sheriff, George Peppin, and Dolan–Riley supporters from throughout the county, all of whom Sheriff Peppin had sworn in as deputy sheriffs, including fifteen Doña Ana and Grant county gunslingers hired by Dolan.

Both the "McSween Crowd" and the "Sheriff's Party" shot at one another for the next three days, but the battle was a stalemate until 19 July, when the army joined the fray. Receiving word from Sheriff Peppin that a soldier had been wounded in Lincoln, the commanding officer at Fort Stanton sent troops into Lincoln. The army's avowed purpose in entering the town was to protect women and children, but the effect of its presence was to turn the fight in favor of the sheriff's forces. Securing a warrant for McSween's arrest, the sheriff and his men set the McSween house afire on the night of 19 July, and although McSween still refused to surrender, he no longer had any hope of winning. In the fighting that followed, McSween, shot five times at close range, died with three of his followers and one of the sheriff's deputies. Bonney escaped unhurt from the McSween house, living to fight another day.

While the battle for the control of Lincoln was over, the Lincoln County War lingered on. At the same time, Colfax County in northeastern New Mexico was also experiencing the lack of law and order, as land and cattle companies on one side and new

Billy the Kid

settlers on the other fought a bloody battle to determine who would control the county's public land. The lawlessness in Lincoln and Colfax counties affected not only those involved in the fighting but countless others as well, some of whom moved elsewhere to escape the violence. Lawlessness in these two counties also demonstrated that Governor Axtell was not in control, prompting President Rutherford B. Hayes to remove Axtell from office in September 1878 and to appoint Lew Wallace in his place. Already famous for his military roles in both the war with Mexico and the Civil War, Wallace became even more famous for his novel *Ben Hur,* part of which he wrote while living in the governor's palace at Santa Fe.

Having hoped for a more prestigious office, Wallace was not happy about his appointment as New Mexico's governor, nor for that matter was his wife, Susan Wallace. Indeed, she spent little

Governor Lew Wallace

time in New Mexico, and she echoed the sentiment expressed earlier by Civil War General William Tecumseh Sherman when she suggested that Mexico should be forced to take back the territory. The governor, however, had to deal with the reality of Lincoln County, and while he felt strong measures were needed there—perhaps including the imposition of martial law—he never went that far. Instead, President Hayes sent a proclamation to New Mexico advising lawbreakers to return to peace or to face the possibility of armed force. Pleased by the calming effect of the president's proclamation, Wallace took the next step toward bringing the situation under control by offering amnesty to those

Old courthouse at Lincoln

who would testify about events in Lincoln as well as remain at peace.

The people of Lincoln were ready for peace, but there was to be one more victim of the Lincoln County War, a lawyer by the name of Huston Chapman. Chapman had made enemies for himself by daring to suggest that McSween had not been solely to blame for what had happened and that Wallace should take actions against both sides. For his temerity Chapman died, gunned down on 18 February 1879, as he stood in front of the Lincoln post office—a year to the day after the Tunstall murder. The two killers were well known gunmen, probably hired by James J. Dolan, and William H. Bonney was an eyewitness to the murder. It was Chapman's murder that brought Wallace, along with a cavalry escort, to Lincoln. Arriving on 6 March, Wallace remained in the town for about six weeks, interviewing most of those who had been involved in the county's war. He even had a secret meeting with Bonney in the hope that the Kid would testify at the trial of the two gunmen arrested for Chapman's murder, a hope dashed by the escape of the two men from jail.

Having done what he could in Lincoln, Wallace returned to Santa Fe. Bonney, on the other hand, turned to a truly lawless life and was finally arrested in San Miguel County, eighteen months after his meeting with Governor Wallace. Moved to Santa Fe for safekeeping, Bonney appealed to the governor for help, but Wallace ignored all three of his appeals. Transferred to Mesilla to stand trial on 8 April 1881 for the killing of Sheriff Brady, Bonney was found guilty and was sentenced to be hanged in Lincoln on Friday, 13 May 1881. Even so, he managed to cheat the hangman's noose, for on 28 April he escaped from the jail at the Lincoln County Courthouse, killing his two guards in the process. He shot J. W. Bell with Bell's own pistol and then grabbed a shotgun to kill Robert Olinger, who was running across the street to the courthouse. To this day, a bullet hole in the wall of the old Lincoln County Courthouse reminds visitors of Bonney's daring escape. A hunted man with a price on his head, Bonney remained at large for just two and a half months, a brief lease on life that came to an abrupt end just after midnight on 14 July 1881. Having entered Fort Sumner late in the evening of 13 July, Bonney was killed in a friend's house by Pat Garrett, who was then the sheriff of Lincoln County. With the death of Billy the Kid, the Lincoln County War was at last over.

The Lincoln and Colfax county wars were the best evidence of lawlessness in territorial New Mexico, but they were not the only evidence. Consider, for example, the famous October 1884 gunfight involving Elfego Baca. Baca is said to have alone held off eighty Texas cowboys for thirty-three hours at Frisco, now Reserve, New Mexico. Consider, further, the gangs who terrorized San Miguel County in northern New Mexico during the early

1890s. Las Gorras Blancas, the White Caps, so named because they wore white hoods over their heads and faces when they rode out on their nighttime raids, cut the fences and burned the property of the large landowners, usually Anglo-Americans, who enclosed the community grazing lands of the Las Vegas land grant. A second gang, which emerged from Las Gorras Blancas, was the gang of Vicente Silva and his forty bandits. For three years the Silva gang robbed and murdered throughout San Miguel County, before Silva was shot to death by one of his followers. Finally, consider the disappearance of Colonel Albert Jennings Fountain and his son as they rode along a road near Las Cruces in 1896. Three men stood trial for the murder of the Fountains, but all three were found not guilty; for while it was widely believed that the Fountains had been murdered by their enemies, the bodies of the father and son were never found.

By the time of the last Indian raids and the trouble in Lincoln County and elsewhere, New Mexico had been a territory of the United States for more than thirty years; yet the overriding facts of life in New Mexico remained isolation and a frontier existence. New Mexico's long history as a frontier meant that law and order was late in arriving, and until something happened to break down New Mexico's isolation, life in the territory would quite simply remain hazardous.

8
The End of Isolation

In 1850, when New Mexico became an organized territory of the United States, its economy did not change much at first. Most New Mexicans continued to farm the land in much the same way as the people before them. Like their predecessors, they were primarily subsistence farmers, growing grain, vegetables, and fruit as well as raising some sheep and cattle. They, too, cultivated lands in parts of New Mexico where water was available for irrigation. In 1850 the New Mexico Territory, which included both New Mexico and Arizona until 1863, officially contained 3,750 farms; and ten years later, the number had risen to 5,086, reflecting a growth similar to the territory's population growth during the 1850s. With more acreage under cultivation, farm production also increased. Corn production nearly doubled during the decade, and wheat production was much greater in 1860 than it had been in 1850.

During the 1860s, however, New Mexico farming did not show similar growth because the Civil War and the subsequent Indian unrest disrupted economic life. Indeed, the number of farms actually decreased between 1860 and 1870, and while corn production increased slightly during the decade, wheat, cattle, and sheep production declined. Nor did farming attract many newcomers to the area during that period. The continual upheavals caused by sectional and Indian conflict, coupled with the inherent shortage of water and the difficulty of getting crops to market, deterred new settlement. Besides, settlers still had access to good farming land in parts of Minnesota, the Dakotas, Nebraska, and Kansas.

Compared to other parts of the trans-Mississippi West, then, New Mexico did not become an important farming area during the immediate post–Civil War years. Cattle raising, on the other hand, became increasingly important to New Mexico's economy as the demand grew steadily after the war for beef to feed miners, soldiers, and reservation Indians. The supply of beef initially came from Texas, with Charles Goodnight and Oliver Loving combining their herds in 1866 and beginning at a point west of Fort Worth, driving their cattle into New Mexico. The route they followed ran southwest to the Pecos River, entering New Mexico just south of present-day Carlsbad, and then followed the river valley toward markets at Fort Sumner and the Bosque Redondo Reservation. What was known eventually as the Goodnight–Loving Cattle Trail, and its successful movement of cattle to the marketplace, fostered other trails, and soon cattle trails crisscrossed New Mexico in all directions, running north into Colorado and Wyoming and west into Arizona.

Texans also soon responded to the demand for cattle by moving some of their cattle-raising operations to the Llano Estacado in eastern New Mexico and into the territory's western valleys. Turning their tough Texas longhorns loose to graze, they simply used the open range, the unfenced public lands that encompassed the grasslands of the trans-Mississippi West. The cattle required little care until it came time to drive them to market, and then those responsible for tending them—the legendary cowboys—rounded up the cattle, branded any unmarked calves, and drove their charges along the cattle trails to market. The cowboys, who came from a variety of backgrounds, included many blacks who had moved west after the Civil War.

The most famous of New Mexico's early cattlemen was John S. Chisum. He claimed for his ranch an area that extended 150 miles north and south along the Pecos River and from the Texas border westward to Fort Sumner. At the height of his wealth and power, Chisum is said to have raised sixty thousand cattle a year. His fight with Lawrence G. Murphy of Lincoln and others was typical of the days of the cattle kingdoms. Cattlemen fought one another, and they fought the sheepmen and farmers who began to move onto the land that had once been used to raise only cattle.

But the days of the open range were numbered, finally coming to an end for a number of reasons. One was the competition for land among cattlemen, sheepmen, and farmers. Another was the weather, for in the mid-1880s drought and subzero temperatures combined to kill off thousands of head of cattle. Still another was the railroad, which made the long cattle drive a thing of the past. For all these reasons, cattle raising in New Mexico experienced fundamental changes during the late 1800s. The ranchers now began to fence in their land with barbed wire, to utilize windmills as a way of pumping a steady supply of water, and to raise cattle that were carefully bred for the meat they yielded. With some cattle raising occurring in nearly every part of the territory, New Mexico's cattle in 1890 numbered 1,340,000.

George McJunkin, former slave and discoverer of Folsom Man

Sheep raising was also central to New Mexico's economy in the years after the Civil War. In fact, sheep had long been important to New Mexicans, having first been brought to the area by Spanish explorers and raised by subsequent generations of Hispanic settlers. Indeed, New Mexico's dry climate and high plains were actually better suited for sheep than for cattle, partly because sheep need less water than cattle and get some of their water from the grass and other vegetation they eat. About fifteen acres of New Mexico pastureland can support one sheep for one year, while it takes some seventy acres of the same pastureland to support one cow for one year. Thus, New Mexico was sheep country long before it was cattle country.

Before it became a territory of the United States—more particularly, in the years between 1800 and 1850—New Mexico's main markets for sheep were the mining towns of northern Mexico. In an average year 250,000 sheep were trailed to Mexico, and in some years as many as 500,000 were marketed there. Valued primarily for their meat, New Mexico's sheep, even with their thin and hairy wool, also made possible the export of woolen goods. Once it became a part of the United States, New Mexico continued to export its sheep and sheep products; and in 1850, when it led all western territories and states in sheep production, it was known far and near as the nation's sheep nursery. New Mexico sheep by the thousands were trailed to Mexico, California, the Midwest,

The End of Isolation

and the North. By the 1870s sheep bred from New Mexico sheep were being raised in the Great Plains and Rocky Mountain states and territories.

The sheep boom of the postwar years also brought an expansion of the sheep raising industry within New Mexico. For example, sheepmen from the Las Vegas area moved to the eastern plains, and there they were joined by other sheepmen from Mora, Anton Chico, and other settlements along the Pecos River and the lower Rio Grande. Hilario Gonzales was known as the richest of all sheepmen during the 1870s. Settled at San Hilario on the Canadian River, Gonzales was said to have run sheep on a thousand hills. Ten miles from San Hilario, at the town of San Lorenzo, there lived another giant of the sheep raising industry, Francisco Lopez. Others whose flocks on the eastern plains numbered in the thousands included Trinidad and Eugenio Romero and Tomas D. Cabeza de Baca.

The success of these men on the eastern plains lured still other New Mexico sheepmen to the plains of Texas as well as of New Mexico. Most of these newcomers also raised some cattle, but their main concern was grassland for their sheep. By the late 1800s the desire for grazing land brought the sheepmen and the cattlemen into sharp competition. At first, sheepmen had the advantage, for sheep were more easily trailed long distances to market, but the arrival of the railroad shifted the advantage to cattle, which could be transported by train to distant markets, thereby filling the ever increasing demand of Americans for more beef.

New Mexico's cattle and sheep production figures in the late 1800s reflect the altered fortunes of the territory's livestock growers. In 1884 New Mexico accommodated approximately one million head of cattle and five and a half million sheep. In 1889 the territory numbered a quarter of a million more cattle and two million fewer sheep than its total five years earlier. In the 1880s, in an effort to reverse their fortunes, sheepmen from northeastern New Mexico began to crossbreed better wool-producing sheep with native sheep. However, this effort was not enough to stop the continuing decline in an industry that generated only falling profits. Not until the 1950s did the decline in New Mexico's sheep growing industry finally end.

Another dimension of the territory's economy that was important during the post–Civil War years was mining, but the real growth of New Mexico's mining industry was slower than in most other parts of the West, even though New Mexico had long been the site of various mining operations. Even before the Spaniards arrived, Indians mined turquoise at Cerrillos, an area south of Santa Fe, which Spanish and later settlers continued to work. In 1828 the first known gold fields in what is now the western United States were found in the Ortiz Mountains south of Santa

Early Mining in New Mexico

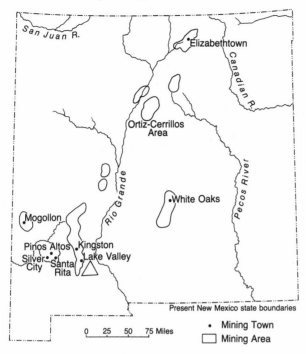

San Juan R.

Elizabethtown

Canadian R.

Ortiz-Cerrillos Area

Pecos River

White Oaks

Rio Grande

Mogollon

Pinos Altos Kingston
Silver Lake Valley
City   Santa
       Rita

Present New Mexico state boundaries

0 25 50 75 Miles

• Mining Town
☐ Mining Area

Fe. More gold was discovered eleven years later at the base of the San Pedro Mountains, also south of Santa Fe. Hispanic miners worked these gold fields just as they had worked the copper deposits they discovered in the 1700s at Santa Rita, east of present-day Silver City.

Copper mining at Santa Rita continued off and on after United States acquisition of the territory, while gold mining, too, was periodically revived. In 1860, for example, the discovery of gold at Pinos Altos by miners newly arrived from California had caused a brief sensation. Located north of Santa Rita and Silver City in the Black Range, Pinos Altos became the focal point for a new outbreak of gold fever, which had set off a rush of people to California in 1849 and to the Colorado Rockies in 1859. In 1860 people from California, Texas, Missouri, and the northern Mexican states of Chihuahua and Sonora flocked into what is now southwestern New Mexico. However, New Mexico's gold rush did not last long, for Apache raids and the onset of the Civil War so effectively discouraged mining that by the end of 1861 mining in the Pinos Altos area had stopped.

Mining in New Mexico was also discouraged by the warfare against the Mescalero Apache and the Navajo during the postwar years. Renewed interest in mining surfaced only with discoveries of silver and gold, especially in southwestern New Mexico. Almost overnight new mining towns sprang into existence, often to become ghost towns as soon as the strikes played out. Silver City,

The Henry Clay Mine near White Oaks

an exception to the fate of so many such towns, grew up with the discovery of silver there in 1869. Elsewhere gold was discovered in 1866 at Elizabethtown, near present-day Eagle Nest, and in 1879 close to White Oaks, located northwest of Lincoln. Still other strikes followed, including the discovery of gold at Hillsboro near Pinos Altos in 1877 and the discoveries of silver at Kingston in 1883, at Lake Valley in 1887, and at Mogollon in 1889. The skeletal remains of these once thriving towns are all that remain of New Mexico's gold and silver mining boom days.

New Mexico's brief history as one of the West's mining colonies was virtually preordained by conditions that were beyond the control of the miners themselves. The shortage of water limited placer mining because there was not enough water to separate the gold from the lighter substances found in gold-carrying dirt. In addition, the difficulty in tracing ore veins in New Mexico's rock made lode mining difficult. And further adding to the woes of miners was the lack of a reliable transportation system. Before the coming of the railroads, mine owners were forced to use primitive overland routes to transport bulky supplies and equipment as well as the mined ore.

Thus, while New Mexico's economy, both agricultural and nonagricultural, experienced some growth in the territory's early years as a part of the United States, such growth was neither steady nor sizable. The limitations in internal conditions—lack of water, lack of arable land, and lack of transportation—remained unchanged, as did the territory's isolation from other population centers and its continued status as a frontier area riddled with Indian warfare. The coming of the railroads in the 1880s was bound to provide a watershed in New Mexico's history, for not only did they give the territory its first truly usable transportation system, but they also broke down its isolation and frontier conditions.

The railroads' arrival in New Mexico was the result of an era of railroad building that occurred everywhere in the United States after the Civil War, but especailly west of the Mississippi River. From a total of 3,272 miles of railroad track west of the river in 1865, the mileage increased to 72,473 by 1890 because westerners felt they needed better contact with the East and also because of the extensive railroad assistance programs initiated by the federal government. In turn, the railroads reduced the isolation of westerners and spurred both economic and population growth. As railroad tracks were laid across the New Mexico territory, new towns sprang up, old towns underwent changes, and trade became possible on a much broader scale. At the same time, the railroads opened up new mining, ranching, and farming opportunities and brought a steady stream of new residents to New Mexico.

Railroad building in New Mexico flourished between late 1878 and early 1881. In fact, almost one-third of all the railroad track laid in New Mexico was put down in just slightly more than two years. During this period workers sometimes laid one and a half miles of track in a single day. The first and probably the best

An A.T.&S.F. train at Glorieta, 1880

known railroad to enter the territory was the Atchison, Topeka & Santa Fe, which followed the mountain branch of the Santa Fe Trail westward from Kansas into Colorado, before swinging south at Trinidad and crossing into New Mexico over Raton Pass. It had won the right-of-way to the pass in a race with another railroad company, the Denver and Rio Grande. As the A.T.&S.F. continued along a southward route, it changed the face of New Mexico: the town of Raton sprang to life in 1879, and farther south in an area already settled by farmers, two other towns—Maxwell and Springer—came into being as major cattle shipping centers. Wagon Mound, a fourth town along the railroad, lay where the two branches of the Santa Fe Trail met. Called Santa Clara until about 1859, the town afterward became known as Wagon Mound because of the covered-wagon-shaped mesa to the east. Still farther south along the A.T.&S.F. line was Watrous, an old Spanish settlement called La Junta until just before the Civil War.

South of Watrous came Las Vegas, the first major New Mexico town to be affected by the railroad. Las Vegas residents welcomed the arrival of the railroad with a gala celebration on 4 April 1879. Before 1879 Las Vegas had been a thriving town, and it prospered even more as a railroad town, but henceforth as two towns rather than one—a division that took place when the A.T.&S.F. decided to lay its tracks across the Gallinas River from the old plaza. Along these tracks a new town grew up, creating in its wake a Las Vegas divided for decades into an old town (West Las Vegas) and a new town (East Las Vegas).

By 1880 the A.T.&S.F. had extended its line far beyond Las Vegas, laying track through Glorieta Pass and building a depot some eighteen miles south of Santa Fe at Galisteo Junction, later renamed Lamy. By taking this route, the railroad deliberately bypassed Santa Fe and its mountainous location. Left without a railroad, the unhappy residents of Santa Fe set out to show the officials of the A.T.&S.F. that they were going to have a railroad even if they had to pay for it themselves. They floated a 150,000-dollar bond issue, which was duly approved by the voters, and used the money raised by the sale of the bonds to pay for a branch line from Lamy to Santa Fe. The first train to travel this line reached Santa Fe on 9 February 1880, bringing to an end the days of the Santa Fe Trail.

While the people of Santa Fe were crusading for their cause, the A.T.&S.F. was laying track westward to the Rio Grande and southward to Santo Domingo. From there the company laid track along the east side of the river, and when it reached Albuquerque, it swung far enough east of the river to avoid Old Town. Thus, like Las Vegas, Albuquerque became two towns. The town that grew up around the railroad became known as New Albuquerque, where the train arrived on 22 April 1880. The original part of Albuquerque became known simply as Old Town.

Soon after the A.T.&S.F. entered New Mexico from the north, other railroad companies also came to the territory. The Southern Pacific Railroad Company arrived from the west, originating in California and crossing Arizona. Just east of the Arizona–New Mexico border, a new town—Lordsburg—sprang up along the tracks in October 1880. Settled by people from Shakespeare, an old mining center that had stood two miles to the south, Lordsburg became one of several towns along the Southern Pacific line as the company continued laying its track in an eastwardly direction. The Southern Pacific and one branch of the A.T.&S.F. met at Deming on 8 March 1881. The A.T.&S.F. had reached Deming by constructing a route that ran from Albuquerque down the Rio Grande Valley, along the way passing through the towns of Los Lunas, Belen, Socorro, San Marcial, and Rincon. At Rincon, north of Las Cruces, the A.T.&S.F. had followed two routes, with one bypassing Mesilla on its run southward through Las Cruces, where the town's residents welcomed its arrival on 26 April 1881, and ending in El Paso; the other branch of the railway went from Rincon westward to Deming.

The meeting of the two railroads at Deming was highly significant for New Mexico because its residents could now travel and ship goods by train to both the east and the west coasts. A

Las Cruces, Main Street looking south (1890s)

transcontinental railroad route—only the second of its kind—was now in place across New Mexico. However, the meeting of the two railroads in Deming did not please either railroad company, and they became bitter rivals. Each occupied a separate wing in the depot at Deming, and each operated its schedule according to a different time zone. Yet the rivalry actually benefited New Mexico because it encouraged additional activity by both companies. In its continued expansion eastward, the Southern Pacific acquired a railroad line in Texas and laid track to New Orleans. Completed on 12 January 1883, this route brought New Mexico into the middle of a line that connected New Orleans with San Francisco.

For its part, the A.T.&S.F. laid tracks from Deming to Silver City, making the task of hauling goods to and from the mines in the area both easier and less costly. And the A.T.&S.F., in reaching Albuquerque, encouraged yet another railroad company to construct a line running westward from Albuquerque to Needles, California. Gallup with its nearby coal mines became a major point along this line. When the A.T.&S.F. acquired this route in 1897, it also possessed a direct link between mid-America and the West Coast that ran through New Mexico.

Other railroad routes encouraged the development of New Mexico as well. In northern New Mexico the narrow-gauge railroad company, the Denver and Rio Grande, completed a route that stretched in 1880 from Antonito, Colorado, southward to Española; and seven years later, the company extended its line to Santa Fe. A second Denver and Rio Grande line, built in 1880 and 1881, linked Chama, New Mexico, with Durango, Colorado. Today that part of the narrow-gauge running between Chama and Antonito operates as the Cumbres and Toltec Scenic Railroad, a joint venture of the states of New Mexico and Colorado.

Workers laid tracks across northeastern New Mexico in 1887 and 1888, giving birth along the way to the towns of Folsom, Des Moines, and Clayton. Folsom prospered for a time as the main livestock shipping point between Denver and Fort Worth, while Des Moines grew up as a small farming and ranching town and Clayton stood at the center of a busy cattle ranching region. Farther south workers constructed a railroad in the 1890s that followed the Goodnight–Loving Cattle Trail into the Pecos Valley. The railroad arrived at the cowboy campsite known as Loving's Bend in 1891, transforming it into the town of Eddy, now Carlsbad.

Three years later, the railroad arrived at Roswell. Both the Carlsbad and Roswell areas were already settled, but both grew more rapidly once the railroad linked them to the outside world. By 1910 Roswell would grow into the main city in southeastern New Mexico. South of Roswell a new town—which took its present name of Artesia in 1903—grew out of a railroad construction

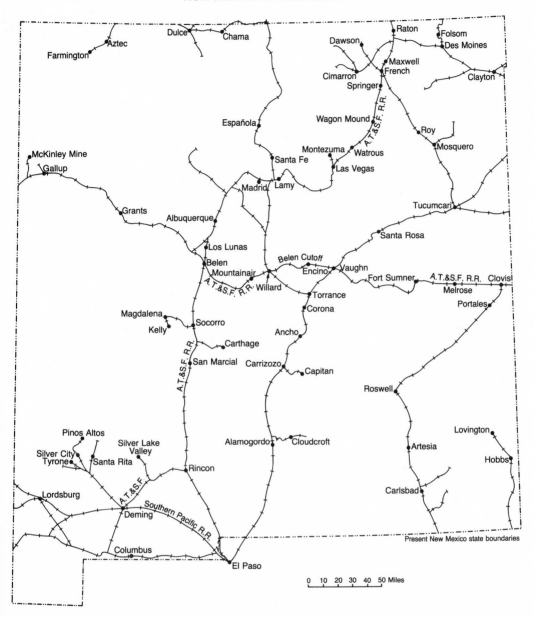

camp. From Roswell the railroad left the Pecos Valley, running
northeastward to Portales and then to Riley's Switch, a point that
in 1906 became Clovis.

Clovis was also the end of the A.T.&S.F.'s so-called Belen
Cutoff. From Belen this route ran south of the Manzano Mountains
and into the Estancia Valley, giving birth along the way to Moun-
tainair (in approximately 1900), Willard (in 1903), and Encino
(in 1904). Farther east the Belen Cutoff ran through Fort Sumner
and the old cattle town of Brownhorn, later named Melrose, and
finally, before crossing into Texas, it reached Clovis. As a town

The End of Isolation 147

located on two railroad lines, Clovis rapidly grew into a trading center for the eastern plains.

Railroads continued to be built around the turn of the century, often with very specific goals in mind and always with the result of changing the face of New Mexico. For example, at the end of the 1800s, the Phelps-Dodge mining company began to lay track into New Mexico from El Paso for the specific purpose of reaching the coal fields near Raton. The first stretch of track connected El Paso and Santa Rosa, and in the process, it aided in the development of the Tularosa Basin. Alamogordo, established in 1899, was the first New Mexico town to grow up along this railroad line; others included Carrizozo, Ancho, Chico, and Torrance. At the point where the Phelps-Dodge line crossed the A.T.&S.F. Belen Cutoff line, Vaughn sprang up, evolving in a short time into an important shipping center for cattle and sheep. The Phelps-Dodge company also built spur lines to special sites in the Tularosa Basin. One spur ran from Alamogordo into the Sacramento Mountains, giving rise to the resort town of Cloudcroft and to lumbering in the nearby forests. A second spur ran from Carrizozo to Capitan and its nearby coal deposits.

Eventually, the Phelps-Dodge company reached its goal of controlling a railroad line that extended to the coal fields of northeastern New Mexico, shortcutting its need to lay tracks along the way by leasing a railroad line that already operated between Santa Rosa and Tucumcari. From Tucumcari Phelps-Dodge laid its own track northward to French and from there to Dawson— at last giving the Phelps-Dodge company the access to rich coal deposits. Along the way the company's line helped to develop northeastern New Mexico by giving rise to the towns of Mosquero and Roy, on the route between Tucumcari and French, and especially by helping Tucumcari grow. Tucumcari's growth was also spurred by a second railroad line that originated to the east. In 1901 the town had been merely a construction site for the railroad line that crossed from Texas into New Mexico. Originally called Six Shooter Siding, the construction camp took on the name Tucumcari in 1902, and it was formally organized as a town in 1907. Located along two railroad lines, Tucumcari became a major shipping center, as coal from the north and cattle and sheep from the nearby ranches were routinely shipped through the town.

Railroad mileage across New Mexico reached its peak total of 3,124 miles in 1914, just two years after New Mexico entered the Union as its forty-seventh state. Along the routes that crisscrossed New Mexico, the appearance and the identity of the land changed. Countless new towns appeared on the map, and the railroads made possible much new economic growth and development. During the heyday of the railroads, moreover, travel across the West took on a special flavor that lingers today only as fond remembrances of a bygone era. It was a time when train

Harvey Girls

passengers moving westward across New Mexico watched land-scapes change from mountainous terrain near Glorieta Pass to the distinctive red cliffs near Gallup. Passengers could renew themselves at such popular stopping-off places as the Harvey Houses, introduced into the Southwest by the enterprising Fred Harvey.

Travelers along the A.T.&S.F. railway network could count on the meals the Harvey Houses served, but it was perhaps the Harvey Girls more than the food that brought weary travelers to the Fred Harvey establishments. According to Fred Harvey standards, the attractive Harvey Girls were women of good moral character. Attired in black dresses with white aprons, the girls earned $17.50 a month plus tips and received free room and board in supervised dormitories. All Harvey Girls began their jobs by promising not to marry for at least a year, but many of them failed to keep this promise. Indeed, one story has it that the Harvey Girls who married their customers gave birth to some four thousand babies named Fred or Harvey, or both.

In addition to comforting travelers, Fred Harvey helped to promote the Southwest by prominently displaying Indian arts and crafts in his establishments and by reproducing paintings of

The End of Isolation   149

Southwestern scenes on menus, placemats, and postcards. Harvey Houses prospered as long as the railroads prospered, but they began to close as fewer people traveled by train. Today no Harvey Houses remain in New Mexico, and only the Fred Harvey Restaurant at the Albuquerque International Airport—under different ownership—even bears the Harvey name. Still, memories remain of that bygone era of railroad travel and its more slowly paced life.

The true significance of the railroad era lay in the fact that the railroads brought New Mexico's centuries of isolation to an end. And with the end of this isolation came many changes, including, first and foremost, the arrival of many newcomers who followed the railroads into New Mexico for a variety of reasons. Many came seeking a new place to live and to earn a living, and New Mexico's expanding economy offered ample employment opportunities. For example, new jobs opened in the mines that were now linked to outside markets by rail. So it was that some miners found jobs in the silver mines at Silver City, while others went to work in mining silver, lead, and zinc at Kelly. Still others worked in the coal mines in the Raton and Gallup areas or in the smaller coal mines at Madrid, Carthage, and Capitan.

Other newcomers found jobs in lumbering, an industry new to New Mexico and born with the railroads wherever mountains offered fine timber; and for the most part, the lumber industry prospered in such northern New Mexico towns as Cuba and Chama. Still other newcomers were attracted to the area by developments in New Mexico's agriculture. In the Estancia Valley and on the northeastern plains, for example, farmers grew beans on a large scale for later shipment by rail to market. In the Pecos Valley farmers moved to irrigated land that had been developed and promoted by Charles B. Eddy and James J. Hagerman; and growers shipped their produce to markets in Texas over the railroad line that Eddy and Hagerman had brought into the valley. Generally speaking, newcomers found New Mexico an attractive agricultural area because of the amount of land that it offered for new settlement.

Most of the farmers who arrived in New Mexico in the late 1880s and early 1900s settled on the eastern plains. Most of them came in search of 160-acre homesteads, and they stayed even though the cattle ranchers tried to convince them that 160 acres were too few to provide a good living in New Mexico. Roosevelt County in eastern New Mexico is one example of the homestead boom. From a county-wide population of about three thousand in 1904, the population had more than tripled by 1910, when homesteaders had already laid claim to almost all of the 160-acre plots of the county's public land. The Roosevelt County story held true for most other counties in eastern New Mexico. On the other side of New Mexico, farmers also settled land that seemed suitable

A farm near Bloomfield (c. 1885)

for farming, and as early as the 1880s the Farmington region in northwestern New Mexico began to prosper.

Wherever they settled, the farmers of the late nineteenth and early twentieth centuries frequently had to farm without the benefit of irrigation water. At first, they were fairly lucky, for the rainfall was sufficient for the farmers, especially those on the eastern plains, to grow crops in much the same way that they were grown in the Midwest. But too little rain fell on the eastern plains from 1909 to 1912, and as a result, many small farmers, including two-thirds of those in Roosevelt County, lost their farms. The farmers who remained in eastern New Mexico became dry farmers, adjusting their methods to the less reliable rainfall and learning to prepare the soil to hold what moisture existed, as well as planting crops of sorghum, corn, and other grains which were suited to the growing conditions. In addition, the dry farmers began to raise some cattle to ensure an income even in bad crop-growing years.

Some towns in the farming and ranching areas existed primarily to provide goods and services for local farmers and ranchers. And as their populations grew, the towns experienced many changes, as new stores, houses, churches, and schools appeared, seemingly overnight. Towns located along the main railroad lines attracted the greatest number of newcomers and, in turn, experienced the most changes. Las Vegas, the first major New Mexico town reached by the railroad, is a case in point.

Shortly after the railroad arrived, New Town, or East Las Vegas, became the site of three hotels, four restaurants, and two real estate offices, and it could boast of three building contractors, three retail merchants, and three doctors. Even Old Town, or West Las Vegas, which was bypassed by the railroad, grew. Before long, the two towns were connected by a bridge built by the townspeople across the Gallinas River. The telephone, invented in 1876, even made a brief appearance in Las Vegas in 1879, and even

The End of Isolation   151

though the experiment with the telephone was short-lived, its very presence in Las Vegas introduced New Mexicans to the new wonder of modern communication.

Five miles up the Gallinas Canyon from Las Vegas, the A.T.&S.F. encouraged still further growth by building the Montezuma Hotel, and soon a trolley line ran between the town and the hotel. Gaining notoriety as an exclusive vacation spot, the Montezuma Hotel played host to people from all over the country, featuring the first building in New Mexico to possess electric lights. Las Vegas and its environs prospered for forty years, and only the coming of highways and cars brought to a close its story as one of New Mexico's fastest growing and most prosperous cities.

However, New Mexico's main railroad town would not be Las Vegas, but Albuquerque, which took longer to get started but became far more permanent. Located in central New Mexico, Albuquerque became not only the territory's leading railroad center but its leading city as well. Reached by the railroad in the spring of 1880, New Albuquerque began its growth spurt in 1881, initially catering in the best western boomtown tradition to gamblers, gunfighters, con artists, and other drifters. These wayward souls found themselves entertained both day and night in the fourteen new saloons and gambling halls that sprang up between First and Third streets on Railroad (now Central) Avenue. Although Old Town remained stagnant, it was nonetheless linked to the new part of town by a horse-drawn streetcar connecting the Old Town plaza with the railroad depot in New Albuquerque.

Eventually, the city grew in both area and population, and among those who arrived from other parts of the United States were many health seekers, including people who suffered from asthma and tuberculosis. These newcomers found relief in New Mexico's clear, dry air and in the centers for tubercular patients that soon appeared in New Albuquerque. The first tuberculosis sanatarium, founded in 1902 by the Sisters of Charity, marked the birth of what was to become St. Joseph's Hospital. Because most of the sanataria were located along the town's main thoroughfare, one stretch of what has become Central Avenue was known as "T. B. Avenue." The growth in population was accompanied by the appearance of Albuquerque's first housing development. Under the direction of longtime Albuquerque business leader Franz Huning, houses were built on the high land east of the railroad tracks, and they were consequently said to be a part of Huning's Highlands.

All those who followed the railroad into New Mexico had a story to tell, but most importantly, they helped to shape modern New Mexico. Bringing their cultures with them, they could not have done otherwise. Italians represented the largest group of foreign immigrants, and second were people from Lebanon. Among those who migrated from elsewhere in the United States, large numbers especially came from Texas, Oklahoma, Missouri, and Arkansas.

Newcomers to New Mexico caused the territory's population to increase markedly. Totaling 91,874 in 1870 and 119,565 in 1880, the population jumped to 160,282 in 1890, to 195,310 in 1900, and to ever greater numbers in the years that followed. Indeed, New Mexico's population grew by 67.6 percent during the first decade of the twentieth century, reaching 327,301 by 1910. In 1910 most New Mexicans could still be counted among the nation's rural population, but nonetheless, New Mexico could boast ten towns with populations in excess of 2,500; the largest were Albuquerque (11,020), Roswell (6,172), Santa Fe (5,072), and Raton (4,539).

New Mexico also felt the presence of its newcomers in terms of the question concerning who owned millions of acres of its land. The issue of landownership had long been a complex problem, for while the 1848 Treaty of Guadalupe Hidalgo had confirmed existing land titles, the land grant titles themselves had continued to cloud the issue. During the Spanish and Mexican periods, grants of land had been awarded not only to private parties, but to whole communities of people as well; and the boundary lines of the land grants were often only designated by such landmarks as trees and arroyos. In one effort to settle the question of landownership, the U.S. Congress set up the Office of Surveyor General in 1854, but while succeeding in reaffirming Pueblo Indian land titles, the surveyor general failed to settle the matter concerning ownership of Spanish and Mexican land grants.

When the railroad arrived with more newcomers, land values in New Mexico rose and attracted investment capital from as far away as the East Coast and Europe. Some investors speculated in land grant titles in the belief that land values would continue to rise, even managing in some instances to claim more land than had been provided in the original land grants. A case in point is the Maxwell Land Grant, which had originally included 97,000 acres of land. In 1879 the owners of the Maxwell grant became beneficiaries of an award of nearly 2 million acres of land by the U.S. Land Commissioner. Because continuing speculation in New Mexico land had become a national concern, Congress reacted in 1891 by setting up the Court of Private Land Claims. Charged with settling land questions once and for all, this court heard lawsuits brought by land claimants, and by 1903 it had ruled on all land grant claims.

Those who gained most from these land cases were Anglo-American lawyers, who often collected their legal fees in land, and Anglo-American settlers who had recently arrived in the territory. Indeed, about 80 percent of the Spanish and Mexican land grants ended up in the hands of Anglo-American lawyers and settlers. The one person who profited most was Thomas B. Catron,

Thomas B. Catron

a land grant lawyer whose involvement in seventy-five grants netted him outright ownership of 2 million acres of land and a share or legal interest in an additional 4 million acres. Those who lost most were Hispanic-Americans, who came to feel that the legal system had taken land that was rightfully theirs because much of the land that was lost had once been held in common for grazing by the whole community. The losers found little comfort in the legal reality of a U.S. court system that simply did not recognize the concept of community ownership of land.

The presence of newcomers in New Mexico brought other changes as well. First, more and more non-Catholic churches appeared in the territory until all the largest Protestant groups had churches in New Mexico by 1900. Second, New Mexico got its first public colleges as the result of an act passed by the legislature in 1889, setting up the University of New Mexico in Albuquerque, the School of Mines in Socorro, and the Agricultural College in Las Cruces. Third, free public education became a matter of law in 1891 after having previously been solely in the hands of churches or private individuals; and schooling received an additional boost in 1898, when Congress passed a bill sponsored by New Mexico's delegate to Congress, H. B. Fergusson, which set aside public lands for the support of the territory's public schools and colleges. Fourth, new building styles appeared in New Mexico, along with other cultural trappings brought by those newcomers in the territory. Fifth, daily newspapers made their debut and were five in number by 1900. Sixth, New Mexico's first public library opened as the result of work by Julia Asplund, who arrived in the territory in 1903 and thereafter became active in public affairs, pushing for the right of women to vote, among other things.

Yet in the midst of all these changes, some life-styles changed very little. Life in New Mexico's northern Hispanic and Indian communities was virtually untouched by the railroads and the newcomers and went on much as it had in past years. However, during this period the Navajo, facing competition from the introduction of machine-made blankets, stopped making blankets and began to weave the rugs for which they are so famous. Also during this period, the Navajo and Pueblo peoples—with the latter continuing their tradition of pottery-making—began to develop as fine jewelers and silversmiths. Thus, new life-styles took root alongside the old during New Mexico's final years as a territory.

During its status as a territory, which lasted more than sixty years, New Mexico was bypassed for statehood fifteen times. Three efforts to attain statehood, which occurred in 1850, 1872, and 1889, involved New Mexicans meeting in convention to draw up state constitutions, but on all three occasions Congress turned down the territory's request for statehood. Although not all New

The daily newspaper at Kingston, 1886

Mexicans favored statehood, the majority of residents did, as did most newcomers who followed the railroad into the territory.

The statehood movement received another boost from the Spanish-American War. The intent of the United States in declaring war against Spain in 1898 was to help Cuba win its independence from Spain; and because Spain had been New Mexico's original mother country, the six-month war became for New Mexicans a kind of test of their loyalty to the United States, which they passed with flying colors. Governor at the time was Miguel A. Otero, Jr., who received his appointment to office from President William McKinley in 1897. Serving ably until 1906, Otero held the dual distinction of being New Mexico's first Hispanic governor since 1846 and of serving the longest of any governor during New Mexico's history as part of the United States.

As a proponent of statehood, Otero reacted to Congress's war declaration by calling for volunteers to fight in the war, a call that both Hispanos and Anglo-Americans answered in great numbers. In fact, more New Mexicans volunteered than there were places for them in the armed forces, and many served in the Rough Riders cavalry unit commanded by Colonel Leonard Wood and Lieutenant Colonel Theodore Roosevelt. As one who had spent time in the West, Roosevelt believed that cowboys from the western states and territories would make the best fighters in Cuba; and in response to Roosevelt's request, Governor Otero offered to send 340 New Mexicans. Among other towns that received a call for volunteers was Clayton, a prairie cowtown in the far northeastern corner of New Mexico. The assignment of collecting Clayton's quota of thirty volunteers fell to Albert Thompson of the U.S. Land Office, which was located next door

Governor Miguel A.
Otero, Jr.

Rough Riders taking the oath of allegiance before the Palace of the Governors, 1898

to the Favorite Saloon. Thompson went to the saloon to read the governor's request, but few men signed up that first day. The next day, however, brought better results, for Jack Robinson, who was roundup boss for the huge Bar T Cross ranch and one of the most respected riders around, enlisted, and after that, Thompson had no trouble signing up the thirty men he needed. Altogether, New Mexicans made up about one-third of the Rough Rider unit.

The New Mexico volunteers and their horses traveled by train to San Antonio, Texas, and from there to Florida. On one occasion railroad delays left the Rough Riders' horses without water and feed, prompting the New Mexicans to force the train to a water-stop. This brash action brought an official reprimand, but Roosevelt applauded the move and only asked why the cowboys had waited so long before acting. The men went on to Cuba by ship, but lack of transports forced them to leave their horses behind and to fight on foot. As one New Mexico Rough Rider later said, "I was born in a dugout right here in Las Vegas, raised a cowboy, enlisted expecting to do my fighting on horseback as all the boys, but landed in Cuba afoot; marched, sweated, and fought afoot; earned whatever fame afoot." One of the first to die in the famous charge up San Juan Hill was Clayton's Jack Robinson, who was shot by a Spanish sharpshooter because the cowboy refused to keep down during the charge. Also serving at San Juan Hill was Captain Maximiliano Luna, who survived the fighting in Cuba but not his subsequent service with U.S. troops sent to the Philippines to crush the Filipino freedom fighters of Emilio Aguinaldo. A bronze bust to Luna's memory stands in the capitol building

The End of Isolation

President William McKinley at Deming, 1901

in Santa Fe. And in 1899, in honor of his troops and New Mexico's many volunteers, Roosevelt held the first Rough Riders reunion in Las Vegas, New Mexico, a town particularly well represented among the Rough Riders and which became the permanent home for its annual reunions.

As a result of the bravery and loyalty of the soldiers from New Mexico during the Spanish-American War, many people in the United States were convinced that New Mexicans had earned their right to statehood. During his 1899 visit to New Mexico, Roosevelt, who was elected vice-president in 1900, said that he, too, favored statehood. Yet the wait for statehood was longer than most New Mexicans wanted or expected it to be, for New Mexicans initially received little backing from officials in Washington, D.C. When a train carrying McKinley, elected to a second term in 1900, stopped in Deming in May 1901, the president would not commit himself on the issue of statehood; and even Roosevelt failed to promote New Mexico for statehood when he became president upon McKinley's assassination in September 1901. A president's support might have expedited statehood, but what New Mexico needed was an enabling act passed by Congress. Here, too, the lack of wholehearted support made it possible for a few obstructionist members of Congress to block New Mexico's statehood bid.

The statehood process stalled until 1910, when serious opposition at last dimmed, and Congress passed an enabling act that invited New Mexico to become a state. Under this act New Mexicans could frame a constitution with the assurance that Congress would be favorably disposed to accept it and to grant statehood. The constitution, which was to spell out New Mexico's government, would have to be acceptable to the voters and to the president as well as to Congress. Once it had received the approval of all concerned, the president would proclaim New Mexico's entry into the Union as a state. With the end of their long struggle for statehood in sight, New Mexicans eagerly embarked upon the task of writing a constitution.

9

Politics and Prosperity, 1910–1929

Once Congress passed the enabling act for New Mexico, the people of the territory took the next step toward statehood. In early September 1910 they elected one hundred delegates to draft a constitution at a convention scheduled to open in Santa Fe on 3 October. Seventy-one delegates, including all thirty-five Hispanic delegates, were Republicans; twenty-eight were Democrats; and one belonged to neither party. In addition to mirroring the relative strength of the territory's political parties, the delegates also reflected a cross-section of New Mexico's economic special interest groups: railroads, coal mining companies, copper mines, the sheep industry, cattle interests, and land grants. Lawyers represented the largest single occupational group, with thirty-two in attendance.

Leadership in the convention fell to a group called the "Old Guard" Republicans, conservatives who were determined to protect their economic interests and their control of New Mexico's politics and who succeeded in dictating the provisions of the constitution that emerged from the convention. The two most prominent Old Guard Republicans present were Charles A. Spiess, an A.T.&S.F. lawyer from Las Vegas who served as president of the convention, and Solomon Luna, a wealthy land and sheepowner from Valencia County. Perhaps the single most powerful delegate, Luna chaired a special committee on committees which decided all committee assignments. Among other influential Republicans at the convention were Thomas B. Catron, Charles Springer, Albert B. Fall, and Holm O. Bursum.

Leading the Democrats at the convention was H. B. Fergusson, a longtime spokesman for liberal causes, who wanted to give New Mexicans a progressive constitution that would include such features of popular democracy as the initiative, referendum, and recall. Democrats engaged in heated debate with the Old Guard

Solomon Luna

New Mexico Constitutional Convention, 1910

over these and other issues, but were outvoted at every turn. Sometimes the atmosphere on the floor of the convention became tense. On one occasion Albert Fall became so outraged at a Democratic delegate's speech that he rose from his seat, shook his fists, and verbally attacked the offending party. Knowing that Fall was always armed, the delegate left the convention floor, never to return. On another occasion the delegates conspired to keep one particularly obnoxious member away for a few days by reporting to the Santa Fe health authorities that the unwanted individual had been exposed to smallpox. The delegate was placed in quarantine for the incubation period, much to the joy of the remaining members of the convention.

The Old Guard Republicans drafted a plan of government that was very much to their liking. They gave New Mexico in 1910 a most conservative constitution, one that protected their perceived economic and political interests. The Old Guard also protected the rights of Hispanic New Mexicans, who were nearly universally Republican throughout New Mexico. Specifically, the constitution guaranteed Hispanos the right to vote and to receive an education. At the same time, the constitution included only a very weak referendum and did not include provisions for either the initiative or recall. Other progressive principles were missing as well—such as the right of women to vote in all elections and the direct election of United States senators. In fact, New Mexico's constitution was the most conservative adopted by any state, new or old, between 1889 and 1912, and it was far more conservative than the constitutions of the other western states. Nonetheless, this constitution, with amendments, remains in effect today, providing New Mexicans with the basic framework of government under which their state still functions.

Once written, the constitution went to the voters for almost guaranteed approval, for most New Mexicans so favored statehood that they were willing to accept any constitution. Some, however, felt that the constitution should be turned down by the voters, and they worked hard for its defeat. Led by Fergusson and other Democrats in public debates and rallies, the anticonstitution forces voiced their opposition to the document's protection for special interest groups as well as its lack of progressive principles, but to no avail. On 19 January 1911 voters approved the constitution by the overwhelming margin of 31,742 to 13,399.

Congressional approval for New Mexican statehood was at long last forthcoming on 19 August 1911, and on 6 January 1912 President William Howard Taft signed the proclamation making New Mexico the nation's forty-seventh state. Between the acts of congressional and presidential approval, New Mexicans held their first election for state offices on 7 November 1911. This initial election campaign was particularly hard fought between the Republicans and Democrats, with the Democrats doing surprisingly well by electing both the governor, William C. McDonald, and the lieutenant governor, Ezequiel C de Baca. However, the Republicans gained the upper hand in the other state races. They controlled the supreme court and both houses of the state legislature. The legislature was particularly important because it chose New Mexico's first two U.S. senators. Meeting on 11 March 1912, legislators selected Thomas B. Catron and Albert B. Fall, both staunch Old Guard Republicans. Ironically, in the following year the Seventeenth Amendment became a part of the U.S. Constitution, giving the direct election of United States senators to the people.

At the next statewide election in 1916, Ezequiel C de Baca won election as the state's first Hispanic governor. However, C de Baca died shortly after being sworn in as governor, and the lieutenant governor Washington E. Lindsey, a Republican, took office, giving that party control of the governorship for the first time. elected governor in 1918 was Octaviano Larrazolo, a leading member of the Hispanic community and the Republican party. This election reflected the prevailing trend in New Mexico politics during the early years of statehood, for Republicans largely controlled the government, and the key to their success was the majority Hispanic population.

While New Mexico was undergoing the transition from territory to state, events were taking place outside the United States which would have an impact upon its citizens. In 1911 revolutionaries ousted Mexican President Porfirio Diaz, who had been in power for more than thirty years. The overthrow of Diaz plunged Mexico into a decade of revolution and civil war, in which various leaders hoped to seize power for themselves. In the north was Francisco "Pancho" Villa, former bandit and now a general with considerable power in the state of Chihuahua. Villa's role in the Mexican Revolution soon brought him into conflict with the United States, for officials in Washington, D.C. blamed Villa for the deaths of U.S. citizens in northern Mexico and for the destruction or theft of their property. On the other hand, Villa was angry with Mexico's neighbor to the north because he believed that the United States should have supported him in his fight to take control of Mexico. Instead, President Woodrow Wilson had recognized as leader of Mexico one of Villa's foes, General Venustiano Carranza.

In an attempt to change his fortunes, an angry Villa planned an attack on U.S. territory at Columbus, New Mexico, a small town that lay just two miles north of the United States–Mexico border. Situated along the Southern Pacific Railroad line, Columbus housed four hundred permanent residents, along with elements of the Thirteenth U.S. Cavalry. Villa believed that a raid on Columbus would embarrass the Carranza government and so anger the United States that it would enter the fighting in Mexico, thus turning the tide of battle in his favor.

Villa attacked Columbus at 3:45 A.M. on 9 March 1916, surprising civilians and soldiers alike, as Villa's men filled the town and began shooting and setting homes afire. Still, the men of the Thirteenth Cavalry responded quickly, and the battle raged on toward daylight before the Mexicans retired southward, with U.S. soldiers in pursuit. During the raid ten U.S. civilians, eight

Columbus after Villa's raid, 1916

cavalrymen, and ninety Villistas died. As news of the attack spread, an angry U.S. government and its citizens expressed outrage.

Responding quickly, President Wilson ordered General John J. Pershing to lead a force of six thousand soldiers into Mexico to punish Villa. The punitive expedition failed, however, for Villa and his men, knowing the terrain, avoided Pershing's troops with ease. Furthermore, the expedition into Mexico revealed the sad state of preparedness within the U.S. Army. Equipment proved unequal to the task at hand, as trucks overheated and horses continually lost their shoes. For Villa, the only real outcome of the unsuccessful chase proved to be heightened resentment toward the presence of the United States in Mexico. At the same time, the raid on Columbus and the subsequent expedition into Mexico did nothing to aid Villa's cause.

Within a year of the Columbus raid, the United States found itself again concerned with its neighbor to the south, but for a different reason this time. On 27 February 1917 President Wilson learned the contents of a telegram sent by Arthur Zimmermann, the German foreign minister, to the German minister in Mexico. The Zimmermann Telegram, as it has since been called, invited Mexico to become a German ally in World War I, which had been raging since August 1914. In return for joining the German side, Zimmermann promised Mexico the return of New Mexico, Arizona, and Texas. The U.S. government actually learned of the telegram from the British government, which had intercepted, decoded, and quickly turned it over to American officials, with the intent of damaging United States–German relations. When the telegram's contents were published on 1 March 1917, the American people reacted angrily, for in January, just two months earlier, Germany had announced its intention to sink all ships found in the war zone around Britain, including those of the United States. U.S. neutrality in the war, carefully maintained since 1914, soon came to an end. On 2 April 1917 Wilson asked Congress for a declaration of war against Germany, and Congress obliged four days later. As a result, the United States entered World War I on the side of the Allies (Britain, France, Russia, and Italy).

Entry into the war brought a wave of excitement and activity to New Mexico. Governor Lindsey immediately committed New Mexico wholeheartedly to the war effort, declaring, "Good Friday 1917 will long be remembered in New Mexico, for on that day New Mexico was summoned to combat at home and overseas. April 6, 1917 our people passed from a status of profound industrial peace to a status of universal war." Following the governor's lead, state officials took steps to secure vital installations against supposed German saboteurs operating from Mexico, while increasing vigilance along the border. Furthermore, they welcomed the army's construction of Camp Cody, a training facility with a capacity for thirty thousand troops, near Deming. As for New Mexico's manpower, on 21 April President Wilson called up the New Mexico National Guard, and by June it was at full strength. Contributing valiant service to the American intervention, New Mexico servicemen fought in France during the crucial battles of 1918 that turned the tide of conflict against Germany. All told, 17,251 New Mexicans served in all branches of the armed forces, with 501 dying in combat or from other causes during the course of the war. These deaths exceeded the national average per capita losses of the forty-eight states.

New Mexico's resources aided the war effort as well. Answering the greater wartime demand for foodstuffs, farmers in

World War I soldiers march past the Governor's Mansion

1918 produced 3,334,000 bushels of wheat and 1,276,000 bushels of potatoes, a significant increase from the 1916 prewar levels of 2,104,000 bushels of wheat and 816,000 bushels of potatoes. Also, ranchers grew and shipped more cattle, profiting greatly during the war from the doubling of beef prices. Mining, too, saw a surge, as coal production, topping 4 million tons, led the way. In addition, the Kennecott Copper Company, new owner of the Santa Rita mines, used large open-pit mining methods to increase production to meet wartime needs. World War I thus spurred economic growth in New Mexico. In turn, New Mexicans contributed materially to the financing of the war. Individual New Mexicans answered war bond appeals with purchases worth 17,952,000 dollars, and the state government bought bonds worth another 750,000 dollars. Both figures exceeded the national government's expectations for New Mexico.

With the coming of peace in Europe in November 1918, New Mexicans soon shed their role as citizens of the world and joined the rest of the nation in its return to isolation. Like most United States citizens, they wanted to forget that there had been a world war. In the words of President Warren G. Harding, they wanted a "return to normalcy," and for New Mexicans normalcy meant partly a return to intense political party rivalry. In the 1920s the Republicans still dominated state politics, controlling both the legislature and the majority of seats on the state supreme court. They also won three of the five gubernatorial elections of the 1920s, electing Merritt C. Mechem in 1920 and Richard C. Dillon in 1926 and 1928, thus making Dillon the first New Mexico governor to win election to two successive terms. However, the Democrats were not without triumphs of their own. James F. Hinkle won the governorship in 1922, and Arthur T. Hannett won in 1924, albeit by a margin of 111 votes.

Aiding the Democratic victories of the 1920s was the support given some Democratic candidates by Bronson Cutting, who at that time was perhaps the most dominant politician on the New Mexico scene. Cutting arrived in New Mexico in 1910, becoming acquainted with the area while his father was director of the Southern Pacific Railroad. He was soon involved in New Mexico politics as a progressive Republican. To support the candidates and the issues that he favored, Cutting bought the *Santa Fe New Mexican*. Very quickly, he made a name for himself in state politics, and just as quickly he angered the Old Guard, who despised his progressive views. During World War I Cutting served in the army and afterward founded and financed the American Legion in New Mexico. With the twin power bases of the newspaper and the seventeen thousand legion members, Cutting became a force to be reckoned with in state politics, throwing his support first to one party and then to the other. Cutting and his faction became so important that his support for one or more candidates in major races was usually enough in itself to get them elected. Cutting himself became a U.S. senator, appointed to the post in 1927 and promptly winning election in 1928.

Another prominent political figure in New Mexico during the 1920s was Albert B. Fall, one of Cutting's Old Guard political enemies. Initially sent to the U.S. Senate by the state legislature in 1912, Fall won reelection to the U.S. Senate in 1918 and three years later quit that post to become secretary of the interior in the Harding administration. By 1924 Fall found himself swept up in the wave of political scandals that shook the Republican administration. The public learned that Fall had used his position at the interior department to lease naval oil reserves at Teapot Dome, Wyoming, and Elk Hills, California, to private oil companies controlled by Harry F. Sinclair and Edward L. Doheny. In return for these leases, Fall received "loans" from the two men, which he used to make extensive improvements on his ranch at Three Rivers in Otero County.

When the Teapot Dome scandal became public knowledge, Fall was arrested and tried in federal court for accepting bribes in exchange for leasing the oil reserves. Found guilty and sentenced to one year in jail in 1929, Fall because of his failing health was allowed to serve his time in the New Mexico state penitentiary rather than in a federal prison. He thus became the first cabinet member in U.S. history to be sent to prison for wrongdoing while

Albert B. Fall

Carl C. Magee

in office. By an odd coincidence, while Fall was found guilty of accepting bribes, neither Sinclair nor Doheny was ever convicted of having bribed Fall.

Among those who helped to bring Fall down was Carl C. Magee, muckraking editor of the *New Mexico State Tribune* and yet another figure central to the state's political scene during the 1920s. Originally a lawyer by profession, Magee came to New Mexico from Oklahoma in 1917, seeking a more healthful climate for his wife. In 1920 he purchased from Albert B. Fall the *Albuquerque Journal,* an outspokenly Republican daily with the largest circulation in the state. Magee, however, changed editorial policy and soon embroiled himself in what was to be lengthy political controversy. He began by calling for a clean sweep of the Republican-controlled state land office which, he charged, operated solely for the benefit of large ranchers. He went on to call for a cleaning up of the powerful Republican party. These remarks angered party leaders and prompted a visit by Fall, who warned Magee to lay off or be broken. Magee refused to back down, and the Republicans responded by denying the financially strapped editor the funds needed to keep control of the paper. As a result, Magee lost control of the *Journal* in 1921 and subsequently began the *New Mexico State Tribune,* with its masthead proclaiming, "Give Light and the People Will Find Their Own Way." This eventually became the masthead set on all Scripps-Howard newspapers.

Magee ran the *Tribune* as a pro-Democratic paper, with its

editorials attacking the Republican party and its leaders at every turn. In 1923 Magee traveled to Three Rivers to check on reports that Fall, supposedly short of funds, had undertaken major renovation projects at the ranch. When Magee saw Fall's newfound wealth, he informed his readers and thus became one of the first to expose Fall's impropriety in the Teapot Dome affair. Now more determined than ever to rid themselves of Magee and his newspaper, state Republican leaders saw their chance in the summer of 1923, when the editor suggested that state supreme court justice Frank W. Parker, a Republican, had mishandled court funds. Although Parker lived in Santa Fe and Magee resided in Albuquerque, the Republican leadership simply manipulated the state's court system so that Magee would be tried for libel before the court of the fourth judicial district in Las Vegas. There Judge David J. Leahy could guarantee a conviction, and in the process, Magee would be silenced.

The libel trial was brief, and as anticipated, Magee was convicted. At the same time, the clearly partisan nature of the trial became obvious to observers when Leahy concluded his remarks in court by stating that Magee was "a greater menace to civilized society . . . than is the cow thief or horse thief." But these were not the final words on Magee, for not content with just one conviction for libel, Magee's Republican antagonists planned to break him financially and put him in jail. Leahy ordered Magee back to court to face charges of contempt stemming from four Magee editorials attacking the Las Vegas court. Again found guilty, Magee was fined and sentenced to 360 days confinement in the San Miguel County jail. At this point, Governor Hinkle, a Democrat, thwarted the court by granting Magee a full pardon.

Another year of legal maneuvering saw Magee tried and acquitted in Santa Fe on the charge of libeling a former supreme court justice and convicted and pardoned for contempt before Leahy's court. In the course of the struggle, Magee found time to travel to Washington, D.C., to testify before the Senate committee investigating Fall and the Teapot Dome scandal. In 1924 he also tried his own hand at politics, seeking, but not securing, the Democratic nomination for the U.S. Senate.

The end to the sordid Magee affair came quite tragically on the evening of 9 August 1925. In Las Vegas to chair a meeting of the state hospital board, Magee was sitting in a hotel lobby when Leahy entered. Leahy had lost reelection as district judge in 1924 because of the political manner in which he had conducted his court. Now, Leahy attacked Magee, knocking him to the floor and continuing to beat him. Managing to free one hand, Magee pulled out his gun and fired it three times. Two shots hit Leahy in the arm; a third hit and killed a bystander who was trying to restrain Leahy. Magee was subsequently tried again before the Las Vegas court, this time on a manslaughter charge, but the new judge directed a verdict of acquittal because of Leahy's largely self-incriminating testimony. In 1927 Magee quit New Mexico and returned to Oklahoma, where he pursued various ventures, including the invention of the parking meter. The Magee trials illustrate in caricature the highly charged, rough and tumble, no-holds-barred nature of New Mexico partisan politics during the 1920s.

While politics divided many New Mexicans during the 1920s, New Mexico's Pueblo Indians grew united in a common cause—for the first time since the Pueblo Revolt of 1680—against government actions which they perceived as threatening their land and way of life. Although the Treaty of Guadalupe Hidalgo had promised that New Mexico's Indians would retain their land, and the office of surveyor general had confirmed Pueblo land titles, the U.S. government had generally ignored the Pueblo peoples. In 1876, however, the U.S. Supreme Court handed down a decision that eventually threatened Pueblo lands. In reaching the conclusion that the Pueblos were more advanced culturally than other Indian groups, the Court declared that the Pueblo peoples were not dependents of the federal government and therefore had the authority to handle their own lands as they saw fit. The result of this decision was that individual Indians sold 30 percent or more of Pueblo lands to non-Indians during ensuing decades. Then, in 1913, the Supreme Court again spoke on the issue of Pueblo lands by reversing its earlier decision and declaring that the Pueblo peoples were indeed dependents of the federal government and that non-Indian claims to Pueblo lands were consequently illegal.

The Court's new ruling created the immediate problem of what to do about the three thousand non-Indians who owned Pueblo land in 1913, especially since some of the non-Indian families had lived on this land for two or more generations. In 1921 Albert Fall, as secretary of the interior, sought a solution to the problem by asking his successor in the U.S. Senate, Holm O. Bursum, to draft an Indian land bill. Bursum's bill gave non-Indians ownership of Pueblo lands they had gained before 1902, and it permitted state courts to settle all future disputes over Pueblo land titles. If it had passed, this bill would have spelled disaster for the Pueblo peoples because it would have meant the permanent loss of some of the best irrigated Indian land, turning all future problems over to state courts that had long been unfriendly to the Indians.

Support for the Pueblo cause in response to the Bursum Bill came from a group of artists and writers who had settled in Taos, inspired by John Collier, a young poet who took it upon himself to let the Pueblos know what was being proposed for them. When the Indians learned of the contents of the Bursum Bill, they were stunned. No federal or state leader had even informed them that an Indian land bill was being considered. As Collier rallied support for the Pueblo peoples among his artist and writer friends throughout the country, the Indians themselves began to unite, and Pueblo leaders traveled to Washington, D.C., to appear before Congress. Widespread support for the Pueblo cause drew national attention, and the immediate result was the defeat of the Bursum Bill.

The attention aroused by the furor over the Bursum Bill also brought improvements in federal Indian policy. In 1924 Congress passed the Pueblo Lands Act, which recognized once and for all the land rights of the Pueblo peoples and provided compensation for the property which, under the law, non-Indians were to give up to the Pueblos. In the same year, Congress passed a second act that addressed the rights of Indians; and this law provided American citizenship for Indians born in the United States. Arizona and New Mexico, however, did not allow Indians to vote in national and state elections until 1947, when a federal court ruled that all states had to give Indian peoples the right to vote.

While New Mexico's Pueblo peoples were fighting to retain their land, other New Mexicans were watching changes at home as well. Like the rest of the West, the state's population continued to grow, increasing from 327,301 in 1910 to 360,350 a decade later. This was a relatively small increase, but these were troubled years, disrupted by World War I and a worldwide epidemic of Spanish Flu. Spreading across the globe at the end of World War I, this flu killed 21 million persons, with 550,000 victims in the United States and about 5,000 victims in New Mexico. Those hardest hit were between the ages of twenty and forty-five, and most New Mexico victims lived in small towns and rural areas. With the war and flu epidemic over by 1920, the state's population grew at a faster pace, reaching 423,317 by 1930.

The reasons behind the newcomers' migration to the state had not changed much; some came for a more healthful climate, while others sought a new livelihood. Most arrived from different parts of the United States, but there was also an increase in immigration from Mexico. Indeed, the number of immigrants from Mexico had begun to grow even before 1920, with refugees from the Mexican Revolution seeking safety north of the border. Later arrivals from Mexico were attracted by job openings in the United States, which were created by increased industrial activity. New Mexicans welcomed the immigrants as a source of cheap labor for work on the railroads, construction sites, and farms. The number of Mexican immigrants in New Mexico grew from 6,649 in 1910 to 20,272 in 1920 and to 59,340 by 1930.

In general, the 1920s saw a surge of development within the state. With the increased use of the automobile, the state built more and better highways, and New Mexico's isolation diminished. From 1921 to 1931 the money spent on road construction increased fivefold, and by 1932 the total mileage of improved roads within the state was 5,700. Like the railroad, highway construction had an impact on New Mexico's towns; as new roads were built, some towns grew, while others, bypassed by the highways, lost population or became less important economic centers. At the same time, trucks began to challenge the railroads as a major carrier of goods, and some short-line railroad routes were closed.

Ever increasing numbers of cars and roads resulted in the steady growth of the New Mexico tourist industry. By 1925 more western tourists traveled by car than by train, and to house travelers, a new type of lodging, the motel, emerged. New Mexico's first motel was the Apache Inn at Valley Ranch on the Pecos River. Many different attractions drew tourists to New Mexico, including the increasing number of national and state parks and monuments. Among these were the Bandelier National Monument, opened to the public in 1916, and Carlsbad Caverns, which opened as a national monument in 1923 and became a national park in 1930. Other tourist attractions included special activities and events, notably the Santa Fe Fiesta, begun in 1919 to celebrate the reconquest of New Mexico by Don Diego de Vargas, and the Inter-Tribal Indian Ceremonial, first hosted by Gallup in 1922.

Two new industries, petroleum and natural gas, also got their start in the 1920s. Although New Mexicans had located oil in the

New Mexico's Parks and Monuments

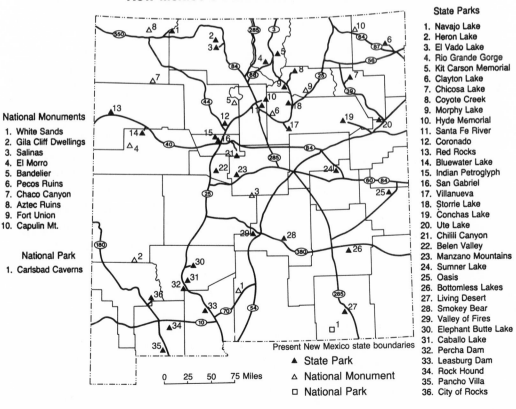

National Monuments

1. White Sands
2. Gila Cliff Dwellings
3. Salinas
4. El Morro
5. Bandelier
6. Pecos Ruins
7. Chaco Canyon
8. Aztec Ruins
9. Fort Union
10. Capulin Mt.

National Park

1. Carlsbad Caverns

State Parks

1. Navajo Lake
2. Heron Lake
3. El Vado Lake
4. Rio Grande Gorge
5. Kit Carson Memorial
6. Clayton Lake
7. Chicosa Lake
8. Coyote Creek
9. Morphy Lake
10. Hyde Memorial
11. Santa Fe River
12. Coronado
13. Red Rocks
14. Bluewater Lake
15. Indian Petroglyph
16. San Gabriel
17. Villanueva
18. Storrie Lake
19. Conchas Lake
20. Ute Lake
21. Chilili Canyon
22. Belen Valley
23. Manzano Mountains
24. Sumner Lake
25. Oasis
26. Bottomless Lakes
27. Living Desert
28. Smokey Bear
29. Valley of Fires
30. Elephant Butte Lake
31. Caballo Lake
32. Percha Dam
33. Leasburg Dam
34. Rock Hound
35. Pancho Villa
36. City of Rocks

Present New Mexico state boundaries

▲ State Park
△ National Monument
□ National Park

0   25   50   75 Miles

1880s, the first well to go into production in 1922 was located on the Hogback field in northwestern New Mexico, and it was followed two years later by production from a well in the nearby Rattlesnake field. Soon thereafter, the discoveries of big fields near Artesia, Hobbs, and Eunice yielded additional petroleum resources. The recognition of natural gas as a state resource dates from 1922, when the first commercial natural gas field at Ute Dome in San Juan County began to produce.

While new industries such as tourism, oil, and natural gas prospered, farmers and ranchers—who made up over 40 percent of the state's population—fared less well. Leading the list of problems that kept New Mexico's agriculture in a depressed condition during the 1920s was a decline in the demand for food crops and livestock after World War I, which, in turn, forced a drop in farm and ranch income and values. Overproduction of farm products only depressed the condition of the farmers by lowering prices, and drought added still further to the farmers' woes. For example, while the state's winter wheat crop in 1926 totaled 4,876,000 bushels, dry weather dropped the output to a mere 150,000 bushels in the following year. In addition, most New Mexico farms and ranches were simply too small to provide a steady income year after year, a condition graphically illustrated by the fact that nearly 30 percent of the farms contained fewer than fifty acres. Finding it more and more difficult to make a living, less successful farmers and ranchers were forced to sell out. One result was that New Mexico's agricultural units tended to become larger.

In the 1920s New Mexico underwent cultural changes as well, in part because the state became a major center for literature and the arts. Albuquerque was home to Harvey Fergusson and Erna Fergusson, brother and sister writers whose ancestors had entered New Mexico over the Santa Fe Trail. From his new home in the East, Harvey Fergusson wrote novels about New Mexico and the West. Publishing his *Blood of the Conquerors* in 1921, Fergusson then wrote four regional novels, including *Wolf Song,* which described life in Taos at the time of Kit Carson. Erna Fergusson, unlike her brother, continued to make her home in Albuquerque. One of her earliest works, *Dancing Gods,* detailed the Indian ceremonials of New Mexico and Arizona. She became the recognized first lady of New Mexico letters.

A new cultural development for New Mexico was the growth of colonies of writers and artists at Santa Fe and Taos. Alice Corbin Henderson, one of the first writers to settle in Santa Fe, came to New Mexico in 1916. She wrote several books and edited *The Turquoise Trail,* an outstanding collection of southwestern poetry. Another newcomer, Mary Austin, arrived in Santa Fe in 1918, founding the Santa Fe writers' colony. Her *Land of Journey's Ending,* published in 1924, contrasted Pueblo Indian culture with the life-

Erna Fergusson

style and culture found elsewhere in the United States and concluded that the culture of the Pueblos was superior. Through the years other distinguished writers came to Santa Fe, including Willa Cather, who, while visiting Austin, developed and wrote most of her famous novel *Death Comes for the Archbishop*. Published in 1927, this novel was based upon the life of Archbishop Lamy and his conflicts with New Mexico's native clergy. Another writer attracted to Santa Fe was Witter Bynner, who became famous for

Mary Austin

his writings on Indian life. Also lured to the Southwest was Oliver La Farge. A New Englander by birth, La Farge won the 1929 Pulitzer Prize for his *Laughing Boy,* a novel about Indian life.

Artists also settled in Santa Fe. One of the first to come was Robert Henri, who stayed only a short time but persuaded John Sloan to move to Santa Fe. Arriving in 1921, Sloan spent his summers at a house on Delgado Street, where he painted pictures of pueblos and Indians. Other artists who later came to Santa Fe were Marsden Hartley, Andrew Dasburg, John Marin, and Russell Cheney. However, the most famous artists attracted to New Mexico did not gather in Santa Fe, but rather at Taos.

The founders of the artists' colony at Taos were Bert G. Phillips and Ernest L. Blumenschein, who arrived in Taos together in 1898, with a wagon and team of horses they had bought in Denver. In the northern New Mexico village, Blumenschein immediately felt the impact of the different New Mexico cultures. He said to Phillips, "This is what we are looking for. Let's go no farther." Blumenschein and Phillips saw in northern New Mexico "one great naked anatomy of majestic landscape, once tortured, now calm." That year these two artists, joined by other painters, founded the Taos Art Colony. To send paintings to the East for exhibition required that the artists travel thirty-five miles by road across the Rio Grande Gorge to Tres Piedras, where they loaded their paintings aboard the narrow-gauge railroad that joined the A.T.&S.F. line near Lamy.

In 1915 the Taos artists formed the Taos Society of Artists. Joining Blumenschein and Phillips were J. H. Sharp, Oscar Berninghaus, E. Irving Couse, Victor Higgins, Walter Ufer, and Kenneth Adams. These painters specialized primarily in New Mexico landscapes and scenes depicting Indian and Hispanic culture. At first, the Taos Society exhibited its paintings anywhere on request, charging only the costs of transporting and insuring the works. After a dozen years, however, the society had outlived its usefulness, and the members agreed to end their association. The artists were now free to arrange for the showing of their own paintings.

Also showing her own work in the 1920s was the great twentieth-century painter Georgia O'Keeffe. Arriving in New Mexico shortly after World War I with the photographer Paul Strand and his wife Becky, O'Keeffe settled in Abiquiu, where she painted distinctive canvases of her new homeland. Her New Mexico paintings—displayed in New York by Alfred Stieglitz, a famous photographer and O'Keeffe's husband—established O'Keeffe's reputation as one of America's greatest modern painters.

Alongside the art colony in Taos, there grew up a colony of writers founded by Mabel Dodge Luhan, a wealthy New Yorker who arrived in Taos in 1916. After her marriage to painter Maurice Sterne ended, she married Tony Luhan, a Taos Indian. She invited

The Taos Society of Artists, 1932 (*standing left to right,* Walter Ufer, W. Herbert Dunton, Victor Higgins, Kenneth Adams; *seated left to right,* E. Martin Hennings, Bert G. Phillips, E. Irving Couse, Oscar E. Berninghaus; *front row left to right,* Joseph H. Sharp, Ernest L. Blumenschein)

writers from around the world to visit her roomy adobe home in Taos. Among those who came were John Collier, the young poet who led the fight against the Bursum Bill, and D. H. Lawrence, a famous English writer, who spent the fall and winter of 1922–23 and part of the spring of 1924 in New Mexico. Lawrence was so taken by New Mexico that he wrote:

> I think New Mexico was the greatest experience from the
> outside world that I have ever had. It certainly changed
> me forever. . . . In the magnificent fierce morning of New
> Mexico one sprang awake, a new part of the soul woke
> up suddenly, and the old world gave way to a new.

Lawrence's New Mexico home was a ranch located in the mountains about twenty miles north of Taos, and his presence in New Mexico attracted other writers and artists who found the Luhans' doors opened to them. Writers and artists alike developed a feeling of kinship with New Mexico's Indians, and whether settled in Santa Fe or Taos, they established New Mexico as a major American cultural center.

The growth of Anglo-American art colonies fostered, in turn, a new awareness of and respect for the work of New Mexico's Indian artists and craftspeople. The construction of the Art Museum in Santa Fe in 1917 provided Native American artists, among others, with a place to display their creations. Also aiding Indian artists was the Indian Tribal Arts Association, a group dedicated to encouraging Indian craftspeople to produce high-quality work and informing the public about Indian crafts. Among the Pueblo Indian painters of the 1920s were Awa Tsireh, Crescencio Martinez, Velino Shije (Ma-pe-wi), Tonita Peña, and Alfonso Roybal. Appreciation for their work soon spread beyond New Mexico to the nation.

The 1920s also witnessed the revival of superb Indian pottery-making. The Pueblo Indians in particular made fine pottery, and the most notable was fashioned by San Ildefonso potter Maria Martinez, who rediscovered the forgotten, thousand-year-old technique of black-on-white pottery. While Maria Martinez carefully fashioned and fired her pots, her husband Julian and other San Ildefonso men painted on the designs. In time, her pottery was sold in elegant shops along Fifth Avenue in New York City.

In addition to the revival in pottery-making, the Navajo began to weave higher-quality rugs. After 1890 Navajo weavers, unable to compete with machine-made blankets, had concentrated on rugs rather than blankets, but with disastrous results, for their craftsmanship had declined noticeably and their native designs had nearly disappeared. However, mainly because of the demands of traders and collectors in the 1920s, weaving began to improve with the reappearance of native designs and dyes made from native plants, fruits, and berries. At the same time, Navajo and Pueblo silversmiths continued their highly skilled work, relying primarily on the Mexican peso for silver until its export was halted by the Mexican government in 1930.

Hispanic artists and craftspeople also received greater recognition in the period after World War I. Hispanic folk art had flourished as long as New Mexico was isolated, but local folk art had been in less demand once outside arts and crafts reached New Mexico. Lithographs from Europe and Currier and Ives prints from the United States found a market in New Mexico after 1850, as did manufactured crafts brought in by the railroads in the late 1800s. However, some New Mexicans were determined to prevent the disappearance of local folk art.

During the 1920s artist Frank Applegate and writer Mary Austin organized the Spanish-Colonial Art Society, dedicated to the preservation of objects of folk art; and the New Mexico State Department of Vocational Education actively promoted a revival of Hispanic arts and crafts. As a result, the carvings and paintings of *santeros* gained new respect, and this, in turn, stimulated whole families to revive the nearly lost art of woodcarving. One such family was the José Dolores Lopez family of Cordova, a small village between Chimayo and Truchas.

At Chimayo the lost art of skillful weaving was rediscovered,

Maria and Julian Martinez of San Ildefonso

and weavers learned to make lovely Rio Grande blankets on the looms of their talented ancestors. As a highly developed Hispanic art form, weaving dated back to the early 1800s, a time when master weavers from Mexico had moved northward to teach their skill to New Mexicans. Two of these Mexican weavers, brothers Ricardo and Juan Bazan, turned Chimayo into the center of the New Mexico weaving industry. Using homespun wool and vegetable dyes, New Mexico weavers made their finest blankets about 1850. The patterns of the blankets were varied, and one of the most popular was the zigzag pattern, which was most likely borrowed from Indian pottery designs.

However, after New Mexico became a territory of the United States, the weaving craft declined, and the only demand for Chimayo blankets was found in the tourist trade. By the 1880s these blankets were made with machine-spun wool and commercial dyes. Then came the revival of weaving in the 1920s, but since the knowledge of earlier practices had all but disappeared, the revival was slow. Only when the demand for quality Chimayo blankets increased did village weavers again produce handspun, vegetable-dyed blankets equal to those of 1850.

Politics and Prosperity

Two other crafts honored during the 1920s were the wool embroideries of Hispanic women and the tincrafts of Hispanic men. Embroidery had always been part of a wealthy Hispanic woman's education, but now it became prized as an art worthy of preservation. Fashioned with long stitches and featuring plant and animal forms, the most popular woolen embroideries were *colchas* (bedspreads) and *sabanillas* (altar cloths). Tinsmithing, a craft with many practical applications, had been one of the few Hispanic art forms not to suffer from the arrival of arts and crafts from outside New Mexico. After 1850 New Mexico tinsmiths stayed busy in framing the prints from Europe and the United States. The frames were made in the form of birds, stars, and leaves, and they were decorated with thinly cut tin strips twisted into spiral ropes. Just as they had done in the 1800s, Hispanic tinsmiths continued to make both practical and decorative items, including lanterns, candleholders, candelabra, crosses, pitchers, and mirror frames.

Hispanic folk drama and music also revived in the 1920s. During this decade patrons of the arts encouraged the preservation and performance of folk plays, some of which had been almost forgotten for a generation. Also gaining new audiences were the *canciones populares,* or popular songs, whose rhythms and lyrics had kept them in vogue even when other forms of Hispanic folk art were suffering from neglect. Then, in the 1930s, Hispanic music received further support when teachers at the University of New Mexico undertook the formal study of Hispanic folk music, which had developed as an art form in the first quarter of the nineteenth century. This continued interest in Indian and Hispanic art forms, given impetus in the period after World War I, is one of the reasons why New Mexico has gained recognition as a major cultural center within the United States.

Along with developing an appreciation for the arts, New Mexicans had undergone numerous changes in the period from 1910 to 1929, from achieving statehood and fighting a world war to sharing in the general prosperity of the 1920s. Newcomers continued to swell the state's population, and in joining the older Indian and Hispanic populations, they helped to bring New Mexico's landscape and cultural heritage into sharper focus. At the same time, New Mexicans learned the valuable lesson that as twentieth-century citizens of the United States, they are subject to the same developments, good and bad, that affect people everywhere within the country and often within the world as well. They would relearn that sometimes painful lesson in the decades that followed.

10

New Mexico since 1929

Just as New Mexicans had enjoyed the country's general prosperity in the 1920s, they fell victim to the disastrous economic conditions that plagued the nation and much of the world during the 1930s. The 1930s were, of course, the decade of the Great Depression, the most severe economic downturn in U.S. history.

While the stock market crash in October 1929 signaled the start of the depression, its fundamental causes ran much deeper than the crash itself and the stock market speculation that precipitated it. Trouble spots appearing in the nation's economy during the 1920s were at the root of the economic collapse, and they included, among others, the overproduction of consumer goods, the economic legacy of the world war, and depressed agricultural conditions. The sad state of New Mexico's farmers and ranchers during the twenties certainly signaled the nation's agricultural woes, for those who kept their land sold less, while others lost their land altogether. Lasting until the United States began to become involved in World War II, the Great Depression threw millions out of work and brought in its wake hard times, misery, and suffering.

One of the hardest hit segments of the New Mexico economy during the depression was farming. In 1931 the state's most important crops were worth only about half of their 1929 value. Dry farmers were especially devastated as they suffered from both continually high operating costs and a prolonged drought that dried up portions of New Mexico so badly that they became part of the Dust Bowl. From Oklahoma to eastern New Mexico, winds picked up the dry topsoil, forming great clouds of dust so thick that it filled the air. On 28 May 1937 one dust cloud, or "black roller," measuring fifteen hundred feet high and miles across, descended upon the farming and ranching community of Clayton. The dust blew for hours and was so thick that light could not be

181

A dust cloud rolling over Clayton, 28 May 1937

seen across the street. Everywhere they hit, the dust storms killed livestock and destroyed crops; for example, in the Estancia Valley entire crops of pinto beans were killed and that once productive area was transformed into what author John L. Sinclair has called "the valley of broken hearts."

In all parts of New Mexico, farm land dropped in value before it bottomed out at an average of $4.95 an acre, the lowest value per acre of land in the United States. Nationwide the average per acre dropped to $31.16. Many New Mexico farmers had few or no crops to sell, and consequently, they fell behind in their taxes and could not meet their mortgage payments. Eventually, they were forced to sell their land, contributing in the process to the overall decline in farmland values. Once they were forced off the land, some farmers became tenant farmers, inhabiting and farming someone else's land while paying rent in crops or money. Other displaced farmers became migrant workers, traveling from place to place to help in harvesting crops grown by someone else. Still others who were forced off their land simply joined the millions of unemployed Americans.

The depression also hurt New Mexico's cattle ranchers, for they suffered from both drought and a shrinking marketplace. As grasslands dried up, they raised fewer cattle; and as the demand for beef declined, so did the value of the cattle on New Mexico's rangelands. Like the farmers, many ranchers fell behind in their taxes and were forced to sell their land, which was bought by large ranchers. As a result, New Mexico cattle ranches tended to increase in size, just as they had burgeoned during the previous decade.

Agriculture's ailing economic condition had a particularly harsh effect on New Mexico's economy, for the state was still primarily rural during the 1930s, with most of its people employed in raising crops and livestock. Yet farmers and ranchers were not the only ones to appear on the list of those devastated by depressed economic conditions. Indeed, high on the list were the miners, who watched their industry continue the downward slide that it had begun to experience in the 1920s. The output of coal dropped to 1.7 million tons in 1936, a total that was two and a half times less than the amount of coal mined in the peak production year of 1919. In addition, many mines became the property of larger companies when conditions forced many of the smaller companies out of business.

As economic conditions worsened during the early 1930s, state and local governments found themselves with too little tax money to provide all the needed services. By early 1933, for example, eight thousand school-age children were unable to attend schools because some school districts simply had no money to keep their doors open. Even successful businesses felt the effects of the depression. For example, the eighty-year-old Charles Ilfeld Company saw profit margins drop from 14.7 percent in 1928 to 2.2 percent in 1931 and finally to a net operating loss in 1932.

New Mexico's northern villagers also suffered. Before 1930 many of the villagers had earned wages through seasonal employment outside their villages, but after 1930 most of these people could not find outside work. Although most families in northern New Mexico raised sheep and farmed, they were often unable to support themselves, like many other New Mexicans.

During the early 1930s help for those in need came from several sources. At the local level churches, the Salvation Army, the community chests, and local offices for the needy provided some help; but as conditions grew worse, local efforts were not enough. As tax revenues dwindled, city and county welfare agencies sometimes faced backruptcy, and some poor and unemployed New Mexicans went hungry. As a result, major efforts to help those in need shifted to the national government in 1933, becoming part of President Franklin D. Roosevelt's New Deal program. Taking office in March 1933, Roosevelt sent a number of New Deal relief measures to a Congress that within months passed most of the acts the president wanted.

New Mexicans welcomed New Deal programs of all kinds. In some parts of the state—most commonly in counties where drought and dust storms made dry farming impossible—more than half of the people were enrolled in relief programs by 1935. In Harding County, for example, 72.8 percent of the people were on relief, while Torrance County had a percentage of 61.4. Catron County, hit hard by drought but not by severe dust storms, placed 58.7 percent of its residents in relief programs. In all, fourteen counties in northeastern and east-central New Mexico suffered from drought, and the percentage of people in those counties who were on relief ranged from a low of 24.3 to a high of 72.8.

Some New Deal programs, such as the Works Progress Administration (WPA), put people to work in many different kinds of jobs. Writers, artists, and musicians practiced their trades as employees of WPA projects, while others who worked for the WPA built schools and other public buildings, including the library and the administration building at the University of New Mexico and the high school in Clayton. By 1936 more than thirteen thousand New Mexicans had found jobs through this program.

Two programs which produced jobs for younger New Mexicans were the Civilian Conservation Corps (CCC) and the National Youth Administration (NYA). The CCC employed young men between the ages of eighteen and twenty-five to work on forest improvement and soil conservation projects. The young men lived in camps near their work sites, and part of the money they earned each month went directly to their families. One notable CCC project in New Mexico, the Spring Canyon dam near Hatch, took 150 CCC volunteers a total of 58,600 man-hours of labor to finish. When completed, the dam was 54 feet high and 408 feet long and trapped enough water to fill a 550-acre lake behind it. Special CCC camps for young Indians provided labor needed in flood control and irrigation projects and helped increase

A CCC project

Senator Dennis Chavez

farm production on Pueblo lands. The NYA, the second program for young people, emphasized job training and paid trainees while they learned. In Clayton, for example, young people learned such skills as woodworking, metal work, adobe work, and weaving, and then they immediately applied their newly learned skills in helping to build the high school. The skilled workers trained by the NYA during the depression years became a valuable national resource when World War II began.

Although the New Deal failed to end the Great Depression, it brought relief to many New Mexicans, and in the process, it helped in producing a major shift in the fortunes of New Mexico's political parties. The long-dominant Republican party began to lose its grip on state politics, mainly because it lost the support of Hispanic New Mexicans, who liked the programs of the Democrats in Washington, D.C., as well as the appointment of Democrat Dennis Chavez to the U.S. Senate in 1935, following Bronson Cutting's tragic death in an airplane crash. By shifting their party allegiance to the Democrats, Hispanic voters helped the party after 1935 in building and maintaining a long period of control over New Mexico politics.

During the 1930s New Mexico continued to experience a population growth. New Mexico was second in the region in the number of families new to one state during the depression decade, and by 1940 the number of residents stood at 531,818. The oil industry, which got its start in the 1920s, remained a bright spot in an otherwise bleak economic picture, for increased oil production provided needed tax money to the state. Tourism also received a boost when the federal government released some federal relief money to create new state parks.

At this time, important rocket research presaged New Mexico's role as a research center during the Second World War. In 1930 Dr. Robert H. Goddard moved to Mescalero Ranch near Roswell to built and test liquid-fueled rockets, a project that he pursued until 1941. His move to the state was precipitated by his early flight tests in Massachusetts, which had alarmed local officials but caught the attention of Charles A. Lindbergh, who made the first solo trans-Atlantic airplane flight in 1927. Lindbergh arranged private funding for Goddard's tests, and Goddard chose Roswell as his test site because of the area's open spaces and good weather. Goddard's work with liquid-fueled rockets progressed rapidly in New Mexico, and in the first test in December 1930 the rocket flew two thousand feet into the air. Testing continued until October 1941, with one of Goddard's later rockets reaching an altitude of nine thousand feet. Altogether, Goddard's research generated 214 patents for designing, powering, and guiding rockets.

Yet the U.S. armed forces saw little value in Goddard's rockets, and as World War II approached, they moved him to the East to develop airplane engines. German scientists, on the other hand, read Goddard's research reports and used his concepts to make rockets of their own, including the deadly V-2 rockets which rained terror on London, England, in 1944. After the war, when American soldiers captured Werner von Braun, Germany's leading rocket scientist, they asked him how the V-2 worked. Von Braun quickly replied, "Why don't you ask Goddard how they work?" However, Goddard had died on 10 August 1945, before he could resume his work at the Roswell test site. In finally recognizing the importance of Goddard's rocket research, Congress honored Goddard in 1959 by posthumously awarding him the Congressional Gold Medal, our nation's highest civilian award.

Goddard's last rocket test in New Mexico occurred in 1941, which marked in Europe the third year of World War II. The war had begun formally on 3 September 1939, two days after German armies invaded Poland; and as the war continued, more countries were drawn into the fighting. The Axis powers—Germany, Italy, and Japan—cooperated with one another in overrunning much of the world, and after the fall of France in June 1940, Great Britain stood alone in Europe against Germany and Italy until the German invasion of the Soviet Union brought that country into the war in June 1941. The United States, the last major power to maintain its neutrality, then joined the fight in late 1941, although President Roosevelt and Congress had earlier lent aid to Britain and other countries opposing the Axis powers. The war itself came to the United States on 7 December 1941, with the Japanese sneak attack on the U.S. naval base at Pearl Harbor, Hawaii. On 8

The Goddard Rocket Collection, Roswell Museum

December 1941 President Roosevelt requested and Congress approved a declaration of war against Japan, and shortly thereafter, Germany and Italy declared war on the United States.

Among the first Americans to see action in World War II were New Mexico National Guardsmen, who were fighting in the Pacific even before the formal declaration of war. They were members of the National Guard 111th Cavalry, which became part of the 200th Coast Artillery, Anti-Aircraft Regiment in 1940. Deployed in the Philippines, then a U.S. possession, in September 1941, the troops of the 200th were assigned the task of defending Clark Field and Fort Stotsenberg, which lay seventy-five miles north of the Philippine capital of Manila. Thus, hundreds of New Mexicans were at Clark Field when the Japanese attacked just ten hours after the strike on Pearl Harbor. For the most part, the New

Mexicans found their job frustrating because their anti-aircraft shells could not hit high-flying Japanese bombers, although the 200th regiment did shoot down some low-flying Japanese fighter planes.

When the Japanese ground forces launched their major assault on the Philippines, New Mexicans fought as members of the 200th regiment and the newly created 515th Coast Artillery Regiment. These regiments covered the withdrawal of American and Filipino troops to the Bataan Peninsula, a thirty-mile strip of land extending from the capital across Manila Bay. The fighting on Bataan was fierce. Battling hunger and disease as well as the Japanese, the defenders of the Bataan Peninsula held on until 9 April 1942, when they at last surrendered. What followed has come to be known as the Bataan Death March, a sixty-five-mile forced march of American prisoners to trains waiting to carry them to a Japanese prison camp. The march took six days, and eleven thousand Americans, including many New Mexicans, died on the way. Those who reached the camps and survived the terrible conditions there remained prisoners of war until 1945, witnessing during their captivity the deaths of thousands of their less fortunate comrades, again including many New Mexicans. Among the eighteen hundred New Mexicans serving in the Philippines, only nine hundred returned home. A Bataan Memorial,

200th Coast Artillery at antiaircraft practice near Las Vegas, August 1940

built at Fort Bliss, Texas, and later moved to Santa Fe, includes our state's eternal flame in honor of the brave New Mexicans who fought and died in defense of the Philippines.

The war lasted nearly four years, with New Mexicans seeing action wherever there was fighting. In fact, New Mexico had the highest casualty rate of the forty-eight states. One group of New Mexicans who played a special role in the war were the Navajo, who served the U.S. Marines as code talkers. Some code talkers translated secret military messages into their native language, while others decoded the messages at their destination. The Navajo language is so unusual that the thoroughly confused Japanese never broke the code. In all, 49,579 New Mexicans were inducted into the armed forces between late 1940 and the end of the war, some as draftees under the Selective Service Act and others as volunteers. New Mexico had the highest volunteer rate of any state.

During the course of the war, New Mexicans watched with pride the actions of the battleship named the U.S.S. *New Mexico*. Commissioned in October 1915 and launched on 23 April 1917, the *New Mexico* did not see action during World War I, but between the two world wars the *New Mexico* came to be known as the queen of the Pacific Fleet. Measuring 624 feet in length and 106 feet, 3 inches in width, she carried a crew of 1,323 men, and her big guns had a range of nearly ten miles. Stationed in the Pacific until 1941, the *New Mexico* was transferred that year to the Atlantic Ocean, and it consequently missed the attack at Pearl Harbor. After the outbreak of war, she returned to the Pacific for the remainder of the conflict, receiving during her tour of duty six battle stars for her outstanding record as well as suffering great damage. In January 1945 the *New Mexico* received a direct hit on her bridge from a Japanese suicide plane, a *kamikaze,* resulting in the deaths of twenty-nine men and the commanding officers. Four months later, hits from two *kamikazes* killed fifty-four men.

Despite the damage suffered, the *New Mexico* stayed in action, and it was present at the surrender of Japan in Tokyo Bay on 2 September 1945. Then, in 1946, the government unceremon- iously sold her for scrap. The only tangible remains of this proud fighting ship—her two bells, her helm, and other mementos— are now the property of the state of New Mexico. One of her bells hangs in the mall at the University of New Mexico in Albuquerque; her helm hangs on one wall in the university's naval ROTC build- ing; and her silver service has been on display at the Palace of the Governors in Santa Fe. The state treasures the remains of the much-decorated battleship and calls the ship its own, and yet, ironically, only one native New Mexican is ever known to have served on board the U.S.S. *New Mexico*.

As the war progressed, New Mexico became increasingly involved in every phase of the nation's war effort. Through its colleges and universities, the state provided training programs for the army and navy, which covered such subjects as weather forecasting and preflight training. The state also played host to special camps built by the national government. One camp near Santa Fe housed Japanese-Americans, Nisei who had been relocated from the West Coast under orders from President Roosevelt after anti-Japanese feelings erupted following the attack on Pearl Harbor. Roosevelt believed that national security required the forced relocation of some 112,000 Japanese-Americans, nearly two-thirds of whom had been born in the United States. Sent to camps in New Mexico and other states, they remained in confinement until war's end. Camps at Roswell and Lordsburg mainly housed German prisoners of war, although the Lordsburg facility sometimes held Italian prisoners and Japanese internees. Throughout the war New Mexico's prisoner-of-war camps ranked among the nation's largest.

New Mexico also played host to a number of army air bases that sprang up around the state. Kirtland Air Base in Albuquerque got its start in 1941, and it was joined the following year by a neighboring base, later named Sandia Base. In 1942 the government also opened bases in Clovis, Alamogordo, and Roswell, bases that eventually became known as Cannon, Holloman, and Walker air force bases. In addition, temporary wartime air bases were in operation at Hobbs, Deming, and Fort Sumner; and in 1945 the White Sands Proving Ground—today called White Sands Missile Range—was established in south-central New Mexico.

The growth of Albuquerque army air facilities during the war exemplified the importance of New Mexico as a national military center. Shortly after the attack on Pearl Harbor, the Albuquerque Army Air Base became the site of an advanced air force flying school, and as such, it was renamed Kirtland Field in early 1942. By 1945 Kirtland had trained 1,750 B-24 pilots and crew members, and on a smaller scale it had also trained aviation mechanics and navigators. For two years during the war—1942 and 1943—Kirtland even doubled as a ground school for glider pilots, and at war's end it was busily training crews for the B-29 bomber. East of Kirtland the Albuquerque Air Depot Training Station was opened by the army in May 1942, specializing in training servicemen in aircraft service, repair, and maintenance. In 1943 this training station became an army air field, and it was subsequently converted into an army air force convalescent center for wounded pilots and crews before it again became an army air field in 1945, officially named Sandia Base.

New Mexico also became one of the country's centers for modern military research, for it was at Los Alamos that scientists assembled the first atomic bomb. Lying twenty miles northwest of Santa Fe, Los Alamos was until 1942 the site of a boys' school whose alumni included J. Robert Oppenheimer, the scientist who

PARA LA DEFENSA

COMPRE USTED

BONOS
Y
ESTAMPILLAS
DE GUERRA DE
LOS ESTADOS UNIDOS

DE VENTA EN SU CASA DE CORREOS O BANCO

A World War II appeal for bonds and stamps

led the team that developed the atomic bomb. At Oppenheimer's suggestion the U.S. government bought the school and surrounding ranch land and established there its military atomic research project, code-named the Manhattan Project. The government sealed off the area in 1943, built research facilities, and brought in many top scientists. By the end of the war some five thousand people lived at the project site, and the town of Los Alamos had been born. Yet the purpose of the project and the very existence of the town were unknown to neighboring residents, for all aspects of the Manhattan Project remained top secret. Scientists and others associated with the project were issued numbers instead of names for their drivers' licenses, and they received all mail at a single address—P.O. Box 1663, Santa Fe. Even those who emptied the trash and collected the garbage had to meet special job qualifications, namely, illiteracy.

The atomic bomb and the idea behind it were so new that not even the scientists who built the bomb, called "the Gadget" at Los Alamos, knew whether or not it would work. To determine the success of their work, scientists detonated a bomb at the Trinity Site on the White Sands Proving Ground near Alamogordo in the early morning hours of 16 July 1945. Signaling the birth of the atomic age, the successful test of the first atomic bomb gave off such a resounding blast and such a brilliant flash that people throughout the state experienced it. A blind girl 120 miles from the test site saw the flash, and those nearby swore that the sun came up twice that morning. Still, the new weapon remained a secret for three more weeks. The people of New Mexico, the United States, and the world learned of the new weapon and its development in northern New Mexico only after an American plane dropped an atomic bomb on Hiroshima, Japan, on 6 August 1945. The Hiroshima blast and a second atomic bomb dropped on Nagasaki, Japan, on 9 August convinced the Japanese government to surrender, thus bringing World War II to an end.

Since the war's end, New Mexico has remained at the forefront of atomic research. Los Alamos Scientific Laboratory, directed by the University of California, carries on research for the Department of Energy, as does Sandia National Laboratories, a private corporation which began as a subsidiary of the Los Alamos laboratory in the late stages of the war. Sandia's main job as a defense contractor has been the research and development of nuclear weapons, while its main nonweapons function has been the development of new and improved sources of energy. Located

Trinity Site excavations at Ground Zero, November 1945

on the military reservation in Albuquerque, where it shares space with Kirtland Air Force Base, Sandia in conjunction with Kirtland led the way in the 1950s in planning U.S. nuclear tests. Since 1963 Kirtland has been the site of the Air Force Weapons Laboratory, engaged in weapons research. The continuing role of New Mexico as a national defense research center has benefited both the nation and the state, through the years bringing to New Mexico both people and money.

While defense became a cornerstone of New Mexico's economy during and after World War II, changes occurred in other segments of the economy as well. The mining industry, which had suffered during the Great Depression, recovered and entered a growth period that helped New Mexico to become one of the nation's leaders in the value of mined mineral products. Of the ninety-one minerals that the U.S. Bureau of Mines lists as vital, New Mexico's mines produce or have produced thirty, including not only copper, gold, silver, lead, zinc, molybdenum, coal, oil, and natural gas, but also large amounts of uranium and potash. The 1950 discovery of uranium in the hills north of Grants by Paddy Martinez, a Navajo sheepherder, set off a major boom in the Grants area and sent prospectors scurrying to find additional sources of uranium, which they soon located near Gallup. In 1977, during the uranium mining boom, New Mexico produced 44 percent of the nation's uranium supply, but the boom unfortunately lasted only until about 1980, when a depression hit the uranium mining industry. Potash, discovered near Carlsbad in 1925, became a mainstay of the economy of that area until it, too, became a depressed industry in the 1980s. Nonetheless, potash, which is mainly used in fertilizer, remains a potentially valuable resource, for in 1978 New Mexico supplied 84 percent of the nation's potash.

Coal mining, which had declined steadily since World War I—with its mines producing, for example, only 117,000 tons of coal in 1958—recovered in the 1960s for three main reasons. First, environmental awareness of the need for air quality control brought greater demand for low-sulfur western coal. Second, mining companies found New Mexico's coal easily extracted through surface mining techniques that are less costly than underground mining. Third, the state's public service company built coal-burning electrical power generation plants in the Four Corners Area. During the 1970s New Mexico's coal production, nearly 90 percent of which is used to generate power, grew at an even faster rate than during the previous decade because the cost of oil, sometimes used to produce electricity, increased radically. With about 550 million tons of coal lying in New Mexico and with state mines producing about 20 million tons of coal each year, New Mexico can count on coal reserves that will last for many years.

Oil and gas production have also been important assets to the state's modern-day economy. In 1977, for example, oil production made up 69 percent of the value of the state's total mineral production, with New Mexico ranking seventh among the nation's oil producing states at that time. In recent years most of this oil—indeed, more than 90 percent—has come from the Permian Basin, which stretches from west Texas into southeastern New Mexico, encompassing and bringing prosperity to cities such as Hobbs. During this same period older oil fields have produced less, leaving oil companies with the dual tasks of exploring for new oil while searching for ways to revitalize older fields. For a time in the modern era, natural gas production also pushed New Mexico high up the list of energy-producing states. Before experiencing a decline in production during the 1980s, New Mexico was the nation's fourth leading producer of natural gas by the late 1970s.

The decline in oil and natural gas production—duplicated to varying degrees by lower production figures in the uranium, potash, and copper industries—has cost the state both jobs and dollars. In 1980, for example, mining employed 6.3 percent of New Mexico's total work force. Four years later, only 4.3 percent of the state's work force held jobs in mineral extraction industries, which were hit hard by a combination of factors, including increased production costs, international competition, and decreased market demand. Reduced mineral production has meant less revenue for a state grown accustomed to collecting severance taxes on minerals extracted from its land.

The trend toward larger farms and ranches, which began in the 1920s and accelerated during the 1930s, continued apace after the depression. The 32,830 farms and ranches in 1940 shrank in number to fewer than 12,000 in the 1970s, while the average size of agricultural units grew during this same period to more than four thousand acres. Accompanying the changes in the number and size of farms and ranches was a shift in the state's population, for more and more New Mexicans found themselves living in urban areas and employed in nonagricultural jobs. Today only about 2 percent of the state's population work directly in agriculture, and two-thirds of the state's agricultural products come from two areas, the eastern and southern plains and the lower Rio Grande Valley. Among New Mexico's thirty-three counties, Chaves County is the leader in agricultural production, with Curry County ranking second. New Mexico's leading products are cattle, sheep, dairy items, and wool, while its other products include cotton lint, hay, sorghum, grain, peanuts, pecans, chili, and poultry.

While agriculture is a relatively less important part of the state's economy today than it was before World War II, tourism is just as vital. With its ski resorts, lodges, guest ranches, camping grounds, and breathtaking landscape, New Mexico offers year-

New Mexico Counties

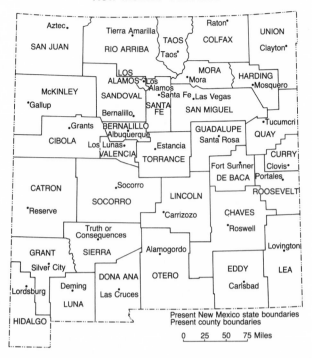

round recreation to those interested in sporting and sightseeing activities. It also offers visitors the opportunity to see Indian ceremonials and to visit parks and monuments such as Carlsbad Caverns, White Sands, and Bandelier. As out-of-state cars swarm over New Mexico's highways in the summer months, locals are often heard to cry, "Texan, Go Home!" This opinion, however, does not eclipse the fact that tourists spend millions of dollars within the state, providing livelihoods for thousands of New Mexicans.

Along with economic changes, the state has experienced an increase in population, which has played a significant role in shaping modern-day New Mexico and its people. The state's rapid growth began with World War II, spurted in the 1950s, slowed in the 1960s, and then increased again in the 1970s. By 1980 New Mexico boasted 1,299,968 residents, a population 207 percent greater than it was in 1940 and one that is significantly different from that of the prewar period. In addition to swelling the state's urban population, the movement of people into New Mexico from other states changed the ethnic makeup of its citizenry; while Hispanos were a majority of the state's people in 1940, the majority today is Anglo-American. Especially since 1970, most of these newcomers have arrived from the East and the Midwest in search of a more moderate climate. Located in the sunbelt region of the country that stretches from North Carolina to southern California, New Mexico has been one of the hosts of

New Mexico since 1929   195

the phenomenal migration of Americans to this area of the United States.

The influx of newcomers eventually brought changes to New Mexico politics, but from the 1930s to the 1960s state politics remained largely under Democratic party control. During this period the Democrats elected the U.S. senators and representatives for New Mexico, controlled the state legislature, and won most statewide races from the governorship on down. The major exceptions to this one-party control of state politics were Republicans Edwin L. Mechem and David Cargo, both of whom were elected governor—Mechem to four two-year terms and Cargo to two two-year terms.

Through their control of New Mexico politics, the Democrats produced the state's leading politicians, and chief among these were Dennis Chaves and Clinton P. Anderson. Holding a seat in the U.S. Senate from 1935 to 1962, Chavez served as chairman of the Senate's public works committee and became the second ranking member of the appropriations committee. From these powerful positions Senator Chavez used his influence to ensure the development of New Mexico during World War II and afterward. Anderson served from 1941 to 1945 as one of the state's two U.S. representatives and from 1945 to 1948 as President Harry S. Truman's secretary of agriculture. In 1948 New Mexicans elected him to the U.S. Senate and subsequently returned him to the Senate in 1954, 1960, and 1966, where he remained until his retirement in 1972. As chairperson of Congress's joint committee on atomic energy, Anderson assured that New Mexico remained a center for atomic and military research.

The fact that neither Chavez nor Anderson ever lost a Senate reelection bid was a reflection of both their popularity and the strength of the Democratic party. Even the popular four-term governor, Edwin L. Mechem, could not break the Democratic stranglehold on New Mexico's seats in the U.S. Senate. Resigning as governor in 1962, with the understanding that the new governor Tom Bolack would appoint him to the Senate seat left vacant by Dennis Chavez's death, Mechem was in 1964 ingloriously rejected at the polls by New Mexicans, who returned Chavez's seat to Democratic control by voting for Joseph M. Montoya. Montoya won again in 1970, but the seventies signaled the beginning of the end of one-party control of New Mexico politics, for in 1976 Montoya lost his Senate seat to Republican Harrison Schmitt.

The shifting political fortunes of New Mexico's political parties during the 1970s occurred for several reasons. Newcomers to New Mexico generally added strength to the Republican party, and westerners were becoming more conservative in their views. Also benefiting the Republican party during the seventies was the crossover phenomenon of registered Democrats voting for Republican tickets. As a result of the increased attraction for Republican candidates, the state's congressional delegation during the 1970s and 1980s has been fairly evenly balanced between Republicans and Democrats, and the state's most prominent politician has been Pete V. Domenici, a Republican. First elected to fill the U.S. Senate seat vacated by Anderson in 1972, Domenici easily won reelection in 1978 and 1984 and rose to the chairmanship of the Senate's powerful budget committee. Then, in 1986, Republicans won the offices of governor, attorney general, and land commissioner, winning the last two positions for the first time since 1928. Since 1968 the Republicans have also controlled at least one of the state's seats in the U.S. House of Representatives.

Yet despite a growing Republican party strength, the Democrats have held their own by continuing to have an edge among registered voters and by winning a majority of state offices. Democrat Bruce King won the governorship in both 1970 and 1978, becoming the first New Mexican ever to serve two four-year terms in that office. Democrats Jerry Apodaca and Toney Anaya also won gubernatorial elections, in 1974 and 1982, respectively; and in 1982 Democrat Jeff Bingaman defeated one-term senator Harrison Schmitt. Today, then, New Mexico politics shows some balance, with both parties winning elections and no one party completely dominating the other, as it has in the past. In 1982 a more populous New Mexico gained a third seat in the U.S. House of Representatives, and in 1976 New Mexicans broke a record that stretched back to 1912. From the advent of statehood New Mexico voters had cast the majority of their ballots for the national presidential winner in every election until 1976, when their preferred candidate, Gerald Ford, lost out to Jimmy Carter.

Transformations in New Mexico's society and culture since the start of the Great Depression were not without effect on New Mexico's oldest residents—the state's Indians and Hispanos. The congressional acts of 1924, which granted Indians citizenship and recognized the rights of Pueblo Indians to their lands, were followed by the passage in 1934 of the Indian Reorganization Act (IRA). A major piece of legislation with far-reaching consequences, the IRA ended the allotment of Indian lands in individual ownership and the sale of unallotted lands to non-Indians; it provided for adding to reservation lands; it restored a limited degree of self-government to Indian tribes; it allowed tribes, if they wished, to incorporate under terms of the act and to elect tribal governments that had some legal powers; it created a 10-million-dollar revolving loan fund for incorporated tribal councils to use in promoting economic growth; it provided a yearly scholarship fund of up to 250,000 dollars for vocational education; and it stated that Indians should receive preference for civil service jobs within the Bureau of Indian Affairs.

Although most Indians saw the terms of the act as an improvement over previous government policy, the IRA did reveal some serious shortcomings, including provisions that denied the Navajo the right to enlarge their reservation and which excluded some tribes (although none in New Mexico) from the terms of the act. In addition, the IRA gave extraordinary power to the secretary of the interior, who had the right to set rules for tribal elections, approve tribal constitutions, veto the choice of tribal lawyers, and make rules for forest and grazing land use. Even though the act set aside monies for the purchase of additional land, economic development, and scholarships, economic resources proved to be totally inadequate.

While the Indian Reorganization Act applied to all of New Mexico's Indians, it had no immediate effect on the various Pueblos, who did not initially adopt constitutional governments; and it had differing effects on the state's non-Pueblo Indians, harming some while helping others. The Navajo, for example, were not only denied the opportunity to expand their reservation, but the size of their livestock herds was also greatly reduced by an order of the secretary of the interior restricting the number of livestock the Navajo could graze on their range units. On the other hand, both the Mescalero and Jicarilla Apache benefited from the IRA, for each tribe—the Mescalero in 1936 and the Jicarilla in 1937—adopted constitutional governments. Each borrowed money under the terms of the act and experienced dramatic economic growth, mostly, at first, in the value of livestock and livestock products.

World War II brought still further changes to the Indians, with some serving in the armed forces while others moved off the reservation to find jobs in wartime industries. After the war additional changes saw more and more New Mexico Indian children enrolled in public school, a trend that has continued since the 1950s. As a result, more now have a college education, with many preparing for professions in law and medicine. Whereas there were only eleven Indian lawyers in the entire United States in 1966, the number since then has risen steadily, in part due to the efforts of the University of New Mexico Law School. In 1967 the law school established a scholarship program for Indian students, and two years later, the American Indian Law Center was opened. Indians also gained power in the political arena by seeking and winning election to state offices. Pioneers in this area include Thomas E. Atcitty, Leo Watchman, and Monroe Jymm, all of whom have served in the state legislature. A Navajo and a Democrat, Atcitty has been a long-time representative and an important member of the New Mexico Human Rights Commission.

Economically, many of New Mexico's Indians still earn their living in the traditional manner by farming and raising livestock.

At the same time, the tribes have diversified tribal economies by developing their own businesses, especially in tourism. The Mescalero Apache own and operate the Sierra Blanca Ski Area in the Sacramento Mountains of south-central New Mexico, a resort hotel three miles south of Ruidoso, and campgrounds for tourists in their forest land. The Jicarilla Apache have also developed tourist sites on their land in northwestern New Mexico, including a lodge at Stone Lake and campgrounds at Dulce and Mundo lakes.

While the Navajo have successfully attracted tourists to their reservation, they have profited more from the discoveries of coal, oil, and uranium on their land. But realizing that mineral resources cannot be replaced, the Navajo Nation has sought to broaden its economy by reviving tribal agriculture. As late as 1936 raising livestock and farming made up more than half the Navajo income, and wages made up less than one-third. By 1958 wages accounted for fully two-thirds of the Navajo income, and by the early 1960s only 25 to 30 percent of the Navajo families did any farming at all, with the income from the sale of their farm products shrinking to almost nothing.

To restore farming to the Navajo economy, the tribe in 1962 began the Navajo Indian Irrigation Project (NIIP). In defining the parameters of the NIIP, a federal act set aside 110,630 acres of land to be irrigated as part of the project, stipulating that 508,000 acre-feet of water from the Navajo Reservoir would be used each year for irrigation. To operate the project, the Navajo Nation set up the Navajo Agricultural Products Industry. Plagued by problems in funding, planning, soil type, water supply, and a lack of trained workers, the project has progressed slowly since the beginning of construction in 1964. Still, the NIIP offers the Navajo the promise of a broader, more productive tribal economy.

Although the modern age has brought changes for New Mexico's Indians, many of their old traditions remain unchanged, and most Indians, Pueblo as well as non-Pueblo, continue to live at home on the lands of their ancestors. Occupation of Pueblo lands has continued for more than four hundred years, although today there is a larger Pueblo population and fewer actual pueblo sites than four hundred years ago. The Indians have also retained their special ceremonies, at times fighting to protect their land and traditions from outside encroachment. In the 1960s, for example, the Taos Indians battled the U.S. Forest Service for control of Blue Lake, which lies in the mountains above the pueblo itself. Surrounded by national forest land, Blue Lake has long been a sacred place of worship for the Taos people, and in the 1930s they received from the national government guaranteed access to the lake and guaranteed protection of the land around the lake.

The guarantees worked well until the 1960s, when heavy public use of the national forest near Blue Lake, including logging, damaged land around the lake and threatened the lake itself. The

Taos people demanded that the national government protect their religious site, and as in the 1920s, the fight for Indian rights gained national attention and encouraged Congress to act. In late 1970 Congress set aside Blue Lake and forty-eight thousand acres of the Carson National Forest for the sole use of the Taos Indians—after an effort by the tribe that was reminiscent of the Pueblo peoples' victory over the Bursum Bill.

The lives of Hispanic New Mexicans have also undergone changes since the end of the Great Depression. During World War II a large number of Hispanos left their homes in northern New Mexico villages to participate actively in the war effort. Then, after the war, large numbers of Hispanic veterans continued their education under the G.I. Bill, which allowed them to enroll in trade schools as well as in colleges and universities. Some gained job skills; others entered professional fields or started their own businesses; and still others entered the political arena to run for elected office. Before the late 1960s New Mexico was the only state in the Southwest in which Hispanic politicians had real power. Dennis Chavez and Antonio Fernandez were members of Congress from 1935 to 1962 and from 1943 to 1956, respectively. In 1968 Manuel Lujan began a long stint as the state's U.S. representative from the first congressional district; and Jerry Apodaca in 1974 and Toney Anaya in 1982 won the governorship.

On the other hand, problems that began for Hispanos in northern New Mexico villages during the Great Depression continued to plague them. After World War II the villages lost population, a phenomenon which made the northern counties unique among those in the United States with a large concentration of Spanish-speaking people, for they were the only such places in the modern period to lose population. The northern communities also lost land, and small farmers and ranchers there suffered problems with the U.S. Forest Service over the use of forest land. Thus, in northern New Mexico many of the people in the mid-1960s rallied behind a new leader, Reies Lopez Tijerina.

A newcomer to New Mexico, Tijerina was a preacher who began to speak out about what he believed to be the root problems of the Hispanic northern New Mexicans, namely, the loss of land, grazing rights, and community spirit. Tijerina argued that Hispanos needed to join together to fight for their rights, and as a vehicle to achieve this end, Tijerina formed the Alianza Federal de Mercedes, the Federal Alliance of Land Grants. Most commonly known as the Alianza, the group grew quicky to five thousand members. Tijerina claimed that the Alianza members were the rightful heirs to millions of acres of land because of land grant titles, which, he said, had been unscrupulously taken from them by the forest service and Anglo-American ranchers and lawyers. In backing rhetoric with action, the Alianza caught the public's attention in October 1966, when Tijerina and 350 followers seized control of Echo Amphitheater on national forest land northwest of Abiquiu. There members of the Alianza announced the birth of a new country on what Tijerina maintained was part of a Spanish land grant.

After gaining extensive publicity when its members arrested forest rangers for trespassing on the occupied land, the Alianza next made the headlines by conducting a raid on the courthouse at Tierra Amarilla in June 1967. The shootout at the courthouse left two law officers wounded and brought a forceful response from state officials. The lieutenant governor, acting in the governor's absence, sent the state's National Guard, equipped with tanks, into Rio Arriba County. The guardsmen arrested some of the area residents, but failed to round up most of those involved in the raid, who escaped. Tijerina himself later stood trial in state court for his alleged participation in the Tierra Amarilla raid and was acquitted. However, when he stood trial in federal court for occupying the Echo Amphitheater and destroying government property, he was found guilty and spent more than two years in a federal prison in El Paso.

Tijerina did not bring about a return of any land grants to the villagers of northern New Mexico; in fact, the Alianza lost much support after the violent raid on the Tierra Amarilla courthouse. However, Tijerina did focus attention on the problems of northern New Mexico, and he voiced the hopes of many of the residents there, who to this day retain their special identity and pride.

On a broader cultural note, New Mexico during the modern period has continued to hold a special attraction for artists in a variety of fields, and among these artists are some whose lengthy careers and talent have helped to bridge the gap between past and present. For example, the great Georgia O'Keeffe fits into the modern period as well as into the period of the artists' colonies in the 1920s, with her work capturing on canvas a timeless New Mexico. Standing alongside O'Keeffe as one of New Mexico's best-known modern painters is Peter Hurd. A native of Roswell who left New Mexico to study with N. C. Wyeth, Hurd later married Wyeth's daughter and returned to his home state, where he remained until his death in 1984. New Mexico landscapes are among his most famous paintings, and Ruidoso Canyon was a favorite subject. Other notable modern-day painters include Santa Clara artist Pablita Velarde, known for her paintings and murals in public buildings; her daughter, Helen Hardin; and R. C. Gorman, who was born on the Navajo reservation and drew his inspiration to take up painting from his father Carl.

Modern-day New Mexico has also continued to inspire accomplished writers, including Paul Horgan, who spent part of his childhood in Albuquerque and later lived and worked in Roswell before moving to the East. A frequent visitor to New Mexico until

Georgia O'Keeffe, 1929

the early 1980s, Horgan includes New Mexico themes in many
of his books, notably in his 1955 Pulitzer Prize–winning *Great
River: The Rio Grande in North American History,* which relates the
history of the people who have lived along the Rio Grande, and
in his 1976 Pulitzer Prize–winning book, *Lamy of Santa Fe.* Still
another writer who unveils life in the Southwest is Frank Waters,
a Coloradan by birth, living today in northern New Mexico. Waters'
The Man Who Killed the Deer is highly acclaimed for its portrayal
of the cultural conflicts encountered by young Indians venturing

Peter Hurd, 1968

into the world beyond the pueblo; and his novel *People of the Valley* tells of life in northern New Mexico's Mora Valley.

In the 1970s and 1980s new writers have joined the coterie of New Mexico's esteemed artists, including among their numbers Rudolfo Anaya, John Nichols, and Mark Medoff. Born in Pastura near Santa Rosa, Anaya has written plays, screenplays, and novels; his best-known novels are *Bless Me Ultima* and *Heart of Aztlán,* both of which are set in and around Guadalupe County. A resident of New Mexico since 1969, John Nichols, also a writer of novels and screenplays, has depicted modern life in New Mexico's northern mountain communities in a trilogy of novels, *The Milagro Beanfield War, The Magic Journey,* and *The Nirvana Blues*—with *The Milagro Beanfield War* being both the first and the best known of the three. Mark Medoff, a member of the drama department faculty at New Mexico State University, is a playwright and writer of screenplays. His *Children of a Lesser God,* a play whose theme is communication between those who can and cannot hear, won a Tony Award as an outstanding production on Broadway. Other writers too numerous to mention also call New Mexico home or include New Mexico themes within their works. Indeed, New Mexico's inspirational influence on literary works lives on in the well over 500 published novels set in the land of enchantment.

Hispanic folk art and drama, revived and revitalized during the 1920s, continues to thrive in today's New Mexico. Patrocinio

George Lopez

Barela, whose *santos* first caught the public eye during the 1930s, created a great many wood sculptures before his death in Taos in 1964, and in the process, he helped to link the past with the present. More recently, George Lopez, in establishing himself as one of the area's finest *santeros,* has carried on the tradition of the Lopez family of woodcarvers in Cordova. After experiencing a revival in recent decades, Hispanic folk plays have also perpetuated New Mexico's Hispanic heritage. At Christmas some communities stage the folk drama *Las Posadas,* which tells the story of Mary and Joseph seeking shelter for the birth of the Christ child. Other dramas performed include *Los Pastores,* the story of the shepherds' search for the Christ child, and *Los moros y los cristianos,* a recounting of the Christian victory over the Moors in Spain.

Indian ceremonials, which have not changed for hundreds of years, continue to aid New Mexicans in reflecting upon their past, providing New Mexicans with a glimpse of living history. Town residents also relive history by observing each year founders' day celebrations and old timers' celebrations, which remind them of their towns' origins. And while the arts, crafts, and culture of New Mexico's past interest many, New Mexicans also support a wide variety of modern cultural activities. Today, then, New Mexico is a state whose people remember the past, live in the present, and prepare for the future.

As a part of the United States, New Mexico and its people will continue to be affected by the events that touch the lives of all Americans, a lesson that the events of the twentieth century have clearly taught us. We also know that New Mexico, now one of the nation's leading centers of atomic and weapons research as well as a leader among energy-producing states, will most likely remain a research center and a producer of energy. Because history provides no crystal ball that allows us to see into the future, we cannot know whether New Mexico, a historically poor state, will continue to attract newcomers, develop new economic enterprises, or find ways to live with a water supply already limited and in danger of being exhausted in some places. Ultimately, we know only that New Mexico is a product of its past, a colorful past filled with the stories of a people who have truly created a "land of enchantment."

Selected Bibliography

Baldwin, Gordon C. *Indians of the Southwest* (New York: Capricorn Books, 1973).

Bannon, John Francis, ed. *Bolton and the Spanish Borderlands* (Norman: University of Oklahoma Press, 1964).

Beck, Warren A. *New Mexico: A History of Four Centuries* (Norman: University of Oklahoma Press, 1962).

Bolton, Herbert E. *Coronado: Knight of the Pueblos and Plains* (Albuquerque: University of New Mexico Press, 1964).

Brown, Lorin W., with Charles L. Briggs and Marta Weigle. *Hispano Folklife of New Mexico: The Lorin W. Brown Federal Writers' Project Manuscripts* (Albuquerque: University of New Mexico Press, 1978).

Cabeza de Baca, Fabiola. *We Fed Them Cactus* (Albuquerque: University of New Mexico Press, 1979).

Dickey, Roland F. *New Mexico Village Arts* (Albuquerque: University of New Mexico Press, 1970).

Dutton, Bertha P. *Indians of the American Southwest* (Albuquerque: University of New Mexico Press, 1983).

Ellis, Richard N., ed. *New Mexico Past and Present: A Historical Reader* (Albuquerque: University of New Mexico Press, 1971).

Fergusson, Erna. *New Mexico: A Pageant of Three Peoples* (Albuquerque: University of New Mexico Press, 1964).

Fergusson, Harvey. *Rio Grande* (New York: William Morrow and Company, 1955).

Hammond, George P., and Edgar F. Good. *The Adventures of Don Francisco Vásquez de Coronado* (Albuquerque: University of New Mexico Press, 1938).

Holmes, Jack E. *Politics in New Mexico* (Albuquerque: University of New Mexico Press, 1967).

Horgan, Paul. *Great River: The Rio Grande in North American History* (New York: Holt, Rinehart and Winston, 1954).

Jones, Oakah L., Jr. *Los Paisanos: Spanish Settlers on the Northern Frontier of New Spain* (Norman: University of Oklahoma Press, 1979).

Keleher, William A. *The Fabulous Frontier: Twelve New Mexico Items* (Albuquerque: University of New Mexico Press, 1982).

————. *Turmoil in New Mexico, 1846–1868* (Albuquerque: University of New Mexico Press, 1982).

————. *Violence in Lincoln County, 1869–1881* (Albuquerque: University of New Mexico Press, 1957).

Lamar, Howard Roberts. *The Far Southwest, 1846–1912: A Territorial History* (New York: W. W. Norton & Company, 1970).

Larson, Robert W. *New Mexico's Quest for Statehood, 1846–1912* (Albuquerque: University of New Mexico Press, 1968).

Lecompte, Janet. *Rebellion in Rio Arriba, 1837* (Albuquerque: University of New Mexico Press, 1985).

Nash, Gerald D. *The American West in the Twentieth Century: A Short History of an Urban Oasis* (Albuquerque: University of New Mexico Press, 1977).

Pearce, T. M., ed. *New Mexico Place Names: A Geographical Dictionary* (Albuquerque: University of New Mexico Press, 1965).

Perrigo, Lynn I. *Our Spanish Southwest* (Dallas: Banks Upshaw and Company, 1960).

Ream, Glen O. *Out of New Mexico's Past* (Santa Fe: Sundial Books, 1980).

Reeve, Frank D. *History of New Mexico* (3 vols., New York: Lewis Historical Publishing Company, 1961).

Roberts, Susan A. "A Political History of the New Mexico Supreme Court, 1912–1972," *New Mexico Law Review*, Special Issue (1975): 1–83.

Sando, Joe S. *The Pueblo Indians* (San Francisco: The Indian Historical Press, 1976).

Simmons, Marc. *Albuquerque: A Narrative History* (Albuquerque: University of New Mexico Press, 1982).

————. *New Mexico: A Bicentennial History* (New York: W. W. Norton & Company, 1977).

————. *Spanish Government in New Mexico* (Albuquerque: University of New Mexico Press, 1968).

Singletary, Otis A. *The Mexican War* (Chicago: University of Chicago Press, 1960).

Spicer, Edward H. *Cycles of Conquest: The Impact of Spain, Mexico, and the United States on the Indians of the Southwest, 1533–1960* (Tucson: University of Arizona Press, 1962).

Szasz, Ferenc Morton. *The Day the Sun Rose Twice: The Story of the Trinity Site Nuclear Explosion, July 16, 1945* (Albuquerque: University of New Mexico Press, 1984).

Weber, David J., ed. *New Spain's Far Northern Frontier: Essays on Spain in the American West, 1540–1821* (Albuquerque: University of New Mexico Press, 1979).

————, ed. *Foreigners in Their Native Land: Historical Roots of the Mexican Americans* (Albuquerque: University of New Mexico Press, 1973).

Wormington, H. M. *Prehistoric Indians of the Southwest* (Denver: The Denver Museum of Natural History, 1973).

Illustration Credits

Courtesy of New Mexico State Records Center and Archives, pp. 117 (B. Farrar Collection), 35 (B. Long Collection), 184 (Civilian Conservation Corps Collection), 154, 168 (C. Olsen Collection), 61 (Cultural Properties Review Committee, Bureau of Immigration, 1905, Territory of New Mexico), 204 (Dale Bullock Collection), 53, 82, 96 (*right*), 188 (Department of Development Collection), 81, 89 (E. Boyd Collection), 62, 67, 115, 121 (*left*), 126 (Frank McNitt Collection), 29 (Ina Sizer Cassidy Collection), 102, 106 (K. Shiskin Collection), 28 (Lucien File Collection), 191 (R. Vernon Hunter Collection), 40, 156, 158, 162 (*top*), 166 (SRC Miscellaneous Collection), 43 (State Parks and Recreation Agency), 133 (*top*) (State Planning Office Collection), 17, 52 (Virginia Johnson Collection).

Courtesy of Museum of New Mexico, pp. 20, neg. no. 8721; 26, *Harper's New Monthly Magazine,* July 1880, neg. no. 71390; 30, Harmon T. Parkhurst, neg. no. 2068; 41, neg. no. 16739; 46, Ferenz Fedor, neg. no. 100297; 57, neg. no. 11409; 71, neg. no. 50828; 73, Illman Bros. Engraving, neg. no. 7757; 76, J. L. Nusbaum, neg. no. 13944; 78, Ben Wittick, neg. no. 15754; 79, F. A. Nims, neg. no. 86959; 80, Mildred T. Crews, neg. no. 66647; 86, Robert Martin, neg. no. 41984; 94, neg. no. 11254; 99, neg. no. 45009; 116, neg. no. 11932; 118, neg. no. 10308; 121 (*right*), neg. no. 50541; 129, Henry A. Schmidt, neg. no. 58556; 139, neg. no. 50884; 143, Ben Wittick, School of American Research Collections, neg. no. 15780; 151, neg. no. 14659; 155, J. C. Burge, neg. no. 14691; 157, neg. no. 5989; 162 (*bottom*), William Walton, neg. no. 8119; 175 (*bottom*), neg. no. 45221; 177, C. E. Lord, neg. no. 28817; 185, neg. no. 57271; 202, neg. no. 9763; 203, neg. no. 43529.

Courtesy of Economic Development and Tourism Department, pp. 10, 13 (*top*), 13 (*bottom*), 14, 16, 21, 47, 51, 60, 88, 96 (*left*), 107, 132, 179.

Courtesy of State Historic Preservation Division, pp. 9 (E. T. Hall, Jr.),

36 (NPS, Fred Mang, Jr.), 59 (Carl Kernberger), 63, 87, 92 (Laura Gilpin), 108, 123 (NPS, Fred Mang, Jr.), 187, 192.

Courtesy of Rio Grande Historical Collections, pp. 127 (Blezer Family Papers), 133 (*bottom*) (De Bremond Collection), 142, 145, 165 (Mares Collection).

Courtesy of Albuquerque Convention and Visitors Bureau, p. 31.
Courtesy of Albuquerque Public Library, p. 175 (*top*).

Courtesy of Collection of the University Art Museum, University of New Mexico, Albuquerque, p. 48 (Adam Clark Vroman).

Courtesy of Ele Baker, p. 5.
Courtesy of Fred Harvey, p. 149.
Courtesy of Mrs. Tony Grenko, p. 169.
Courtesy of Wide World Photos, Inc., p. 182.

Index